SYMBOL AND METAPHOR IN HUMAN EXPERIENCE

Symbol and Metaphor
in Human Experience

BY MARTIN FOSS

PRINCETON, NEW JERSEY

PRINCETON UNIVERSITY PRESS

1949

Printed in the United States of America
By Princeton University Press at Princeton, New Jersey

TO MY SONS

CONTENTS

1

THE VIEW OF THE "SCHOOLS"

Every age has its favorite solutions to its problems. These solutions may be the result of previous research, but they have passed through many brains and have been polished like an old coin. They are repeated again and again and they gather authenticity while they lose depth.

The depth of the answer depends on the intensity of the problem which it contains. An answer is valuable only in so far as it stimulates further inquiry. This holds true even in the exact sciences where the hypothesis serves as a springboard for the searching mind. In a still higher degree it holds true in the realm of philosophy where answers are merely fertile formulations of problems. "Let us know in order to search," says St. Augustine. The favorite answer of an age, however, is often one in which only a minimum of problems is preserved and which has been promoted to its place as favorite because it seems to render superfluous all further questioning. It closes all doors, blocks all ways, and just because of this permits the agreeable feeling that the goal has been reached and that rest is granted.

One of the favorite answers of our age has been the symbol. Man has, as they say, a "symbol-forming power," and it is this power which makes him a man. Consequently everything that man produces is a symbol. Symbol is the slogan, the magic key which opens all doors and answers all questions. In symbolism all our thinking comes to rest. Science is symbolical, art is symbolical, even religion is.

It is useful to arrive at general conclusions of a sweeping character. But it is dangerous too. That our conceptual knowledge and our artistic creation have a common ground is obvious. They grow, after all, out of one and the same root—the human mind. But it should not be doubted that they both cover very different grounds and that what we call meaning in a conceptual formula differs widely from the quasi-meaning of an artwork. One cannot even speak of the "meaning" of a symphony without forcing the issue.

We have to face this difficulty not only in the sphere of art, but also in the sphere of myth and religion. From time to time people have tried to "explain" myths, to state their real symbolic content. They have interpreted myths as symbolic statements of natural events, and mythology emerged as primitive natural science. These interpretations, while casting small light on the nature of myth, do afford us a useful glimpse into the mind of the natural scientist, who is at home only in the world of symbols and must transform all of his findings into symbols. Indeed, it may be that the modern common-sense attitude toward symbolic explanations is only another indication of the almighty power of natural science in our time.

Mythology, however, presents a fascinating paradox: for whereas all symbolical thinking has as its goal the ordering of the world into clear and convenient patterns, mythology on the other hand serves a very different function. So different, indeed, is this function that some scholars, especially the school of psychoanalysts, have regarded the myth-making faculty as an endeavor on the part of man not to clarify, but to hide, to confuse, to disguise, to blur, above all to conceal that which he fears and would not face.

This theory is ingenious, but I do not think it obtains. It is true that myths are akin to mysteries and that mysticism, taken literally, means secrecy and silence. But secrecy is not confusion and disguise. Indeed, secrets may frequently be communicated and shared among those who are eligible to understand them. Philosophy in its youth sprang from mythology—"mystery" in Greece and "upanishad" in India meant secret wisdom. It would be a sad day for humanity, if philosophy were proved to have emerged out of an impulse to confuse and to hide, out of an inclination to create disorder. The enemies of metaphysics might have reason to rejoice, but no serious scholar would.

Although we cannot view the psychoanalyst's interpretation of mythology as pertinent, there is, nevertheless, a serious lesson to be drawn from it, namely, that there are two approaches to knowledge, not to be confused one with the other—the one through myth, philosophy, religion and art, and the other through the symbols of scientific systems—and that they will, indeed, appear to move in opposite directions.

As the word symbol is generally used in connection with scientific knowledge, we must find another word to characterize the very different kind of knowledge we are concerned with in art, myth, and religion. To this end the word metaphor will best serve our uses, for although it has heretofore been used in a narrower sense than it will be here, it is the paradox of metaphor which has given rise, in the history of thought, to the very problems with which we will concern ourselves. The school of symbolism, of course, has claimed the metaphor as a species of symbol. But the fact could not be overlooked that the metaphor, compared to the clear, exact, and useful symbol, seemed unclear, complex, and useless—even as a superfluous luxury in the economy of the human mind. It was regarded as an ornamental addition. But what soon came to puzzle thinking men was how a supposed ornament could exert so dynamic a power in myth and artistic creation.

It is the aim of this work to elucidate the character of metaphorical thinking. For this purpose it will be necessary not only to give to the metaphor its specific place among other forms of thought, but also to show the inter-relations between these forms and metaphorical thinking.

The task is difficult, and one would not dare to enter immediately into the thick of the problem involved. It would be better to begin with a widely held everyday view as a springboard into further investigation. Now, looking over the centuries of the past we shall find two main trends of thought, powerful and widely acclaimed, which again and again supplant each other as dominant in their age. Alternating with each other, fighting against each other, and supplementing each other, these two trends represent, in combined tension, the prevailing attitude of human thought down through the ages. A short survey of these trends may prepare the ground for our investigation, although neither of the two can be regarded as giving the final answer.

One of these two views emphasizes a world of images, a flux of sensuous impressions. There is passivity and surrender to that which imposes itself upon the mind. Very early this school of thought learns to reject all fixations of objects, independent in their boundaries; it refuses to believe in forms, substances, forces, in active organization or any systematic interrelated truths. From early Buddhistic schools to Bergson there have been men of all dispositions, turning against a static world of being; religious champions of a floating, mysterious Nirvana; orgiasts, fleeing from the organized expediency of a scheduled life and losing themselves in the intoxication of mass-feeling; cynics, deriding the balanced pedantry of the social structure, living as anchorites lives of protest; highly cultured skeptics—Pyrrho, Sextus Empiricus, and the English Empiricists like Hume—using the weapons of their opponents in order by logic to destroy the logical tissue which they had tried to avoid.

All these men were, of necessity, inconsistent in that they fought against something which they could not do without and used the very thing they denied in order to prove its nonexistence. Unawares, they spun a tissue of compromises in order to avoid a meaningless Nirvana. They made use of unities in order to refute unity and transformed the stream of images into specially constructed sense data. As educators they addressed the self of man whose existence they denied, explaining it as a flux of vaguely similar impressions. In short they contradicted themselves repeatedly, but remain even yet as powerful as ever. Nor is this surprising since they represent one of the two eternally coexistent principles which perpetually compete.

Isolation and determination are here discarded; distinction and relation are eliminated and replaced by an uninterrupted flux. On the other hand, change in the flux cannot be denied, differences have to be acknowledged, and so separate images have to be detached. This done, the sensationalist philosophers face the new difficulty of bringing these images into flux again and of linking them together in an uninterrupted continuity. It would seem only an escape if, in order to do this, differences were blurred into approximate "similarities" and images melted into each other by a mysterious "association" of these undefined similarities. In doing this the sensationalist has already partly deserted his ground and has adopted the hostile view of detached and separate units which, being unable to connect, he groups loosely and mechanically together in "bundles" of association.

When the sensationalist has once acknowledged an image as a distinct feature, he will not only have difficulty in segregating it from other images and will do this in a merely arbitrary way, he will also be unable to master its inner complexity. Therefore an infinite abundance of details will present itself. It will be an insoluble problem where and how this infinite abundance of details is to be stopped, how a selection of details should and can take place. In fact, there is no stopping and no selection, there is only surrender. There is no firm hold on anything. Man is attracted and captivated by the sensuous experiences which come his way; and when he actually discriminates among experiences, his omissions and selections are arbitrary. Soon he will attempt to make good to himself those experiences which he passed over. The illustrator faces this problem when he attempts to catch life. His series of illustrations is always arbitrarily limited and he tries to make up for this arbitrariness by adding fragment to fragment of life. But his task is hopeless. The more he amasses the more confusing his work will appear. And just as he wants to catch the flux of change by sheer number of his images, so he will also try to hold and preserve in every single image as many details as possible. Here too every selection seems arbitrary, and thus he will add detail to detail in order to be true to nature. Witness the sensationalistic works of the impressionist who, in a pedantic and quasi-scientific way, gathers an infinity of nuances. And yet still feeling his work to be arbitrary and fragmentary, he repeats in endless modifications the same aspect of nature, attempting to make up for what must always be omitted. Or we see the fiction writer drowning his stories in a sea of details which still are disconnected and blurred and so force him to repeat his endeavors in ever new modifications.

When we pass now to the rationalist, the second of the two eternally fighting and compromising schools of thought, we will find him equally one-sided and equally inconsistent. As the sensationalist was forced to cope with certain elements, foreign to his fundamental view, so, indeed, is the rationalist. The rationalist does not surrender to any flux of images. He is active and imposing. He makes statements, and in making them he stabilizes the sensuous flux; he delimits, marks clearly, and connects in a distinct relation what he has defined and differentiated. To make things distinct, means to show their difference, and so the rationalist is concerned with nothing so much as with drawing lines of demarcation and regarding these lines as essential. As the sensationalist was in fact unable to draw any lines of demarcation, so the rationalist can do little else except outline and demarcate. And in order to make these lines clearer than nature presents them, he has to simplify, omit, select—in short he has to do all that the sensationalist does not do or does with a bad conscience. Again as the sensationalist is very reluctant to separate an image, so the rationalist puts his emphasis on the framing of the sensuous images. Indeed, the framework as such assumes the greatest importance. And so framing, organizing, and dividing enters the content of the image itself, cutting it into smaller and smaller units. What cannot be put into this network of dividing lines is stigmatized as mere confusion. It is not only superfluous; it is even highly disturbing. It may have a kind of pseudo-existence as a phenomenon, as appearance or simply as error or deficiency or privation—the rationalist scholar will avoid it as much as possible, as if it were the work of the devil. The rationalist is a fanatic, not of orgies, but of asceticism. He trains himself to overcome the sensuous world, to forget it; he invents sophisticated methods in order to render innocuous the disturbing world which he cannot absorb in his system. He does so as a scientific monk of Pythagorean asceticism; he does it as an Eleatic philosopher who denies and eliminates from his thoughts what he cannot master; he does it as a Platonist, withdrawing to the heavenly Ideas, and he does it at last as a Cartesian master of a mechanical world. There is unquestionably greatness, even sublimity in the sacrifice of these ascetics who burn a half of the world on the altar of rationalism in order to organize the other half and to master it in their lofty framework.

The rationalist's construction is built on discontinuous entities. Empty spaces appear everywhere between the outlines. It is a network of bridges built into the air, a framework without anything to frame. The "horror vacui" enters this system and endangers it right from the beginning, as in the ingenious atomism of Democritus where emptiness plays a decisive role, and even in Descartes's system where God has to fill the gaps which burst open between the neatly defined things. This difficulty, however, rationalism tries to overcome, and it succeeds indeed in merging the discontinuous entities of its system into a unity just as tight and powerful as the uninterrupted continuity of the sensuous flux. It achieves this by an ingenious device which it can hardly explain and which may be called the irrational element in Rationalism: The danger of destroying unity by breaking everything up into self-sufficient parts, is avoided, if the self-sufficiency of the part enables it to stand for the whole, "signifying" the whole. The idea of "signification," of "meaning" is the magic tie between part and whole. The part stands for the whole, and the whole, as the meaning of its parts, assumes the role of a "systematic" whole in which every part has its true reality only in its direct representation of the whole. The parts as such in their relation to each other may remain discontinuous, closed in themselves, self-sufficient in their boundaries, but in their "meaning" of the whole they are welded together and tied into an unbreakable unity.

Meaning, signification is what counts in the rationalistic world. Everything is detached, isolated, but everything has in its detachment and isolation a "meaning," everything is a "symbol." Symbol is the ingenious device of rationalism. Signification and symbolism compensate for the abandoned inner context and continuity. They restore the lost unity of the world.

A new difficulty, however, threatens the world of symbols. If the symbol expresses the paradoxical view that the part is the whole—at least somehow the whole—then every whole is also a part, symbolizing another, greater whole. Here the system threatens to slide away and to dissolve into a flux without end. Therefore an end has to be found, and as it cannot be found in the system itself, it has to be imposed in order to stabilize the system. Wherever a "closed system" is assumed, the closure of the system has to be arbitrarily effected by an element which is not part of the system, but has been taken from outside as an expedient of practical necessity. Here again rationalism has to take recourse to something which is not rational. The system receives its final meaning from something which it cannot symbolize: it has its final end in a purpose for which all symbols are means. We are therefore forced to conclude that for all its self-sufficiency and exactitude, the system owes its ultimate justification to that vague and indistinct, if omnipotent, element which may be called existence or reality or life. All the asceticism and elimination of "life" is only a means to serve life which as a last goal stands behind the system and closes it. This goal may assume all kinds of different forms, never quite distinct, never as exact as the system of symbols which serves it. This systematizing and unifying purpose may be propagandistic or instructive or educational, it may be merely entertaining or it may be turned toward the simplification of our mental efforts, aiding our memory. There are many systems of symbols, some ignoble, others elevated, indeed some so far beyond the expediency of everyday life that they seem to outgrow the world of the merely useful; but essentially we must say that wherever there is a set of symbols, that set of symbols has been devised and directed toward the service of some specific end or expedient. Symbols are tools which make it possible to organize the machinery of social life and to master the complexity of our civilization. There is no small value in the symbolic construction; it makes man foresighted, saves him from being drowned in the abundance of details, from being entangled in the changing moments of life and from tottering around in a useless struggle. It lifts men into the cooler sphere of a clear-patterned schematism.

Therefore all symbolic systems—and especially those which we call scientific—tend to emphasize the immediate relationship from part to whole, from symbol to meaning. What does not serve this goal, is useless and has to be omitted. Where there was an excess of details in the sensationalist view, here on the other hand is a tendency to avoid all unnecessary details. Symbolism is exact the more it succeeds in omitting details and abstracting from everything which could distract from the one and only route to the whole. The tendency to exactitude is a tendency to abbreviation, and at the end of this tendency stands the abstract sign, a symbol so utterly simplified that it in fact denotes nothing but itself and so negates its own destination. Surely, such an extreme symbol is no longer a real symbol; it is an empty abstraction and as such just as insignificant as the crude sense datum in its pure factuality, the detached detail in the sensuous flux. Here, in their extremes, sensationalism and rationalism prove their one-sidedness and the necessity of their mutual dependence. The hypostasis of crude sensuous factuality, worshiped by extreme materialism, would be just as meaningless as a rationalistic Divinity of abstract Being. These results, indeed, lie ahead of both routes when separately followed to the complete end. But it is this very end of a total completeness which will force both of them to find their mutual supplementation in each other. For the sake of completeness the sensationalist will strive for more and more details and so in differentiating and specifying will resemble the analyzing endeavor of the rationalist; and equally for the sake of completeness the rationalist will simplify and abbreviate, and so work upwards to an all-embracing meaning of life, an unquestionable end which carries the whole edifice and enters into every part of it.

The one-sided emphasis on Sensationalism or on Rationalism will therefore lead to a certain ambiguity. All primitive thinking begins in the dust and dawn of ambiguity. Young metaphysics cannot avoid the vagueness of statements which express the wavering between the two hostile movements of thought. And even in later times, when both schools have found their separate language, they still will borrow from each other: the sensationalist will try to stabilize the flux by abstraction, the rationalist will try to give concreteness to his symbols and so open the door to the vagueness of images. Wherever in the history of philosophy the one appears, the other will turn up immediately, and neither of the two in their one-sided interpretation will represent the full truth. Their fanaticism is largely due to their one-sidedness, and the battle they fight against each other has its origin in the fact that neither of the two can live without the other. The sensationalist may deride the abstractions and sophistications of reason, the rationalist may condemn the confusing ambiguity of the senses, yet neither of them alone can penetrate into the metaphysical depth of fundamental problems.

These fundamental problems are beyond mere images and symbols. When, for instance, the sensationalist or the rationalist tries to grasp the problem of continuity: the one describes only the continuity of flux, the other only the continuity of a series—and neither of them really understands the other. It needs true Metaphysicians, like Aristotle and Leibniz, to enter deeply into the profound meaning of such a problem.

The great tradition of philosophical ideas passes beyond the schools of Sensationalism and Rationalism, and points to a sphere where neither images nor symbols suffice, to the realm of the Metaphor.

2

THE SYMBOLIC REDUCTION

SYMBOLISM is founded on the relation of part to whole, a relation much more enigmatic than common sense believes it to be. At the bottom of it is the idea that the part represents the whole, or as Plato and his followers put it: the part participates in the idea of the whole. Proclus says:[1] "We see the form (εἶδος) in each part severally, in the sense that even the part has become a whole by participation of the whole which causes the part *to be the whole* in such a fashion as is proper to a part."

By representation or participation a relation is meant, similar to identity. The part is somehow the whole, identical with the whole. It is the microcosm, representing the macrocosm. It is no accident, indeed, that from time immemorial the microcosm-theory has been linked to the atom-hypothesis. Democritus states both of these metaphysical theories, and Plato[2] adopts together with Democritus' atom also his microcosmic world view. Rightly understood every atom is a microcosm, a symbolic part, representing the whole of the universe. This is the profound truth beneath the atom-theory, the atom not being an empirical object, found by experiment and research. Nobody had ever seen an atom; it was beyond any experience, but it had to be conceived, because it alone made a symbolic organization of nature possible, a systematic view of the universe where every part represented and revealed the nature of the

[1] Proclus, *Elements of Theology*, trans. by Dodds, Prop. 67.
[2] Plato, *Timaeus*, 53Cff., 88Cff., 90D. Already Democritus' predecessor Anaxagoras had acknowledged atoms which, containing all elements of the universe, were, in a way, representations of the universe as a whole.

[13]

whole. Whenever symbolism is at work, atomism is at hand as a device of symbolization. So it was in Stoic times, when symbolism was powerful and the World appeared to be full of "logoi spermaticoi," every one of which represented the infinite Logos, the World-Logos. So it was again in Leibniz' philosophy two thousand years later, when monads as immaterial atoms had to build the universe and every monad as a microcosm "mirrored" the macrocosm of the universe. It is here and everywhere the part which is somehow also the whole.[3]

To be sure, whenever our modern philosophers speak of part and whole, they do not so much think of the foundation of symbolism, of representation and participation: the part does not so much represent the whole, as that it constitutes a whole together with other parts as a summing up and addition. The atom is here generally understood as an additive element, and the scholar is asked either to construct the whole out of a multitude of atoms, or to divide it into these last parts as its constitutive elements. Descartes's Rules for the Direction of the Mind recommend this kind of analysis and technique: addition and division, not representation, are here the essence of the atom-theory. But then, what does addition mean; what is an entity, the essence of which is to enter into a unity with others and to form with them a whole? Is this conceivable, without the whole being anticipated in the part? In fact, addition presupposes as its foundation the idea of symbolic representation or participation. And here we enter the field which, indeed, has always been regarded

[3] Whitehead, in his modern revival of Leibniz' monadology uses the same device of symbolization, making part and whole interchangeable: "Actual entities atomize the extensive continuum. . . . But in another sense the actual entity . . . includes the continuum." (*Process and Reality*, 104); see also with regard to pattern and event: *Science and the Modern World*, 159, 181, 183, etc.

as the model of all symbolization: the sphere of the Number.

In the history of thought, number undoubtedly has been a most powerful symbol. Pythagoras bases his symbolic world view on number, and his atomism is an atomism of arithmetic.[4] Descartes, Hobbes, the modern symbolic logicians follow this line and build their theories in accordance with the rules of arithmetical symbolism.

Every number as an "integer" is a "whole" number. But as a "whole number" it, nevertheless, is only a part, stands in equation to others and exists only in its capacity of forming relations in a series. The "whole number," just because it is a whole, is relative and dependent, inclining toward collective grouping, finding its destination in addition as a mere part of a sum. But, on the other hand, numbers could not be added to sums, if every whole number did not anticipate and represent a sum itself. What we call "equation" is possible only because the whole number has as its intrinsic principle the capacity of stretching beyond itself and of uniting with others, tending toward a sum, with regard to which it is only a part of a whole. Mathematical "equality" is not a mere comparison between two detached entities, but a function, residing in the number and manifested only in the "equation" as an active operation.

But here again we have to consider the fact which is essential to all symbolization: What common sense and science emphasize in the number is not so much its capacity to enter into equations and to add up in a sum or to shrink by division, but the fixed, immobile character of its "wholeness"—the independent, detached, and invariable nature of the number as such. This is the paradox of

4 On the kinship between atomism and the Pythagorean number-symbolism see Aristotle, *De Caelo*, 303a4.

symbolism, that the part is fixed as an independent whole, that the part is regarded as if it were a whole.[5] The tendency of the part toward the whole is neglected in favor of a part which is somehow itself already a whole. In this way, number is conceived as detached and self-sufficient, and even when it is related to other numbers, even when it enters an equation, an arithmetical proposition, it is primarily the number as such upon which the interest is concentrated. Number is conceived and so is another number, both in isolation, and the inconspicuous $+$ merely connects these self-sufficient numbers in an external manner. Addition becomes thus a mere togetherness of disparate wholes; the sum a collective entity, complete, total, and self-sufficient. Symbolic logicians enclose every number in a separate class and in this way mean to understand its essential character. The number-proposition, the arithmetical function, has vanished into the background.

This interpretation of the arithmetical proposition has

[5] "Pars pro toto" as the principle of number is shown by the simple equation $1 = 1$ and by the addition $1 + 1 = 2$. The equation $1 = 1$ would be a paradoxical statement, if it meant that 1 is in every regard and absolutely equal to 1. Absolute equality would mean identity and not equality which is only a partial sameness on the ground of differences. Peter and John are equal and can be added as equal, if we abstract the partial element which they share in spite of being different. This partial element (that they are citizens of New York) can be abstracted and can, although only a part, stand for the whole man, and so Peter and John are addible as equal (two citizens of New York). What we call here abstraction is the treatment of a part as if it were the whole, omitting the infinite differences which make up the real whole. But these infinite differences are silently included in the numbers and their equality. The Pythagoreans rightly called number a unity of definite and indefinite; or better, a definite sameness on the ground of an indefinite infinity of differences. This infinity can never entirely be swallowed up by the definiteness; there is no last and absolute total number because number always will be carried from one to the next by the infinity which lies behind and works in the process and operation of the unending series.

its parallel in the field of logic. The logical proposition has very often been compared to the arithmetical proposition in also being a kind of equation, a kind of addition between fixed and detached terms, the sum of which forms the whole proposition. Hobbes, especially, treats the logical proposition as a mere calculation. But what distinguishes the one from the other and makes a special consideration necessary with regard to the logical proposition, is that the latter contains an element which defies the simple summing-up of addible parts and which has troubled logicians from time immemorial: the difference of weight between subject and predicate. One cannot simply add subject and predicate. The subject is on a different level than the predicate. Aristotle calls it the ὑποκείμενον, the fundamental entity, while the predicate is only a categorical statement with regard to the fundamental subject.

The relation between subject and predicate has never ceased being the most crucial problem of logical research. Relying on our grammatical form of speech which juxtaposes subject and predicate and seems to sum them up in a kind of equation, symbolic logicians have tried to minimize the importance of the subject or even to eliminate it entirely, in order to bring the logical proposition down to a mere arithmetical equation of predicates.[6] But this attempt has never quite succeeded. The symbolical juxtaposition of the two fixed terms may justify the logi-

[6] Lask (*Lehre vom Urteil*, 1912) tries to solve the crucial problem by regarding both of the two terms of the equation as subjects, not predicates, while the only predicate is seen in the category of their relation. Similarly with regard to relational propositions: Couturat, "La structure logique de la langue" (*Revue de Métaphysique et de Morale*, 1912, p. 5). Leibniz, however, had already rejected this view, because the predicate could not possibly have one leg in the one subject and the other leg in the second subject of the relation (*Philosophische Schriften*, ed. Gerhardt, VII, 401).

cian in regarding both of them as equal, both of them as mere predicates. But then there remains the problem of what makes the unity and necessity of these fixed, detached, self-sufficient predicates. The mere togetherness of predicates is always only relative, fragmentary, hypothetical. But every relativity asks for something absolute, every hypothetical relation for something categorical. The mere word implication which logicians use, in order to explain the necessity between the terms, is only a vague pictorial repetition of the old whole-part relation, and often even the whole and the part may be interchangeable, allowing now the one, now the other term to inclose as a whole and to imply its counterpart.

Relation and implication of predicates do not suffice— the subject is wanted, it is wanted for the unity of the terms, as a necessity of their togetherness. The subject— the true "subjectum," the ὑποκείμενον—is, and can only be, the ground on which the terms meet, the unifying function and process of the proposition itself. The process of the proposition is the *subjectum*, and as such it not only carries the fixed and detached terms towards each other, but also—in unifying them—transcends every single term, and in transcending, destroys their independent status in a unity of meaning which is the meaning of the proposition and leads to further and further propositions, linking them together in the higher unity which we call conclusion.

Static symbolism has no use for the dynamic function of the propositional process. It has found a refuge in a compromise which language and common sense have sanctioned: The *subjectum* of the proposition, the unifying function has been closed into one of the fixed terms, has been made a subject *in* the proposition. As such it has lost its carrying and forward-driving character and has become a static, symbolically reduced entity, a predicative term, a part which merely represents the whole. Every predicate can become a subject in a proposition, and this compromise between process and term has given birth to the hybrid concept of the "universal." The paradoxical character of the universal has kept the schools in doubt and turned them fighting against each other. Stigmatized by the nominalists as a mere word, a *flatus voci*, it has on the other hand been hypostatized as being the true essence of the world. It is in fact neither the one nor the other, it is a compromise: it is the predicate, raised to the role of subject—or better it is a term of the proposition which represents and encloses the creative tendency of the propositional process.[7]

Tendency, function, process is the essence of the universal, as it is the essence of the subject. Subject is function, and the subjectification of the predicate makes it into an equally dynamic universal. Only tendency is what we call "general" or "universal," because only tendency stretches beyond a multitude of predicates. The universal is the tendency of expansion, it anticipates as tendency its predicative fulfillments, which can only be conceived in the process of propositional thinking. The Arabian philosophers—and following them the philosophers of the Christian Medieval era—rightly understood and characterized the universal as an *intentio*.

The basis of all intentional interpretation of the universal is Aristotle's ingenious concept of the entelechy. Without wishing to enter here into an explanation of this

[7] The universal, standing for the necessity and unity of the propositional process, is, indeed, able to change the hypothetical into a categorical proposition. "If X is human, then X is mortal" could now take the form: "Man is mortal." Logicians are wrong when they deny importance and a special meaning to this change.

extraordinary concept, this much may be said: the entelechy stretches beyond a multitude of predicates, not as
a merely relative connection of parts, but as a constitutive
necessity, a tendency of development and at the same time
an anticipation of the developed.

Entelechy and universal are both the source of countless contradictions and insoluble problems. As to the
universal, it is on the one hand fixed and reduced to a
predicative statement and as such finite, complete, and
self-sufficient; but, on the other hand, it surpasses this
predicative finiteness, is infinite in its tendency, general,
"universal" in its functional character and as such is inexhaustible and never complete. The universal, in other
words, is the prototype of those philosophical antinomies
which gave to Kant the clue to his whole system: it is the
infinite process, reduced to a finite object. As a finite object it takes its place in the proposition as a mere predication; as tendency and process it becomes subject, carries
as *intentio* the propositional drive. It is a "regulative principle," to use another Kantian term, restricted to a fixed
thing, detached and self-sufficient apart from the propositional process in which alone it fulfills its destiny.

By transforming the infinite process into a finite object, symbolism has to substitute for the loss of univer-
sality. This substitution is done by introducing the static
concept of completeness and totality. The universal, instead of pointing to a process of predication and instead
of anticipating, as a framework to be filled, the ever-grow-
ing content of its clarification, now perpetuates an empty
framework and tries to stabilize it in some kind of boundaries. These boundaries will most efficiently be drawn by the
enumeration of all cases which actually exhaust the frame-

work, now called a "class."[8] Or, if the enumeration is not possible, the class will be established by a more or less accidental predication which distinguishes this framework from others. That such an arbitrary and accidental classification is "incomplete," logicians have well understood.[9] It is not more than a vague description and simplification for practical use, and may at any time be replaced by another more adequate and more expedient one. Classification, therefore, is always contingent and deficient. Statistics may step in as an aid to this classification in which symbolism has lost its connection with process and has resigned either in factual enumeration or in a vague description of some similarity. The member of such a class, the thing, will in its empirical factuality triumph over the tendency of a unifying function, and this triumph of the object was foreshadowed already in the unfortunate formula of the "universale in re," where the "res" swallowed up the universal process and became its substantial ground. Aristotle's[10] uncertainty about the weight and substantial reality of the universal was partly responsible for this development by which genus or class became the prototype of law. Process seemed to vanish and had to be rediscovered in modern times, when law was freed from the fetters of arbitrarily fixed classifications and restituted as the law of process. The necessity of this law is not the necessity

8 But enumeration can never lead to the necessity of law. The enumeration of cases, even a totality of cases, cannot constitute a lawful truth. Totality is always limited if only by the manner of investigation. "All" will turn out to be merely "some." Induction, based on enumeration, therefore, asks for a leap from single cases and their enumeration to the entirely different realm of necessity and law. This leap is a risk and, therefore, scientific laws, grounded in induction, are hypotheses. On the limited nature of totality see Aristotle, *Physics*, 207a 10ff. and Foss, *The Idea of Perfection in the Western World*, p. 33ff.

9 Russell, *Introduction to Mathematical Philosophy*, 1920, p. 182.

10 Aristotle, *Metaphysics*, 1035b, 1038b, 1042a.

of the object, but a necessity in which objects are involved and transcended. It is movement with which our laws of nature are mostly concerned, not static things.

The symbolic endeavor to reduction and fixation, however, has found refuge even in the lawful realm of process and has here introduced the crucial concepts of fixed causes and fixed ends. Cause and end are symbolic representations of the process. Their true nature has been the object of discussion since the early times of philosophical thought. Already Socrates has his doubts with regard to "causes." Descartes and his followers despair even to solve the problem and appeal to God's assistance. It is only a continuation on this road of escape when Locke, Hume, and their disciples—repeating to a great extent the old paradoxes of the Greek skeptics—reduce causality and power to mere relation, succession, and habitual expectation.[11]

What, after all, is the "cause"? The paradoxes connected with this concept resemble very much the antinomies which we mentioned before and which rose out of the symbolic transformation of tendency and process into a fixed object, the reduction of the underlying *subjectum* into a limited subject as part and side of an equation.[12] Just as the ὑποκείμενον, the carrying function of the propositional process, was pressed and fixed into a part and term *in* the proposition, lending itself to an addition with other terms in a propositional equation, so here, the tendency of the causal process, the substantial ground, is pressed into one

[11] Plato, *Phaedo*, 96. Descartes, *The World*, chapter 7. Locke, *Essay concerning Human Understanding*, ii, chapter 13, sect. 7. Hume, *Inquiry concerning the Human Understanding*, sect. 7.

[12] Meyerson, when separating law and cause, and stating that cause adds to law the concept of the fixed object, seems to have a similar point of view, but his interpretation is influenced by Bergson's stabilization of time by space. (*Identity and Reality*, chapter 1.)

side or term of a causal proposition, into a fixed, so-called cause and is added to another similar term—the effect—in an equation of causal relativity. And, just as the propositional subject, after having undergone this symbolical transformation, *has* its predicate, so the cause *has* its effect. And now, indeed, the Skeptics are in a position to ask where the cause, as a finite entity, ends and where the effect begins; whether cause and effect are simultaneous and how, if so, they are discernible; and if not simultaneous but separated in succession, how can the one influence the other and belong to the other in a mysterious unity.

In fact, it is not that the subject *has* its predicate, but that the subject *is* the process which is conceived in a series of hypothetical predicative fixations; and it is not that the cause *has* its effect, but that the causal process, as such, is hypothetically thought of as consisting in a series of fragmentary symbolic reductions, causes and effects which grow out of and vanish into the process. To be sure, it is essential that the *subjectum*, the process, is interpreted in distinct and relational symbols; this analytical interpretation, however, does not constitute but presupposes the unity of the undivided process. The analytical interpretation will even be merely hypothetical and arbitrary as to the mode in which the division is made: where cause ends and where effect begins; and it is this element of arbitrariness which led to skepticism. The skeptics, instead of limiting the arbitrariness of cause and effect to the various possibilities of dividing the process in the reflective mind, ridiculed the process itself in putting it together out of bits of fixed causes and effects, just as Zeno had ridiculed the process of movement in showing that it could not be, if understood as a mosaic of fixed points of rest. Hume repeated Zeno's fallacy in the field of causality in trying to show that none of the arbitrarily fixed impressions which he added in a Zenonian way contained causal necessity. For Zeno, movement was an appearance of blurred places of rest; for Hume, causality was an habitual growing together of fixed situations. Rationalist and sensationalist met in the same fallacy.

Who attempts to understand the world as a togetherness of fixed symbolic entities can impose unity upon them only from outside or above. Just as the symbolic logicians understood the terms of a proposition as an equation of predicates, separating them from the carrying function,[13] so symbolic science stabilizes, indeed, cause and effect into an equation between fixed and detached entities, detached from the *subjectum* of the process which now assumes the character of an equally stabilized and imposed necessity of "law." Left to themselves, the fixed and detached entities, cause and effect, become discontinuous facts, contingent in their atomic isolation, and the working of the necessary law upon this contingent material appears as a miracle from above. A miracle, indeed, is this scientific view which is determinism and contingency in one, connecting two worlds, the world of the unchangeable necessity of law with the world of a contingent matter of fact.

The revolt against this view began early. In the field of human life the split between a necessity above and a mere chaotic contingency below seemed unbearable. The rebellion against this philosophy found expression in the Aeschylean tragedy where an iron law of fate, a divine predetermination ruled over the human playthings which in vain struggled to avoid their destiny. This revolt being appeased to a mere resignation in the Sophoclean tragedy, philosophy now takes the lead to smooth down the paradoxical unity of necessity and chance. It is the rationalistic

[13] p. 17.

and symbolic part-whole solution which from now on seems to satisfy man: The world down here in its variety and concreteness is, according to this philosophy, only an image of the lawful necessity above. Analogy connects both worlds: that which seems contingent participates in the necessity of the world-order, as part participates in the whole, stands for the whole, represents the whole. Thus the two worlds are united by analogy, that is, by proportion— a miraculous proportion, indeed, between the necessary and the contingent, the absolute and the relative. But in spite of its paradox, this Platonic solution gives confidence and tranquillity of mind to the coming ages, and enters as an "infinite analogy" the system of Thomas Aquinas, where the "infinite wholeness" of God is related by analogy to the finite world. In this infinite analogy part is whole, but it is this in a mysterious way which surpasses the limits of understanding.[14]

As expedient as the scientific construction and its Platonic interpretation may be, it avoids the compromise between process and object only by eliminating the process entirely and by substituting for it a fixed order of law which is, in a mysterious way, connected with the contingent matter of fact. It is not to be wondered that, under the leadership of Aristotle, our understanding of nature had to turn to the contradicting and problematic unity of tendency and object mentioned above,[15] which at least preserves something of the process, although it involves antinomies. Now cause again carries the effect, absorbing the dynamic power of the process necessary with regard

[14] See the beginning of this chapter on Democritus and the microcosm-macrocosm-analogy. Similar are all the part-whole-analogies which we find even in oldest times, such as the Atman-Brahma-analogy, or the analogy between individual soul and world-soul, the one in the many as a symbol of the all-comprising "one."

[15] p. 20.

to the effect, which in its turn appears as conditioned and, therefore, contingent itself. Necessity and contingency are here not placed in different worlds, but alternate with each other. Every cause is necessary in relation to its contingent effect; and even more than that, every station on the way is both necessary and contingent, conditioning and conditioned, actual and possible, because every effect turns into a cause and so assumes necessity and actuality, and every cause has once been an effect and, as such, merely possible. What we conceive as the process in time has this paradoxical character, where every station of the way is actual and possible, necessary and merely contingent, and where the turn from one to the other keeps the process on the move.

Paradoxical as this attitude towards nature may be— a mere compromise caught in antinomies—it asks for its supplementation because the arbitrariness of closing the causal process in the first of its stations is obvious. A different interpretation, counterbalancing the first, has to form together with it a more adequate view of nature. This is the teleological interpretation, which throws the weight of the *subjectum* not upon the first but upon the last entity. Here the change does not run from necessity and actuality towards the contingent and possible, but, on the contrary, from the merely possible and contingent toward its actualization and necessity. The effect, the result, is here the meaning of the process: the causes, as merely potential means, lead up to the necessity of the goal. Here too, there is movement, development, process of time; and here too, every station of the way is potential as well as actual, contingent as well as necessary, for every stage of the way changes from means to end and from end to a mere means for another end.

Aristotle as well as Kant felt the necessity of this double

aspect of nature; Kant in his cautious manner accepted
the teleological view only reluctantly and with limitations,
because his time regarded it as unscientific. But, teleology
does not surpass the exact symbols of science to any
greater extent than does simple causation. To be sure,
teleology anticipates the end and thus mixes the necessity
of the end with previous stages of merely potential means.
But simple causation has a similar paradox; it looks back
to the start, pushing back to this start the necessity which
it contributes to the following stages, regarding these
stages as possible effects of previous necessary causes. The
one leaps to the future, the other stretches to the past.
Both views have the tendency to seek the necessity of the
process beyond its arbitrary enclosure in one and only one
station of the way and to find it everywhere that reflection
comes to rest. This tendency, however, has to remain a
mere tendency, because if it were to achieve its goal of
necessitating every station of the way, the process would
be turned into a totality of fixed, necessary, actual parts,
and these parts would constitute a whole, an all-actual
totality of facts which as a totality would be its own cause
as well as its own effect, its means as well as its end. This
totality would have lost the flow of process in time; it
would form a stable and unchangeable scientific system or
be hypostatized to a pantheistic divine totality where first
cause would be identical with last end. This, however,
would show the fallacy of turning a process into an accomplished objective system. The totality of the fixed system
would be a dead totality with regard to which nothing
would come into being. It would not even be absolute, but
only exclusive to other totalities. Its necessity would be de-
ceptive: being only a possible totality, it would have to lead
beyond itself to the infinity of the process, which alone is
able to procure life in its moving and creative aspect.

The emphasis has to stay with the process, and this, indeed, has given rise to a new and powerful concept with which modern times have tried to state and clarify the paradox of necessity and chance: the concept of force. Force is restricted neither to the causal nor to the final process; it enters the scientific field as well as the ethical realm of action. Force is necessity, but a necessity which manifests itself, realizes itself in events which have not the necessity of the force itself. They are with regard to the underlying force merely contingent, but this contingency means a reality too, the reality of becoming, when understood as the realization of this its underlying force.[16]

Becoming is not change. Change merely abstracts the contingent differences and stresses their relation, without taking the substantial ground of necessity into account. When we speak of change, we are reflecting upon the discontinuous series of differences, isolating them and relating them as the contingent element in nature. Sophists and Skeptics, denying necessity, emphasized, therefore, the merely changing aspect of the world, without being aware that it was their own reflecting and abstracting mind, their own "subjectivity" which excluded necessity and gave birth to the chance-character of the universe. Nature in its concrete reality is not merely changing, but "becoming," and in the movement of becoming, as in all movement, is a necessity of direction. Direction in change, tendency in change is what we call becoming, and it is the idea of force with which we grasp this necessity of direction.

Causality and teleology find their truth in the concept of force. In this force and its direction the contingent differences of change are comprehended as stages of the way, always surpassed by the necessity of direction which an-

---

[16] Leibniz (*Schriften*, ed. Gerhardt, iv, 523) stresses the reality of force. "Le reste n'est que phénomènes et rapports."

ticipates future differences, even if it does not close these future stages into the exact formula of a final cause. Anticipation is essential for direction, movement, and time. The anticipation of stages cannot be discarded from the necessity of direction. In the direction of our question as well as in the direction of our striving, this anticipation is realized before answers or goals are clearly fixed, and often these answers or goals are only inadequate and transitional symbols of the direction which points beyond them. It may, therefore, happen that our will as a striving tendency feels its own necessity more intensively as long as it remains a direction than when it has fixed and detached a finite goal. The most essential decisions of our life are in reality only directions, although they may take the shape of ends—as our ideals do—and they lose the necessity of their character the more they are turned into exact and limited goals, having again and again to be taken back into the process in order to regain vitality. In the same way our laws are only working hypotheses, stating the direction for the searching and questioning process, remaining always open to correction.[17]

But, to be sure, the tendency and anticipation of force cannot do without the fixation of causes and goals and will give to these symbolic fixations the character of totality, as mentioned above. The dynamic process will be in danger

[17] Laws of nature, causal laws of movement are always hypotheses, and essentially connected with contingency. The hypothesis is necessary with regard to its tendency towards truth, as towards an ideal; but it is contingent in its fixed formulation. A law of nature which would be more than an hypothesis would have to concentrate on the force itself and not on the specific manifestations, as e.g. the law of conservation of energy. Such a law is really no law but a tautological analysis of that which by definition energy is apt to mean. Just as in the field of ethics, Kant's law of lawfulness is an absolute law only because it restricts itself to a tautology: the statement of the general validity of the infinite will.

of being lost in these totalities: cause will always appear as "the whole," it will swallow up the process. Whenever we know the cause, we presume to know everything essential. "Cause" puts an end to the searching process, for every cause is, rightly understood, the first and last cause. Causes are often sought for not because of a thirst for knowledge, but in order to quench this thirst and to give man the good conscience of "having done with" and of being at rest in the explanation reached. And equally, he who has fixed a purpose is fully satisfied and at rest; the "end" restricts and limits the tendency, catches it in a fixed frame. Purpose as "end" is indeed an "end" of a tendency, it brings it to a standstill. We set a goal as we set a limit, and this is not so much done as a springboard, but as a haven. In doing this we surely mark out a certain space, but we do it in order to rest contented in these boundaries. Who chooses a profession, settles down in it and outlines once and for all certain limits to his activity. To be sure, his profession gives him room to move, but he wants this room in order to concentrate on fixed and prescribed activities. The end is, therefore, not so much turned toward the future, as that it negates future in transforming it into a closed present. Very often the reason for this transformation and negation is the fact that the future is disquieting and disturbing. We "care" for the future in eliminating it as a future and transforming it into the well-known present. In caring for our future we dispose of it as if it were present, and in fixing it as a model for action we look back on it as on a past experience. We follow the end, imitate instead of discovering, repeat instead of creating. Repetition is not the cause of our ends, as Hume thought it to be. Habit is not so much the mother of our actions, but on the contrary, our actions, under the imitative restraint of our purposes, under the fixation of our ends, give birth to repetition and the formation of habits. Every virtuoso confirms this as the secret of his "training." The goal, the profession, the care makes us repeat, makes us to be virtuosi, and so the symbolic reduction becomes the source, not the result of habit and imitation.

But, on the other hand, although cause and end absorb and eliminate future and past and close them into a limited whole, common sense is right in attributing to them an expanding tendency too, for the functional process is not entirely extinguished. Just as the *subjectum* of the proposition preserved itself in spite of all predicative fixation, and just as the universal was, rightly understood, not merely an empty frame, but an *intentio* and thus kept the functional process alive, so every cause is understood as stretching beyond into the past, and every end is also regarded as an extension into the future. Cause may be complete and end may be complete, but cause and end nevertheless become alive as a widening power, as all completeness and perfection of Pantheism wants to be understood as a process of life. And it is this ambiguous element in cause and end, this survival of the functional process which made causality and finality suspect to the pure empiricist.

The pure empiricist, therefore, is eager to eliminate cause and end from his scientific system. They are "inexact," they disturb his symbolic fixation in introducing some element of process and tendency. He wants to abolish these rests of an "unempirical" attitude and replace them by a plain series of detached data. He believes only in a sum of parts, maybe a "total" sum—every sum is total—but not in an extending necessity of law, of function, of force, and of will. For him there cannot be any cause necessarily pointing to an effect, no means stretching to an end. This consistent purist will only acknowledge the existence of detached effects—or better, of mere facts—because an effect without the necessary connection to a cause is what the empiricist would regard and worship as a "pure fact." Unable to connect these detached facts, he will be compelled to the minimum of just adding them, "associating" them to statistical sums, which in a limited field may be regarded as total sums. These statistical totalities of facts may substitute for a scientific system. As a fanatic empiricist he may at the most permit himself to fill certain gaps between facts by producing artificially new facts in a set-up of experiments specially constructed for that purpose. But he will think it unscientific to go beyond the total addition of his facts. Repetition of facts and the summing up of them will be the main source of scientific order in a purely empiricist world.

But the pure empiricist will have a still greater difficulty in understanding and analyzing the sphere of human life and finality. Here too he will consider the pure facts which will be the result of suppressing the necessary connection between means and end. Means without ends are obviously not "means" any more, but "facts"; and just as the purist who detached the effects from their causes had to introduce a minimum of interpretation by adding them into a material of statistics, so here also the purist has to unify the means into a totality of means without end, that is, into a totality of technique, of method. But as a technique or method will always be in want of a goal, the purist will fool himself in believing that the technique as such may serve as its own goal, the method itself as its own truth. In this way the task of man will be reduced to the perfection of technique, to the systematization of interconnected means, i.e. to a machinery which runs for its own sake. The machine age, if there is anything of the kind, would indeed be the consequence of this purism; the machine would rule over life and would tell man what to do and what to be. The machine as an object without a meaning and function beyond itself would, in its factuality, become an infatuation, enslaving man by its mere meaningless existence, a caricature and loss of the symbolic task. Whenever objects as such become powerful, money in the hand of the miser, things in the hand of the collector, then they infringe upon life and crush it by their brutal and nonsensical existence. The symbol, at least, serves to organize and by organizing to master. But the meaningless thing, detached and isolated, will turn mastership into mere possession. And he who wants to possess will himself be possessed.[18] The thing, not guided and subordinated by meaning, grows beyond its master and enslaves him. To serve the machine, to perfect it, and to construct a totality of means without a goal would be the blurred ideal of such a time. It would be a mere abstraction, an extreme reduction, extreme in its one-sidedness and absurdity—yet somehow life that cannot ever be completely crushed would creep in as a hope: it would be the absurd hope that goals, ideals, some creative process may, as a by-product, be born out of the deadening service of the machine.

[18] See p. 113.

3

TRANSITION TO THE METAPHORICAL
SPHERE

THE symbolist who indulges in the reduction and fixation of concepts extinguishes the true subject of the propositional process. He has, therefore, some difficulty in passing from one symbol to the other and he may consider a mere statement of the connection sufficient. He may be contented to call this connection, vaguely, implication, using again the part-whole relation on which all symbolism relies. Microcosm and macrocosm in symbolic reference, monad and central monad, atom and sytem of atoms—this is all that symbolism can do to clarify the problem.

Pythagoras, however, saw already that there is an "ἄπειρον" (infinity) behind and beyond the finite symbols of numbers. And Democritus likewise recognized an infinity, an emptiness, in which his atoms flowed. Infinity and emptiness or nothingness are in all future thought the most vital problems, and even mathematics cannot do without the crucial symbols 0 and ∞ which will forever stand in the way of a purely symbolic interpretation.

The symbolic concept of "being" is limited as every symbol is; but from what is it delimited? From nothingness, from "naught"? And if so, what is this naught? Is it "being" all over again? Plato asks the question[1] and others have continued to ask. This problem is avoided and may be happily forgotten when men turn to the proposition of identity. This proposition concentrates entirely on a symbolically fixed entity and connects this entity merely with itself. It realizes the principle of all symbolism in declaring

[1] Plato, *Sophist*, 257 ff.

that the whole is the part: that "A" as subject is exhaustibly explained in "A" as predicate. The true *subjectum*, the functional process, as such, is made obnoxious and even superfluous by leading it in a circle. What the process of thought achieves here is the confirmation of the unchangeable and all-sufficient nature of the symbolically reduced term.

Rationalism has always glorified the proposition of identity. Identity is the meaning of the Aristotelian divine thought which thinks itself and nothing but itself. It is the meaning of Spinoza's "amor intellectualis" in which love turns toward itself. And both have called this identity God. Even Jehovah's sublime words: "I am that I am" (Exodus 3, 14) were regarded as a glorification of the divine principle of identity.

The law of identity, however, has never been a sufficient foundation of rationalism. Besides its positive form it has at least sought expression in a negative way and has given rise to the law of contradiction: "A is not non-A." With this non-A something emerges which had been hidden in the proposition of identity: the problem of the "naught" which tortured Plato, the "ἄπειρον" and emptiness which had crept into the system of the symbolists Pythagoras and Democritus. The non-A keeps the A in its bounds: the A is no longer all, as it had been in the identical proposition, it is a part beside something else, it is delimited and distinct with regard to the non-A. And this non-A is the other, the different, a rather vague and indistinct otherness, to be sure, indistinct because it represents the infinity, the ἄπειρον. This proposition can rightly be named an "infinite proposition," because it leads from A to an infinity of different entities. It opens up the closed shell of identity, and this may be the true value of the negative proposition.

Not as a fixed symbol of contradiction, but as the open door into the infinity of differences, the non-A, the negation is important in the process of thought. Plato[2] already discovered that "non-being" means the difference in being. And Aristotle[3] clarified the issue in revealing the positive character of this realm of differences: it is the "possible," the potential which rises out of the negation. A world of possibilities opens up in the movement of propositional thought as it carries beyond the limited and fixed symbols. It is the functional process which gains recognition and which, linking term to term and proposition to proposition, forms as an infinite tendency the continuity of thought. Continuity, as a problem, arises and remains in the focus of philosophical discussion.

The problem of continuity, as mentioned above,[4] has been broached in vain by Rationalistic and Sensationalistic thinkers, mostly in connection with the problem of movement. For Descartes,[5] Hobbes,[6] and other mechanistic Rationalists, continuity means an adding up of a series of disconnected places, between which the necessary connection remains unexplained. For Bergson[7] it is the gushing forth and flowing of differences in a stream of uninterrupted, indiscernible, and therefore, in fact, indifferent unity. Aristotle,[8] however, had already broached the problem of continuity in an ingenious manner. In explaining the Zenonian paradoxes of movement he states clearly that Zeno confused division and divisibility, the actual and the possible. Continuity means a possible and therefore unlimited divisibility, not an actual division which would

[2] Plato, *Sophist*, 257.　　　　[3] Aristotle, *Metaphysics*, 1033a.
[4] p. 12.　　　　[5] Descartes, *Principles of Philosophy*, ii, 25.
[6] Hobbes, *De Corpore*, vi.
[7] Bergson, *Evolution Creatrice*, p. 2ff.
[8] Aristotle, *Physics*, 231b 15; 232b 20-25; 233a 15-30; 262a 23ff.; 263a 29; b6f.

have to end in an actual last part. But, surely, for a
Greek, even for Aristotle, the possible meant never more
than the shadow of the actual. And when Aristotle raises
the definite question whether the possible or the actual is
fundamental,[9] he is inclined to give preference to actuality[10] and, therefore, to the actual division into detached
parts. And so the problem of continuity disappeared into
the background. It was Leibniz[11] who, following the great
scientists Galilei and Fermat, drew the problem of continuity once more into the focus of philosophical interest.
He did so by connecting this problem, just as Aristotle had
done, with the problem of infinity. And just as Aristotle
had distinguished between division and divisibility, division
being essentially finite and divisibility being infinite, so infinite divisibility again became the ground for investigation. Infinite divisibility was very different from actual
and finite division; infinite divisibility does not stop with
parts and wholes. Part and whole are both overcome by
the continuity of the process with regard to which parts
and wholes are merely transitional stages. The dividing
boundary between the parts is, therefore, here no actual
boundary and does not really separate. It "articulates,"
that is, it unites and intensifies the unity beyond the parts
because its meaning is the emphasis on the undivided process which passes beyond. It is not enough to stress with
Aristotle[12] that in continuity the parts have a common
boundary, as long as these parts remain independent entities. The main difference is the underlying and undivided

9 Aristotle, *Metaphysics*, 1019a and 1049bff.
10 Aristotle, *Metaphysics*, 1051a.
11 Leibniz, *Schriften* (ed. Gerhardt), II, 475.
12 Aristotle, *Physics*, 227a. But Aristotle goes further than that in
228a, b, where he investigates the continuous process of movement,
and also in 222a, where he describes the "now" in time not only as a
divider, but also as a unifier.

process in the course of which the division assumes a contingent character. Even if the division has been actually made, it still remains a merely contingent division with regard to the underlying process.[13]

Although it is again the crucial difference between the potential and the actual, the situation has fundamentally changed: the emphasis is now on the potential; infinite divisibility is potential, but its potentiality is the "actual reality" of the process, and in the light of this reality the division as such, the so-called actual division, weakens into a mere possibility. So the actual and the potential have interchanged roles. The infinite continuity as potentiality is real, is actual, it is the substantial ground of an infinite process out of which parts and wholes rise and into which they disappear as mere manifestations of a transitional character.

Even mathematics shifts its ground: not only the detached number and the series of these added numbers count, the function and process of developing the series grows in importance. Every number assumes now a functional character itself, leading to other and always other numbers, permanently on the verge of changing and disappearing into the realm of mere possibility, carried away by an infinite and continuous process.

So the atomic view of symbolic purism loses its exclusive and dominant position, and cedes its place to a process which, with regard to the changing aspects of its phases and their being overcome by a continually growing unity, can be called a *metaphorical process.*

[13] Aristotle's statement that continuity is mostly where the division is potential, but can also be found in actual division (*Metaphysics*, 1023b), may be thus interpreted. See also Leibniz, *Schriften*, ii, 282: "continuous quantity belongs to possibles, but also to actuals, considered as possibles."

Symbolism, however, partially holds its ground and achieves a compromise which combines the characteristic qualities of the symbolic and the metaphorical sphere, and which, although a wasp-nest of contradictions, assumes the most important role in our understanding of world and nature: the "continuum." The continuum which is neither just a symbol nor only a process is on the one hand continuous, but on the other hand a series of parts and a whole of parts. This hybrid entity of a continuum assumes with its part-whole character also the quality of an object, and so all the paradoxes appear which in the following systems of thought are essentially connected with the continua of time, space, and world. They are wholes, objects, and therefore finite—but at the same time they are continuous and infinite. Kant's ambiguous attitude toward time and space has its root in the hybrid concept of the continuum: Now time and space are functions, now they are objects—now the world is infinite, now it is finite. The Kantian antinomies have their source and their solution in the character of the continuum as a compromise between symbol and metaphorical process.[14]

Space and time as well as the world are continua. Our great philosophical systems have wrestled with the paradoxical problem of the continuum and have decided, unable to close its paradox into one single concept, to express its ambiguous nature in two separate, but in spite

[14] "Organism" may also be mentioned here as such a hybrid concept: it is a process, infinite and continuous, but this process is interpreted as a finite object, a whole with parts, the cells which build each other mutually. But what is overlooked is the fact that the cells also destroy each other mutually, that the organism grows in consuming and dissolving itself. "We live our death" says Heraclitus, in order to express the vanishing of the discontinuous in the continuity of the process. This dialectic or metaphorical character of the organism Kant did not consider when he emphasized exclusively its purposive nature. (*Critique of Judgment*, §65.)

of their separation, dependent entities: matter and substance. Matter emphasizes the object-character, the limited, fixed, predicative element which in spite of its fixation changes in the process of continuity. Matter is the "totality" of symbolic fixation, but as an infinite totality it is indefinite and at the same time it contains a discontinuous manifoldness. It is even the principle of discontinuity, which in itself is a "contradictio in adjecto." As discontinuous it is deficient, wanting, passive, unstable, contingent, and even inconceivable; it rejects any conceptual formula, and is, nevertheless, the material for form, the readiness for form. It is resistance against and at the same time surrender to form, a paradox which Plato already expressed in his *Timaeus*, where matter resists form and nevertheless has an inclination and disposition for form, so that the "demiurgos" has merely to persuade it towards fulfilling its destiny.[15]

Substance, on the other hand, stands for the active, forming power which necessitates the passive matter and transforms its contingent nature. Substance is indivisible, continuous, it is process, function, creative; it is the *subjectum*, the subject, and has—in the medieval era—assumed as divine substance the character of a spiritual subject. But, in spite of this, substance as a continuum, like the subject in the proposition, is objective, builds itself up in a series of inherent accidents, becomes a totality of finite qualities, total although infinite. Even Spinoza could not extricate himself from ambiguous statements with regard to his Divine Substance, which led his followers to interpret the Divine Subject as a system of mechanism.

Substance and matter in their close relationship, which

15 Plato, *Timaeus*, 48ff.

even an Aristotle was in danger of turning into identity,[16] represent the paradox of the continuum which, indeed, is both and neither of them: time and space as continua are neither substantial nor material, and yet are somehow the one as well as the other. They are complex and simple, stable and in process, contingent and necessary, finite and infinite, concrete and abstract; in short, they are contradictory and a true example of the Kantian antinomies.

The identification of substance and matter is fallacious and has, wherever it was made, resulted in a confusion. But just as wrong as the identification of substance and matter is the opposing of both as contradicting elements. Identity and contradiction are both symbolic interpretations and have to be left behind when philosophy tries to understand the unique relation between the metaphorical process and the symbolic reduction. It is, therefore, very inadequate to speak of an antagonism between substance and matter. Who regards substance as a continuous infinite force and regards matter with space, time, and other continua as a resistance against this force, should be aware that, in using opposites, he attempts to explain by rational and therefore symbolic terms while trying to transcend the symbolically reduced sphere. But this is exactly what we are used to doing, because all interpretation and explanation takes its start in the sphere of symbolic reduction. We may call it reflection, and this word again pictures the symbolic interpretation as a movement in an inverse direction, so to speak, negating, undoing what the primordial movement did. Can we wonder that the metaphysics of India, Heraclitus, Dionysius Areopagiticus, Scotus Erigena, Spinoza, Schopenhauer, Bergson, and many others is built on this view of two antagonistic ways,

[16] Aristotle, *Metaphysics*, 1070a; but compare also 1029a.

tendencies, forces? Nobody can quite rid himself of this symbolic interpretation. But he can make it clear that what he calls resistance is not a mere negation, that force cannot even be conceived without resistance, nor substance without matter, nor the metaphorical process without the symbolic reductions which have to be exact, fixed, detached, in order to be transcended and overcome in the process which carries them beyond.

Substance, therefore, as the bearer of a resisting continuum, has to be conceived as a force stretching beyond the material resistance. The tension of this process, the ancient concept of *conatus*, is the continuous overcoming of parts and wholes, of sums and series; and the inadequacy of every whole and series is an inadequacy with regard to the functional process which essentially goes beyond any fixation.

Therefore every symbol is fragmentary and hypothetical when seen in the light of the infinite process which carries it and goes beyond it. We may become conscious of this drive in the tension of doubt, in the questioning and searching power of our mind which guarantees the infinite continuity of research, and which may even guarantee our existence as such. Socrates, Augustine, Descartes and Kant have based their philosophy on this truth. And this truth was for them not merely a psychological experience. The functional process, the drive which unites the terms of the proposition and goes beyond the single proposition, the continuity which carries and overcomes the discontinuous series of symbols, is not a psychological fact; it is the condition for all facts, psychological or not; it is the ground on which psychology and other sciences are built. The danger of misunderstanding this process psychologically is great, and even Kant has, in stating this infinite drive as a "regulative principle," lowered it to the

level of a mere subjective method. What he really meant
was much more: the drive is there, and our mind has to
follow in its track.

This regulative principle is, therefore, not subjective;
it is less subjective than the symbolic reductions. Finite,
as they are, they are dependent more or less on circumstances, on the accidental phase and volume of our knowledge, on the purposes which we have set before us; they
are instrumental and expedient. But this regulative process is not. Therefore this process has to undo the symbolic
fixation, has to extend, where the symbol reduced. It extends
not merely to another and greater "whole." If it were
only this, then this process would not be essentially different from the symbolic formation: the symbol would
transform a bigger whole to a smaller one, and the regulative process a smaller whole to a bigger one. But, in
fact, this process transcends the entire realm of part
and whole and by this transcendence enters into infinite
continuity; it is the reality of the potential which is permanently beyond the merely actual. This process, therefore, questions all material interpretations. To be sure,
interpretation is needed as well in everyday life as in scientific systematization. The philosopher also has to interpret.
His interpretation, however, transcends the symbolic
sphere. If he remains entirely in the order of a symbolic
system, he is a scientist among others, maybe a psycholo-
gist; if he, on the other hand, does not at all consider the
symbolic order, he becomes vague and loses the ground
under his feet.

The only course for the philosopher is to start in the
world of symbols, but to negate them systematically.[17]

[17] This explains the paradoxical character of a "system of philosophy." It is a negative system; its principle is the systematic challenge
to the related whole of symbolic fixation. Kant called this systematic

Negation is the narrow path of philosophy. The negative "infinite proposition" was the springboard to the problem of continuity. Out of the "Naught" Plato developed the difference of things; Aristotle, the world of possibilities. Negation is the door to philosophical truth.

Dialectic, therefore, has been and continues to be the method of metaphysical thought. It is not the accidental method of a few philosophers, it is the road which every great philosopher had to take. Dialectic relies on symbolic concepts, but uses them only in order to state their insufficiency, their incompleteness and merely hypothetical character. Whether the destructive quality of dialectic appears in the more subjective form of doubting and questioning, as it did in Socrates, Saint Augustine, Descartes, and even in Kant; whether it detaches itself entirely from the human mind and appears as a self-destructive power, inherent in the symbolic finite concept itself, is of minor importance. The latter view, however, is inclined to hypostatize the dialectic movement and to transform it into God's own development, as Hegel did. But dialectic itself is not the absolute process of truth; it is the humble approach of the philosopher, who is hardly God. He is, on the contrary, very deficient, and his dialectic thinking is merely a way of preparation. Whatever he touches, turns into negation, and the products of his thought have this negative tint which keeps doubt alive and with it the drive of inquiry. Space and time, world and matter become questionable entities, even freedom is, in the dialectic ap-

---

challenge critique. But this critique is not so much a "system of critique"; it is rather a "critique of system," and thus it is superior and, in a way, antagonistic to the system as such. It follows the order of a system, but it does so because it has to undo its rigidity; and it has the power to undo the rigidity of the system because it contains a superior truth.

proach, only the "negative freedom" which leaves man dissatisfied. Thus the philosopher knows himself to be a transition only, a way. His way is not the way of creation but of critique. In his critique, however, a direction is disclosed, and this direction points to something which is not merely negative and which forms itself in the dialectic destruction. The philosopher can grasp it only as a "problem," and only as a problem it stands out on his way. So in transcending the continuum, the problem of continuity arises; in breaking up the resistance of matter the problem of force and substance is raised, in destroying the negative freedom the problem of a positive freedom may be seen, beyond the paradoxical relation of chance and necessity, of the possible and the actual which leaves us in the dialectic position of a mere "ought."

Leibniz mentions "freedom" together with "continuity," and calls both of them "the labyrinths of the human mind."[18] To clarify these labyrinths, he turns to dialectic: in infinity all things become the equivalent of their opposites, movement becomes rest, inequality becomes equality. And likewise Kant turns to dialectic when he tries to disentangle the antinomies of freedom and God. He follows the method of the great Skeptics who also used the dialectical method in order to rise in free inquiry ($\sigma\kappa\epsilon\pi\tau\epsilon\hat{\iota}\nu$) beyond the deficient and contradicting fixation of their symbolic thinking. Even God became the problem of dialectic when "negative Theology" cleared the way toward understanding Him.

Does the philosopher ever reach his goal? What he gains is a world of problems, and this is not little. The problem of continuity is not little when it enables him to lift himself above the contradicting totality of discontinuous sym-

[18] Leibniz, *Nouvelles lettres et opuscules*, p. 178ff. and *Essais de Théodicée*, Preface.

bols. The problem of substance is not little when it makes him see not only an aggregate of added symbols and predicates. The problems of force and freedom are not little when they point toward a sphere where there is more than mere resistance and the mutual determination of finite and fixed influences.

But the dialectic process does even more: it points beyond all these problems to one great problem which links them all together: the problem of a process which is not merely critical but creative. This process may not be entirely deprived of the element of destruction and critique, and, to that extent, may resemble the dialectical process. But essentially it is beyond negation. Here the mere potentiality of force and the mere divisibility of continuity is overcome by something which is the realization of force and an indivisible simplicity,[19] although rich in itself, an abundance of which Spinoza and Leibniz could only dream. As a metaphysical dream it may become reality in the sphere which, in anticipation, we called the metaphorical process and which leads into the realm of art, ethics, and religion.

[19] On simplicity see Foss, *The Idea of Perfection in the Western World*, p. 49f.

4

METAPHOR AND SIMILE

In the atomistic view of a pure and abstract symbolism the fixed entities are detached and discontinuous; so it is difficult to connect them with each other. The early Greek thinkers, Anaxagoras, Empedocles, and others had to face this difficulty. Special intermediaries had to be invented, but even then atoms remained essentially disconnected. Their interaction, if there was any, remained more or less accidental. An element of contingency has always characterized atomic theories and has been a very disturbing factor.

Why are we disturbed when we have to content ourselves with a statement of contingency? What, after all, is an "accidental event"? It is, what is better called "coincidence." Coincidence means a togetherness of facts, a mere togetherness and nothing more. This "nothing more" is what we resent. A mere togetherness is dissatisfying because we expect and ask for more. We ask for a tie that binds them together and this tie is what we mean by necessity. And we only understand that which means to us a necessity, a lawful unity. Where the necessity is missing, we rest in ignorance. Who denies necessity, denies the possibility of understanding.

Therefore nobody, except the cynical skeptic, has ever seriously denied necessity. Hume, forced by his atomic philosophy, goes very far in the denial of necessity, but he too has to compromise and to grant a minimum of necessity and unity. He does so in his concept of association on the ground of similarity. Now, the word association is not much more than a mere statement of togetherness and therefore does not lead far. And "similarity" expresses only a vague and provisional possibility for future investigation with the hope of finding in this similarity a partial sameness which may constitute a necessary unity. As long as similarity alone is experienced, the association is still nothing but a coincidence. Therefore the psychology of associations may be an adequate description in a sphere where we do not get beyond contingency, i.e. in dream-associations and in the association of mentally diseased persons. It is, however, inadequate in a sphere where description alone does not suffice, but understanding is wanted: in the sphere of human thought.

But the objection might be made, is not in every coincidence, in the coinciding of facts at least, a necessary togetherness of time? Is not their simultaneity in the coinciding of facts? And is simultaneity not a kind of lawful necessity? I do not think so. Mere simultaneity is contingent. That two people die at the same moment is a coincidence as long as it is not one and the same causal event in which they die. And whenever we experience any truly necessary connection, the statement of mere simultaneity appears queer, even funny. It is funny to say: I have "at the same time" a soul and a body.[1] On the other hand, it is quite adequate, when Aristotle uses simultaneity in expressing the reflection upon the law of contradiction: "A is not at the same time non-A."[2]

This example leads to the problem with which we are mostly concerned in this chapter, the simultaneity of reflection. All simultaneity can be regarded as a simultaneity of reflection, a symbolic transformation of something which

---

[1] The parallelism of mind and body in Descartes's and Spinoza's systems is justified only if we distinguish clearly between soul and mind. The mind, not the soul, can be regarded reflectively and simultaneously together with the body, and may be considered on an equal footing (see p. 137).

[2] Aristotle, *Metaphysics*, 1005b.

assumes simultaneity only by the act of reflecting.[3] Reflection is contingent with regard to its object and holds this object in the contingent relation of simultaneity. If it, however, did nothing but this and if it stopped at this relation, it would be a perpetuation of contingency and ignorance. But it does not stop there. Reflection relates in order to compare, and it compares in order to find beyond mere comparison the necessity of a lawful unity. To be sure, as long as reflection remains in the state of mere comparison, of mere simultaneous accidentalness, it is contingent itself and may just as well lead into error, losing itself in wrong inferences of analogy. Analogy, as a comparison of reflection, has often enough given rise to the most fantastic and arbitrary constructions of the mind.

Reflection tends toward necessity. And here we grasp again[4] the extraordinary connection between the contingent and the necessary. Contingency is inconceivable without the background of necessity; and the necessary can only be known when connected with contingent facts. But it would be wrong to state a "relation" between both. Relation only relates the contingent to the contingent, never the contingent to the necessary. Necessity, however, is the ground on which contingent relations occur. We mentioned

[3] Bergson (*Données immédiates de la conscience*, 10th ed. p. 84, and *Durée et Simultanéité*, pp. 56 and 67ff.) explains simultaneity as the combination of space and duration; and in this regard Whitehead (*Concept of Nature* 1920, p. 53) follows him. Bergson believes that space, as the principle of stabilization and symbolization, is responsible for the manifoldness of simultaneous facts. It is not space, however, which makes simultaneity possible, but the discontinuity of a mere relationship. Time is not less a form of discontinuity than space. Both are equally continuous and discontinuous (p. 39), and, therefore, as far as they are forms of reflection, contribute equally to the coincidence of simultaneous facts; and as far as they are processes of continuity, lay equally the ground for an indivisible and absolute existence.

[4] See pp. 24-28.

before the rationalistic attempt to relate the contingent to the necessary: it was done by the scientific system where necessary laws were related to a contingent matter of fact. It was equally done in the Platonic philosophy where the relation of analogy connected the necessary Ideas with the contingent world. To escape these paradoxes contingency, as a stumbling-block for our knowledge, was argued away in calling it a mere negation or privation or ignorance. But whoever shares this view should be aware that he debases together with contingency also reflection. Is reflection nothing but an impotence, an ignorance, a privation? Is it not a power, a positive capacity? Freedom of choice is coupled to the contingency of reflection, and freedom of choice has rightly been praised as a widening power of the human mind. Freedom of choice is the positive side of contingency and reflection; it deserves respect, although perhaps not the glorification to which the Skeptics were inclined.

One cannot eliminate contingency without eliminating reflection. Plato's necessary Ideas were bought at this price. But Aristotle saw that these necessary Ideas, detached from reflection, were meaningless. And a similar criticism may be justified with regard to the modern value-theories which revive the Platonic Ideas in the ethical sphere. These objective values are rather problematic entities, detached from the free choice of the reflecting mind. But indeed, with the freedom of choice contingency enters the field, and thus values and truths seem to slide down into the relativity of contingent discoveries or contingent realizations.

There is only one way to preserve the positive character of reflection and freedom of choice. We have to understand that they receive meaning only in their own transcendence and therefore in their own ultimate destruction.

As we have already pointed out, we reflect and compare in order to enter by free reflection, comparison, and simultaneity of coincidence, into a sphere of necessity. This is to discover truth and acquire knowledge. Knowledge makes us see that simultaneity was merely an experimental statement and replaces it by a lawful unity; that coincidence was a fragmentary view, lacking the insight of a lawful connection. The isolated and thus merely related facts of our reflection change in the discovered context of truth.

Free reflection may be a danger because of its element of contingency and may develop into mere play. We can compare anything with anything, connecting in reflection the most disparate things. Nevertheless reflection is indispensable, and our scientists have freely to construct simultaneities, especially in the mechanics of heavenly bodies in order to arrive at measurements in the universe. All measurement, in fact, is based on a constructed simultaneity of the measuring rod and the object which is to be measured. There are different degrees of risk in these reflective comparisons. The risk may become a fallacy when reflective comparisons are too freely used in the sphere of human life and history, as they were by the mathematician Oswald Spengler,[5] who constructed freely historical "simultaneities" in order to bring together in a loose comparison the discontinua of cultural periods. But on the other hand, just here, where life is concerned, the playful freedom of reflection may, more than anywhere else, be forced into the necessary process of the searching mind, driven by the desire for truth. Where this happens, and it should happen in every scientific inquiry, the true destiny of reflection is fulfilled. The split between a free and playful reflection and the necessity of a lawful process is now overcome, a

[5] Spengler, *Decline of the West*, I, 112 and 364.

split which is reflected in the dualism of intellect and will.
The intellect, separated from the process of will, would
only be a playful and contingent reflection; the will separated from the intellect, nothing but a blind force. Their
unity, so often discussed in the fight between the medieval
realists and nominalists, is to be found in the transcendence
of reflection into the process of necessity which is the process of the willing and searching mind. Here the transcending reflection receives the character of necessity from the
process into which it vanishes; and the process in all its
necessity preserves the freedom of the reflective thought.
What we call the freedom of the will is the freedom of
choice transformed into the necessity of process. It rests
on freedom of choice, but it is more than that: it is freedom
which has overcome the contingency of free choice and has
become necessary. Therefore the unity of freedom and
necessity was rightly stressed by Plotinus, Spinoza, Rousseau, and Kant.

Freedom is neither contingency nor necessity as such.
Aristotle seems to identify freedom with the first, Spinoza
with the latter.[6] But these philosophers, in fact, saw rightly
that the miracle of freedom is connected with both of these
problems. It can even be regarded as their metaphorical
unity. Without the contingency of reflective comparison no
free decision can be made, and this decision, although necessary with regard to the contingent comparison, would
nevertheless not be regarded as free, if it were nothing but
necessary. If the God of Spinoza represented only a necessary determination, he would never be a free God. He is
free, because the contingent finiteness of his *modi*, espe-

---

[6] See Aristotle, *De interpretatione*, 18b 31 and 19a 7; and Spinoza,
Correspondence (ed. Wolf), letter 43 (p. 256), 58 (p. 294), 75 (p.
347). But see, on the other hand, Aristotle, *Metaphysics*, 1048a 10ff.
and 1075a 19; and Spinoza, *Ethics,* book v.

cially the "infinite mode," the intellect, are dissolved into his necessity. Seen from this contingency of the *modi* and with regard to them, God is a free, and in his freedom, transcendent necessity; and whenever our contingent reflection is carried over into the necessity of a decision, our will appears as a free necessity.

Where the searching mind is driven by the necessity of truth, comparison and free reflection lose their self-importance and become a transitional and tentative stage. Here man is aware of the inadequacy of mere comparison. He reaches beyond and finds expression in the Metaphor. Metaphors have been defined as comparisons, analogies, similes. Similarity seemed to constitute the metaphor as it constitutes the simile. But it is not always similarity that makes a metaphor a striking element of speech: very often the dissimilarity is so strong that psychoanalysis was inclined to interpret the "sick simile" as an attempt to hide, dissemble, disguise the truth or to shock the audience by the violence and inadequacy of the analogy.[7]

Whoever measures the metaphor by a fixed symbolic standard will indeed have to find psychological reasons for its deficiency. He will find such reasons either in an intentional or in an unintentional confusion. In this way the "sick simile" would be not more than the confession of an intellectual failure. To be sure, similes are often nothing but failures of clear expression. Men who are inclined to use similes, who begin their sentences with "it is as if" or "so to speak" are in so far apt to be a little vague in their mind. Therefore such people will try to make up for the inadequacy of the simile by piling simile on simile, hiding lack of quality by quantity. But the flowery way by which some orators try to convey by numerous similes a full

7 Heinz Werner, *Urspruenge der Metapher,* 1919.

knowledge of their subject means, in fact, a marching on the spot. Where matters are difficult or transcend our rational knowledge, such endeavors are understandable. They manifest the inability of the human mind and are, therefore, to be found wherever men cannot live up to their standards. Man's reflection on God and on the human heart, surpassing the capacity of clear expression, will often be clothed in similes. Early poetry indulges in this form of expression. But caution is here necessary: what seems grammatically a mere simile, may be more. A true metaphorical process may appear in the inadequate form of a simile. What distinguishes the true metaphor from the inadequate simile will be considered later.[8]

Another endeavor to overcome the inadequacy of the simile is the allegory. The lack of quality is here out-balanced, not by quantity as we saw before, but by an elaborate specification of details. Sensual imagery comes to help where rational clarification fails. But the length and copiousness of the details make it more than ever impossible to follow the line of comparison. This endeavor to saturate our imagination is an ingenious way of making a virtue out of a vice. It may develop into a playful satisfaction, covering up the questions which an immature or over-mature age despairs to solve. Here entertainment is substituted for knowledge, and this is even more the case in another form of playful thinking: the riddle. The inadequacy of the simile, forcing to a leap in order to over-bridge its inconsistency, is here fructified by turning the leap into an exciting risk, an amusing gamble. A guess is necessary, and the guess may succeed or fail. In any case, surprise will be the happy reward after having "found out." It is surprising, and we call it a joke when something inadequate nevertheless seems to make sense, something

8 See p. 56.

crooked turns out to look straight. The accidental element
in the comparison has been put to service: surprise, entertainment, laughter is the result.

But not always: the risk may be entertaining, it may also
be disastrous. A wrong guess, where serious values are at
stake, may lead to death and destruction. Young people
and young cultures do not only see the playful aspects and
consequences of their deficiencies: the risk of missing the
answer has often been coupled in folklore with the penalty
of death. The story of Oedipus and the Sphinx is only one
of many versions where the inadequacy of the riddle ter-
rifies.

As a joke or as a threat, the riddle is the expression of
a discontinuous world of gaps, where leaps are necessary
and failure awaits us. The serious riddle, the tragic riddle
of folklore, however, comes close to a very different problem which may lead us a step further away from the simile
and nearer to the true metaphorical process, the Secret.
Secret is not riddle. Who finds the world full of puzzling
riddles, may be amused or horrified, according to his temperament; but who gets at the Secret of the world, will
take a very different attitude. Secrets are not solved as
riddles are unravelled or as nuts are cracked. Secrets are
wooed in wonder and searching, and wondering and searching have nothing of the gambler's way of guessing riddles.
The Upanishads and the Greek Mysteries do not propose
riddles, but they express a secret wisdom. Wisdom does not
solve, it states the problem. In the dawn of civilization
people stored their wisdom in the treasure-book of proverbs. A proverb may appear as a simile, a comparison, but
it is very different. The comparison connects one object
with another in order to procure additional knowledge. But
if we take a proverb like "Among blind men the one-eyed
is king," we many consider it as a comparison between two

groups, the blind and the seeing. If we, however, learn only what the simile tells us: that the one-eyed can be compared to a king when he lives among blind men, then the result of our comparison is rather foolish.[9] In fact, neither the one-eyed man nor the king is the real interest, neither of the two is supposed to profit by the comparison. The true significance of the proverb goes far beyond the blind, the one-eyed, and the king: It points to a wisdom in regard to which the terms of comparison are only unimportant cases of reference.[10] It teaches the relativity and deficiency of all worldly power, and this wisdom, without being expressly stated, rises above the transient analogy and its inadequate formula. It lifts us above these and other cases of an arbitrary selection to a lawful necessity. Although the form of the proverb is still very much like the simile, even like the riddle, witty and surprising, playfully enclosing a general rule into the nutshell of particular cases, nevertheless its transcending character points to the metaphorical sphere. For it may now be stated: the simile and the analogy link the unknown to the known, in an expedient and practical way, closing the problematic entity into a familar pattern. The metaphorical process, on the contrary, raises the problem even there where we seemed at home and shatters the ground on which we had settled down in order to widen our view beyond any limit of a special practical use.

[9] Understood as a simile or as a riddle which has been answered, the proverb could be formulated: What is the one-eyed among men? Answer: a king. Or: Who is the king among blind men? Answer: the one-eyed. Both answers are inadequate and arbitrary.

[10] Here the reader may be reminded of the parallel problem, discussed on page 18 where the shift was made from the mere comparison and inadequate equation between the two fixed terms in the proposition to the lawful necessity of the functional process, as the *subjectum*, with regard to which the terms are only fragmentary perspectives.

Having arrived, step by step, at this general statement, it will be easy to eliminate from the metaphorical sphere all those cases of symbolic reduction, comparison, simile, analogy which go under the name of metaphor. Whether the poet compares his sweetheart to a flower or whether he calls her right away "my flower"; whether we scold a person for behaving like a pig or whether we fling at him the word pig—this grammatical difference carries no difference of meaning. In both cases the one-sidedness and injustice of stressing one quality, one part and enlarging it to the whole is seen: we never do justice by comparison. The so-called metaphor is in line here with all symbolic reduction; the one and only quality of the comparison, the *tertium comparationis*, is exaggerated until it takes the place of the whole thing, is identified with it, stands for it, according to the general symbolic recipe. This gross inadequacy is, rightly seen, always a caricature. It may be an unintentional one, as when adults call each other "honey," "kitten," etc. It will, however, usually be an intentional caricature, as used in political fights, both in word and in picture, when kings, priests, captains of industry, party-chiefs are reduced to asses, pigs, monkeys, etc.

Furthermore, all those forms of speech have to be classified as mere symbolic simplifications of expediency, where complex and unfamiliar experiences are brought under old well-known concepts and images. So symbolism makes things handy by letting the part stand for the whole, a particular for a general, a quality for the whole object: book (beechwood); biblion, bible (bark of tree); terra (dry, meaning earth); γῆ (seedfield for earth); erda (inhabited place, for earth); femina (suckling); arrive (disembark); rival (competitor in the use of a stream or in general: neighbor).[11]

[11] See for further examples Bréal, *Sémantique*, and Wundt, *Sprach-psychologie*.

Out of this same endeavor to feel at home in the small world of a fixed and limited and well-known environment the many similes are derived which very wrongly are classified personification. Our body is surely the most familiar environment, and so things have been compared for expediency to parts of the human body.[12] It may be objected that our campaign of purification scarcely leaves any room for metaphors. If it is true, however, that metaphors break up instead of fixing, keep us on the move instead of letting us settle down, then it is understandable that the single word of language, polished and made a handy tool of expedient use, will scarcely have a metaphorical character. Many words may have been conceived as problematic and expanding entities but they have lost their dynamic function and have turned into a mere symbol of familiarity. Every language is full of "dead metaphors." Only in rare cases, words, mostly complex words, may preserve a metaphorical character. Young languages, still in the problematic process of development, expressing the searching function of language, are richer in metaphors. So the German words *klangfarbe* ("color of tone" or timbre) and *farbton* ("tone of color" or tint) express a problem, the unification of two sensuous spheres; eye and ear are under-

---

[12] Legs of a table, foot of a mountain, head of a bridge, bottleneck, tongue of scales, etc. But this superficial analogy should not be confused with the endeavor to link spiritual inner experiences to bodily material events. If it is not just the lazy attempt to shelve away the new spiritual problem in closing it into familiar bodily reactions, it may very well be the awakening of the truly philosophical soul-body-problem, the insight into the connection of the inner and the outer world which causes these metaphors: So in words like distress, distraction, Angst (tightness used for fear), perverse, decide, comprehend. It is not easy to decide, whether the attempt was made to get rid of a problem by analogy or simile, or whether the opposite urge is at work: to open the mind to a new problem, to express it, and to keep it alive in the tension of a metaphor.

[58]

stood to be branches of one common sense.[13] Two symbols are here brought together, not in a comparison by which the one, as unfamiliar, shall be clarified in its relation to the other as the familiar one. On the contrary, two highly familiar words are brought together in order to question their familiarity and in order to arrive at a problematic insight of a still unknown unity. Very similar are the expressions "high tone" and "low tone" which reveal a profound philosophical problem, the introduction of space into the temporal realm of music, and these metaphorical expressions have, indeed, for a long time been regarded as mere forms of speech, until rather recently our psychologists discovered their truth-value.[14]

It must, however, be granted that it is not so much in the single word but in the process of speech itself, stretching over and beyond single words, in which the metaphorical move towards extension of knowledge is to be found. Only in this process of speech can the metaphorical task be fully achieved, that is, to oppose the tendency of the word toward smooth and expedient fixation in familiar fences, and to draw it into the disturbing current of a problematic drive. In a way every sentence is metaphorical, conveying to the single word a meaning beyond its dictionary sense. Every word loses in the setting of the sentence something of its "general" character, becomes more concrete; but in doing this it gains another kind of generality, the generality of context, difficult to define, a lawfulness which is very individual. This seems paradoxical, and it is this paradox which the mere comparison avoids. But in order to avoid it, the comparison simplifies, becomes one-sided

[13] Compare Shakespeare's graceful words: "To hear with eyes belongs to love's fine wit." (Sonnet 23)

[14] It may not be a mere accident that the above mentioned metaphors belong to the sphere of artistic insight, art being one of the outstanding realms of metaphorical knowledge. (See chapters 6 and 7.)

and unfair to the concrete object. It loses too much and
gains too little. Therefore we do not compare where we are
vitally concerned, that is where we love.[15] The metaphorical
process of speech does not enhance the kind of generality
which is systematic, i.e. which is an addition of parts to a
whole. It is the unique generality of the intentional process
to which the terms are sacrificed, and it is their mutual
destruction in this process out of which a new and strange
insight arises.[16] This destruction of the fixed symbols has
given the impression that the metaphor was a "sick simile"
or a confusion which psychoanalysis had to explain. What
was here misunderstood, was the fact that a unique necessity of intention more than of systematic fixation was
achieved by destroying the familiar distinctions of the
single words. In blasting the symbols and shattering their
customary meaning the dynamic process of the searching,
striving, penetrating mind takes the lead and restores the
truth of its predominant importance. It is what Aristotle
aims at when he calls the metaphor energy.[17] The charac-
terization of the metaphor as energy is excellent and more
correct by far than Wundt's "Gesamt-vorstellung," a word
with which he wants to pass beyond the mere togetherness
of symbols in a comparison. So he speaks of "disparate
parts mixed" in the metaphor.[18] But "mixture" is not the
adequate expression. It is energy-tension, and here we have
the same rationalistic interpretation of tension or force
by substituting for it a mere addition, mixture of parts,

[15] A course in comparative religion or art is very informative, but it
does not always contribute to the deeper understanding of these realms.

[16] These metaphors of speech have always been regarded as highly
confusing, so Shakespeare's words: "take arms against a sea of
troubles"; or Elizabeth Browning's: "Sweeping up the ship with my
despair threw us out as a pasture to the stars." Here is neither a
simile nor a clear image of an allegory to rest on.

[17] Aristotle, *Rhetoric*, 1412a.

[18] Wundt, *Voelker-psychologie; Die Sprache*, II, 600.

as we find it in the old Greek philosophy where "mixture" was the usual weak explanation for a lawful and necessary unity; we find this in Anaximander, Anaxagoras, Empedocles, and even still in Plato's *Philebus*, although here as a mixture of a certain order.[19]

Metaphor is a process of tension and energy, manifested in the process of language, not in the single word. But there is a good reason why the metaphor was usually sought in a word, a single term, and not in a multitude of words. It was the right understanding of the truth that the metaphorical realm is a realm beyond quantity, multitude, and togetherness. The metaphorical sphere transcends the many and realizes a simple and indivisible unity, although not the unity of a total and complete object or symbol or word. It is the unity of tension and process. This unity of process may materialize in a single word if this word is in itself complex and expresses the process, as in *klangfarbe* (tone-color); but far oftener it will find expression in the passing from word to word, not as a summing up and addition, but as a function of indivisible unity. Therefore many terms, even many sentences or scenes and acts—as we will later on see with regard to the drama—may belong to the one metaphorical process. But this process is a metaphorical process only when the many are overcome in a unity which is not numerical—neither one nor many—but unique and simple. This unique unity is by no means a "whole," a totality of parts. Parts and whole are equally transcended. No whole is "new"; it is always laid out in the parts, and in knowing the parts one knows the whole. The metaphorical process, however, is different: here the known symbols in their relation to each other are only material; they undergo a complete change in losing their familiar meaning in each other and give birth to an entirely new

[19] Plato, *Philebus*, 27ff. Also Locke's "mixed modes" belong here.

knowledge beyond their fixed and addible multitude. Creation, judged from the level of fixed symbols, arises out of destruction, out of a seeming conflict and out of a loss of familiarity. And only in this way the "new" can come to life. "Creatio ex nihilo" means just this: that the parts are transformed to a "nothing" with regard to that which has become life. The living creation is born out of destruction of the old, it is not a summing-up of the old parts but their entire absorption in the creation. A creation is, therefore, "new" and "unique" not in comparison only to other objects, but with regard to its own parts or composition which have disappeared by giving way to the unconditioned simplicity of the absolute.

Life, energy, spontaneity is, therefore, indeed beyond symbols and their familiar relation. But it is wrong to seek this life by eliminating all symbols and by plunging into the darkness of nothingness, as some mystics have tried to do. The simple is not the exclusion of the complex, it is the overcoming of complexity. It is never a thing but a process, it is in need of the fixed images as well as of the fixed symbols. Only in transcending symbolic fixation can the energetic process, the substantial function, the subject as a fundamental drive, be realized.

Personification has been regarded by many scholars as the essential element of metaphorical thinking. Jean Paul[20] makes this his main point, and he is right. It would, however, be a very superficial view—we rejected it before—if we are to take as a personification the mere symbolization of an object by parts of the human body. The body and its parts are not the "person."[21] Person, again, is a process, not a thing. Personification, therefore, draws objects into

[20] Jean Paul, *Vorschule der Aesthetik*, §50.
[21] On body see p. 83.

the drive of the process. No description of things can ever be a personification, nor any comparison of an object to another one. All this leaves us in the realm of things, however vivid and colorful the description or comparison may be. Only when the objects lose their independent character and turn into aspects of an indivisible process is personification in the making.

Personification will need objects for its realization, and here it is rather unimportant what kind of objects they are. Too great an emphasis on the object is detrimental: A young girl shown as a fountain in the woods may be an allegory, and when painted as a picture very boring, but this is no personification in a metaphorical sense. The mythological process of transformation as such, described in poetry and folklore, may result in a dynamic metaphorical movement in which the fountain as well as the female are only moments of transition, revealing a creative power. When the storm-wind is shown as a man with blown-up cheeks, as in some allegorical Renaissance pictures, this may satisfy the fashion of the day, but it again does not personify anything. But when the rebellion of the elements is shown, maybe without a human body but as a powerful process, then Nature as a creative force may well appear personified.

The word personification is misleading, when it is associated with the human body. It should not even remind us of anything specifically human at all. If we cling to the human sphere, we begin to think in psychological terms, and then it is only a small step further to identify the metaphorical process with the subjective process which this or that individual undergoes in a certain mood because of a certain temperament. The same psychological misunderstanding has caused people to criticize Kant's aesthetics as a merely subjective approach, and Kant's way of expressing himself has indeed given some incentive to this interpretation. But when Kant emphasizes that the Sublime is not in the object itself, not a quality of the roaring sea, the waves, the clouds, but is, on the contrary, a conflicting movement in the spectator, then he expresses a metaphysical truth; but he does it unfortunately in a psychological form and seems to shift the meaning of Art into subjectivity. What he really is after, however, is the discovery of a new level, a new objectivity, the objectivity of the creative process. The Sublime is objective, it is real, whether Smith or Miller experience it or not; but it cannot be reduced to a mere quality of a fixed object.

Therefore it is also a psychological reduction, to place the essence of the metaphorical process in emotion and feeling.[22] Feeling is to be found in every thought. The metaphorical process is not extraordinary in this regard. What makes people think that metaphors arouse a special feeling is the fact that the conflict in many metaphors may be accompanied by vehement feelings. But the metaphorical process is not always vehement, not in those unconspicuous metaphorical terms which we call verbs. The verb as such is the expression of a process and, to this extent, metaphorical. The verbal metaphors have even the advantage of not petrifying into dead symbols, because the conflicting elements which may be involved are so amalgamated and integrated that an abstraction and reduction by omitting some in favor of others was impossible. The petrifying of language here had to go a different way: it had to drop the verb as such and replace it by a noun, and this indeed is the development which young languages undergo in aging. Languages, grown old, are poor in verbs, but rich in fixed static nouns. Whether historically the verb is the cradle of language, because it carries the process of speech,

22 On feeling and emotion see p. 132ff.

may be questionable. In some Negro languages verbs seem
to appear late and to develop out of the metaphorical
union of fixed symbols. On the other hand we have early
languages which express differences not of things but of
actions and processes first, and only later dissolve these
expressions of processes into nouns and adverbs.[23] The
most fundamental and problematic expressions of our languages, however, have usually the form of verbs and remain verbs, even after they have been superficially transformed into nouns, for instance: l'être, das Sein, being, das
Wesen, das Werden, becoming, das Leben, etc. The form
of the noun only disguises the metaphorical character of
process. The "infinitive" of the verb—être, sein, leben—expresses the problem involved better than any fixed symbol
could. When the Bible names God, the "fountain of life,"
or when Nicolaus Cusanus calls Him, the infinite "posse,"[24]
it is the metaphorical process beyond all symbolic fixation
that is meant.

We mentioned the term "being" as a metaphor. It expresses indeed a metaphorical process, and it does so even
as a merely conceptual "being." The conceptual process
of being, shown in the empty little copula "is," as it connects the terms of a proposition, has been placed by some
philosophers together with the concrete being of existence.
This is by no means a mere confusion. It may become a
confusion when from conceptual being inferences are drawn
with regard to existential being, as it has been done in the
ontological proofs of the existence of God. Conceptual
being manifests itself only in hypothetical entities, and
these hypothetical entities, taken apart, can never be the
foundation of an absolute existence. But the ground of

[23] Westermann, *Ewe-Grammatik*, 95, and *Sudansprachen*, 48ff.
[24] Psalms 36, 9 and Cusanus, *De apice Theoriae* 1463.

all hypothetical fixations is not itself hypothetical and relative. Hegel[25] was right to bring conceptual being into a dialectic relation, into "speculative identity" to concrete reality. Our languages are, therefore, not altogether wrong in using the same word "being" for both metaphorical processes. And the possibility of applying our conceptual thought to the world of existence may have its ground in the unity of the two metaphorical processes of being.[26]

The conceptual "being," as expressed in the inconspicuous copula, is not a mere sign of addition; it expresses unity and so it represents the function of the proposition, the process of its development.[27] It is not itself the *subjectum*, the ground and substance of the varying predicates and relations. If we detach this "being" and abstract it from the process, then we make it a mere empty symbol or sign and place it as a fixed entity at the side of the two other propositional terms. But if we regard the copula as representing not itself but the process of the proposition, as it carries from one term to the other and even beyond the single proposition, if we regard it together with its terms, as the expanding drive of these terms, infinite and inexhaustible in its want of predicative statements, then this being as a unifying power stands for the process of truth. Then conceptual being is not itself a concept, but a metaphorical process which gives rise to concepts and makes them disappear in each other for the sake of an expanding knowledge. And then, at last, the creative ground of conceptual understanding is not entirely different from

---

25 Hegel, *Logic*, translated by Wallace, pp. 329, 331.

26 On this unity as the process of consciousness see p. 73ff.

27 Compare Peirce, *Collected Papers*, III, 277: "Neither the predicate nor the subject or both together can make an assertion. The assertion represents a compulsion which . . . continues and is a permanent conditional force, a law. . . . The sign which signifies the law is the copula of the assertion."

the equally creative ground of existential being in which images and symbols arise and pass away in an infinite series of changes.

As thought presupposes this ground of being, so perception presupposes the process of concrete existence. Our perception is not less a selective reduction into symbols than thought is. Not "impressions," not sense-data, are selected, however, but objects, wholes; and these objects as wholes are merely provisional because they are reduced from the inexhaustible substantial ground of existence which carries them and integrates the one into the other. Causality[28] is the metaphorical process of substance which gives rise to the symbolic articulation of existence and at the same time extinguishes it. The single things exist only in this process of causality; and causality is metaphorical because it appears as the unification of disparate entities.

"Existence" is a process; "being" is a process. The distinction between "dynamic" and "static" is lost in the paradoxical unity of the infinite process. Is existence movement? Is it rest? Existence reveals the metaphorical truth that Being is Becoming; that movement has its necessity only in a resting tension of force. This paradoxical unity of Becoming and Being, of movement and rest is the Heraclitean Logos, and it is Life.

Movement is not detached from rest, and rest should not be regarded as merely that out of which movement starts and into which movement vanishes; neither should rest be conceived as a "Grenzbegriff" (limiting concept) in infinity, as Leibniz did, when he called rest an infinitely small movement. Rest and infinity are not limiting concepts, to be striven and sought for: they underlie all movement as force and conservation of force, carrying and transcending movement. Science may investigate a limited move-

[28] On causality see p. 22ff.

ment, abstracted from its infinite ground; but life is the indivisible unity of rest and movement, of Being and Becoming. It is the infinite tension of the metaphorical process itself.

The Aristotelian concept of the "unmoved mover" may be understood as an endeavor to express the unity of rest and movement as the problem of existence.[29] And here in this unity which is God and the principle of Nature, Aristotle indeed touches on the problem of force. Force is that element which is not itself movement and therefore not drawn into the changes of the moving process but nevertheless is the principle of movement, underlying all change as the remaining and in so far "resting" ground, indivisible and without magnitude. He calls it life, intellect, and will.[30]

As will, intellect, or life, this process of existence can, indeed, be regarded as "resting" in itself, while the phases of this process, as considered and reflected upon, are changing in their relation to each other. What we call rest in the sphere of reflection is only a phase in the changing movement of the searching mind and is not lasting. The symbolic reduction is here resting in a fixed relation of comparison but is transitional and conditioned, and called a "whole" only as long as the mind rests in it. But, at the same time, it is merely a part beside other parts and therefore moving on, taking different meanings in the relations in which it becomes involved. Every whole, therefore, *seems* only to be resting while it, in fact, is related to other wholes, and this changing and moving world comes truly to rest only in the process which transcends all parts, wholes, relations, and changes.[31] "Cause" is such a seeming rest,

[29] Aristotle, *Metaphysics*, book XII and *Physics*, book VIII.
[30] Aristotle, *Metaphysics*, 1072b 29, 1075a 11 and 1072a 26ff.
[31] The "resting" character of the whole may be regarded as an image

a whole, but it changes into a part which together with its effect forms another whole. And whether cause is added to effect as equal to equal, or whether, in a semi-truthful compromise it stretches as a larger whole over its effects, a universal and lawful whole, it always remains only a hypothetical and limited whole.

"Wholeness" or "perfection," therefore, is limited to things, to objects which are whole or perfect only in their relation to other things, but are altogether transcended by the metaphorical tension of the process which is resting because it is the principle of conservation, energy, and existence.

---

of the "infinite rest" of the process, a kind of analogy to it. But all these expressions are not more than vague similes. There is no analogy between the finite and the infinite, between a "whole" and that which is never a whole: the process.

5

METAPHOR AND MYTH

THE problem of existence is the theme of mythology. Myth is troubled by existence, and it states this problem in the crucial concept of the "World." "World" stands out as the great secret of existence and its source of wonder. It is a mythical concept—or better, it is not a concept at all; it is a metaphorical process, it is the existential process as such. All the famous problems of philosophy which are connected with the concept "World," with the "object" World, have grown out of the confusion of symbolic reduction and metaphorical expansion. Is the world finite or infinite? Has the world been created in time and will it vanish in time? Or is the World eternal, and what does eternity mean?

Our symbolic reductions do not know "world." If we had only the capacity for forming symbols, we could not know about "world," we would not live in a world. We would only know of that systematically related sum of symbols which we call environment. Every science as well as the common sense of daily life realizes an environment around us. And environments are symbolic reductions of expediency. Whether we adapt ourselves to the environment as the plant does, which can take only what environment offers; whether we seek our own environment according to our needs, as animals and nomads do, or whether we show the astonishing capacity of shaping the environment according to our purposes and so of modifying it, a capacity which has caused the settling down of mankind in fixed places and the dawn of civilization; all this is still only environment, only a system of purposely selected and reduced means of expediency. The baby has its environment of eatable things, the physicist of measurable things—each individual, as long as it is a finite purposive Ego, a symbolic Ego, stands in relation to an environment, and is just as relative as its environment is. Ego and environment have meaning only with regard to each other and only for the sake of a purpose to be fulfilled. Taken apart, they are nothing. The "world-system" of Newton not less than that of Einstein is not really a world-system, but only a system of a finite, reduced environment, although extraordinarily wide-framed; its reduced concepts of time and space belong to a finite and restricted system of symbolic reduction. Time and space of the "world," world-time and world-space, are not touched by these constructions of an ingenious but conventional expediency. Important and useful as they may be, they are neither true nor false in a philosophical sense. The philosopher—and everybody is in a way a philosopher—tries to live beyond the environment in a world.

World is not a system, but a process, not an object but a function, and this was what Kant discovered when he declared world-time and world-space as functional. World is not an "All," not a totality which could never be anything more but a purposively restricted sum. The Kantian cosmological antinomies have their source in the confusion between totality and process.[1] World as a metaphorical process transcends all totalities, sums, systems, environments—or whatever the symbolic reductions or relational togetherness may be called. World is absolute and infinite, and only the metaphorical process is absolute and infinite. It can, however, only be absolute and infinite in transcending the finite symbols, not in eliminating or denying them. This world-process, driving beyond symbolic systemati-

[1] On these antinomies see p. 39.

zation, acknowledging the fixed symbols and transcending them, is what mythology calls creation.

Mythology begins with the myth of creation, and that which is created is "world." World is not "made." Symbolic systems are made, constructed. Environment is made, but world is created; creation means the paradoxical overcoming and therefore the destruction of the merely relative togetherness of symbols. Who identifies symbol and metaphor makes it impossible to understand the act of creation which is at the same time destruction and birth, a birth which grows out of destruction, a being which needs the naught and transcends it: "creatio ex nihilo" is the medieval formula of the metaphorical process, and in vain the scholastic rationalism of St. Thomas tried to explain it away: for him "nihil" means that there is no logical condition for creation.[2] But on the contrary, there is always a logical, a symbolic condition for creation, but creation turns it into naught in transcending it.[3] In the light of creation the symbolic togetherness of things develops into naught and disappears in the unity of an infinite process.

The naught of creation stands for the totality of relative symbols; it is the naught of matter, and matter was, indeed, regarded as nothingness in the thought of many great philosophers. Matter is not omitted in the process of creation, but is a necessary element. Yet it is this only when transcended, when overcome. To "overcome" is the command which religion asks. But that which shall be overcome is not "world," it is that which in the process of world-creation seems to resist and, as an element of destruction, has itself to be destroyed, although it is essential to creation. Detached and isolated it appears as accident or evil.[4]

2 St. Thomas, *Summa theologia,* I qu. 45a.   3 See p. 62.
4 See on evil p. 94ff.

What is it that overcomes matter? We may call it "form." But already Aristotle saw that the old distinction of form and matter does not suffice in its static isolation. So he added the "external causes" (1070b 23), the efficient and the final cause which, as energy, are essential to the existence of living nature. Life takes the lead and assumes the role of being, becoming and existence. In this process of life it is consciousness which may be regarded as the core of being.[5] Consciousness is real, is being; it may be potential being, but even as potential it is in a process of realization in which no distinction can be made between that which is but could also not be (matter or mere possibility) and that which essentially and necessarily is (form). In this process of realization the potential carries over and beyond itself into an actuality with which it has continuously been united, but through which it, nevertheless, does not ever lose entirely its potential character. We were in the course of this work repeatedly confronted with the contrast of necessity and contingency, and we wrestled with the enigmatic problem of freedom, akin to both necessity and contingency.[6] Here, in the realm of life and consciousness these difficulties dissolve. Potentiality, as the category of life and consciousness, is never merely contingent, as the possibility of things is, but is "free," that is it has only when isolated the character of contingency, but assumes necessity in the process in which it is involved. In

---

[5] Reflection may separate "consciousness" from its object and call only this object of consciousness "being." But then reflection is forced to regard consciousness, detached from "objective being," as non-being, as mere contingency, subjectivity and error. But although this has been done, the varying and changing objects of consciousness should rather than consciousness itself be regarded as "non-being," because they, as merely possible, may possibly be *not*. Life and consciousness, however, are never only possible, but potential.

[6] See pp. 24ff. and 49ff.

this process the necessary meaning lies permanently ahead of the potential consciousness as its direction and future. This meaning appears, therefore, as revealed. But this "revelation" does not originate in a realm foreign to the entity to which it is addressed and does not reach backward from a future, totally detached from the present. The future, although in the course of developing, is somehow already there; it is present, as future can only be understood on the ground of a present which anticipates the future and, in anticipating, carries over into it. The potential realizes an actuality which, in spite of being not yet, nevertheless somehow *is* already.[7] This, indeed, is the secret of life and consciousness that the potential is in a mysterious tension and unity with a never-ceasing actuality; that the communion of present and future is a consciousness which always is present, but always has to realize itself in a future. This inner articulation of the actual and potential, of present and future, is an awareness, not of a detached object but of its own direction and development.

The attempt to describe this awareness by any dualism of relationship is doomed to fail. Even the distinction between "potential" and "actual" is not wholly satisfactory because it can easily be misunderstood as a mere relationship. In order to express the unique character of articu-

[7] See on the problem of actuality and potentiality Aristotle, *Metaphysics*, 1019a, 1049b f. and 1051a.———The Aristotelian discovery of the problem of life and consciousness as a striving toward a future which is already somehow present, was foreshadowed in the ingenious Platonic problem of the question which contains somehow already the answer, and in the problem of love which in its process of longing is already somehow in the possession of the beloved value. (*Menon*, 80; *Lysis*, 218; *Symposion*, 200-203).———In some of his writings Aristotle, however, drops the potential out of consciousness and life, changing the metaphorical and problematic unity of the potential and actual into "complete actuality." (*Metaphysics*, 1048b 23ff.; 1050b 1ff.)

lation which only life possesses, other words should be used, words which, taken from life itself, convey the transcending movement forward from life to a beyond of a fuller life, linked in continuity to this its own future, but at the same time held in the distance which makes awareness possible. Wherever life becomes conscious of its creativity, it is faced by a living entity, the "Thou," and this Thou is to the I a revelation of its own meaning and future. It is always a Thou, and only a Thou, as an expression of life which carries the I forward and makes it aware of its destiny. Not self-consciousness, but consciousness of the Thou is fundamental to life. The I, to be sure, remains the potential, but a potential for the Thou which reveals and expresses the I in its movement upward and beyond. In the process of life, expression means always communication with a Thou which is never fully realized but remains an inexhaustible power, leading on into a meaningful future. This Thou is, if reflected upon, other than the longing and striving I; but it is also that which is in no way other than the I, the "non aliud" of Cusanus,[8] and it is this essentially, because we are here in a realm where consciousness has not an object, not a content detached from itself, but is aware merely of its own drive and destiny. When theology reflects upon this indivisible process of creation then it not only separates the Thou from the I, making them both stand out in distinction, but even gives to the Thou the character of a content, a thing, and calls it the last goal, the "summum bonum." Our religious experience, however, finds a more adequate, although problematic answer: God.

God is the eternal future of life and at the same time its eternal present.[9] The past is foremost reserved for the always surpassed, always deficient and potential I in its

[8] Cusanus, *De Non Aliud* (1462).
[9] See on the present and on eternity, p. 106ff.

limited and fixed status.[10] It is reflection which turns back
to the past and, therefore, to things in their environmental
fixation, to the I as a thing, to the ego in its setting. Kant
was quite right in stating that man can get a reflective
knowledge of his ego only as an object, a fixed, determined
entity, finished off and factual. But what he only partly
acknowledged was that a non-reflective consciousness of
creativity carries our life, never to be closed in the ego
alone, because constantly on the way beyond this ego toward a life of greater scope and richness. We are not per-
mitted to call this fundamental consciousness a "self-consciousness," because it is a process transcending the self,
pushing forward into a Thou. Creativity is not to be found
in the empty circle of self-identity, not in the self-centered
egoism of perfection. But neither is it to be had by stopping short in a merely potential I which then, indeed,
remains, as it did in Kant's system, an empty, if not tragi-
cally empty, X of unification, isolated in the loneliness of
its merely negative infinity.[11] From this I no bridge leads
to any Thou; it became necessary to find the Thou by analogy and thus to construct it by reflection. The Divine
Thou even had now to be understood in terms of a limited
experience, deduced from certain events in our life, instead
of leading creatively into a never-yet-experienced future.[12]

10 Compare Elizabeth Barrett Browning: "As if God's future thun-
dered on my past." (*Sonnets from the Portuguese*, 28.)

11 This lonely and tragic modern Kantian I entered the modern subjective
nihilism of Heidegger and Sartre. A merely potential—and thus
emptied and mutilated—I is, indeed, lost in the world, faces only its
death and can be regarded as "une passion inutile."

12 Maimonides reads this reflective interpretation of the divine
nature into Exodus 33, 20ff.: When God passes before Moses, he
cannot see God's face, but, looking after Him, can only reflect upon
His works; he cannot enter into His process of creation, cannot see
the face turned toward future. (*Guide to the Perplexed*, i, chapter
21.) Reflection, indeed, is a turn backward to the past, an analysis

But the divine life can only be understood as such a future. The Bible rightly calls Him "the living God," "the fountain of life"[13] and makes His prophets emphasize the creative power of future.[14]

Existence is fundamentally consciousness, and as such it carries the twofold aspect of a communion between I and Thou. In this communion it is the I which is wanting and as a free potential has to realize itself in the necessity of the divine Thou. Freedom of the I is not only compatible with the necessity of the divine power, but even presupposes it.[15] In the face of the divine necessity, freedom is not only the capacity to reach upward, but also the mark of deficiency, the source of error and sin. So the movement from the deficient, contingent, and freely potential I toward its divine destiny has again a twofold aspect: it is the awareness of sin and at the same time the confidence in grace, and it is this very deficiency and limitation, this sinful nature which leads toward the Divine, a paradox which can only be stated and understood as an outpouring of grace. Sin and grace in the metaphorical unity of a process of consciousness characterizes that which we call the process of prayer.

According to early Indian philosophy it is the process of consciousness, the praying process which is reality and

---

as well as a summing up of manifold "accidents." Aristotle calls "essence" as the result of reflection, τὸ τί ἦν εἶναι, the being of that which *was*. But all analysis and summing up of reflection presupposes a unifying and substantial power which is never totally given in the analysis, but transcends it and may be found in another Aristotelian concept: the energy or entelechy.

[13] Jeremiah 10, 10 and Psalms 36, 9.

[14] See Isaiah 43, 18, 19: "Remember ye not the former things, neither consider the things of old; behold, I will do a new thing."

[15] See pp. 52, 53.

existence. Brahama means originally prayer, and at the same time World and God. Confession of sin or praise of grace is the eternal theme of those prayers which are put into words. But besides all these prayers which are expressed in words and which have been uttered here and then in space and time there is a fundamental movement of spiritual existence. This fundamental prayer knows no distinction between a praying I and the God. It is one unique movement which carries beyond the one into the other. No relation of difference, no quantitative statement does justice to this creative drive which reflection in vain has tried to close into objective entities and their relation to each other. If one begins to introduce number into the communion of I and Thou, then number will indeed also enter the Divine itself, and a multitude of gods will rise out of this reflective interpretation. To be sure, we know of such religious systems, we even distinguish between monotheism and polytheism. But here the question arises, whether these differences reach down into the depth of the religious myth, or whether they are merely concerned with dogma and ritual. We shall have to investigate later the problems involved in dogma and ritual.[16] Here it may be sufficient to state that wherever a god is worshiped, and this holds true also in polytheistic rites, he is unique and is in the praying act of his believers an only god. In the hymns of early religions the god to whom the hymn is devoted takes and receives all the devotional resources which live in the heart of the believer.[17] In these hymns God may be called by innumerable names, so different in character that he seems to be split into a multitude of persons, but this superabundance of names again is merely a metaphorical way of transcending the single and fixed attribute

[16] See on dogma and ritual p. 93. [17] Heiler, *Gebet*, p. 171.

by uniting it with others and always others in a process
of mutual interconnection which resembles more a mutual
negation: it is the conflict and integration of conflicting
images and symbols which expresses the transcendence of
the Divine. Neither addition nor comparison nor analogy
makes the praying man amass the most contradicting attributes and names: it is the endeavor to transcend any
single name and so to enter into a sphere beyond symbols
and words. The living God of the Bible forbids the fixation
in images and names: but just because of that the faithful
could describe the divine anonymity in an infinite process
of dissimilar and contradicting expressions. God is Father
and Bridegroom, Lord and Judge, He is Life and eternal
Stability. A god who is fixed into a symbol or image is an
idol. But the abundance of contradicting names keeps the
divine process alive and expresses the metaphorical anonymity. St. Thomas, therefore, was wrong when he explained God's attributes as analogies, God's wisdom and
goodness as similar to that of men, although a wisdom
and goodness of a different proportion. Master Eckhart
came far nearer to the religious spirit, when he declared
that if God was wise, he himself was wiser; if God was good,
he himself was better;[18] because wisdom and goodness,
when attributed to God, were either meaningless or stood
for an unknown power, for an anonymity which could only
be expressed by a paradoxical negation. Behind all divine
attributes appears their negation, and this negation, or
better this process of transcendence, was already expressed
by Philo when he stressed the infinite Beyond as the truth
in all religious symbols and attributes.[19]

18 Meister Eckhart, trans. by Evans, p. 246.
19 Philo, *De Mundi Opificio*, 2, 8. Whether the abundance of names
serves a metaphorical transcendence, or whether it is merely the
summing up of supplementing qualities, is not always easy to decide:

The superabundance of divine names has its parallel in the superabundance of occurrences and situations which are expressed and described in the stories called myths. They indulge in concrete products of imagination in order to rise beyond imagination. As the proverb selected familiar and limited experiences in order to break their familiarity and limitation and to point beyond them to a truth of a metaphorical character,[20] so the myths are abundant in concrete and detailed happenings which seem to cancel each other and open our eyes to a new realm of meaning, unfamiliar and deeply disturbing. The "miraculous," as it appears in these myths, is not a breach of law—of a law which is familiar and holy only to our modern mind—but, on the contrary, it is the establishment of a higher lawful necessity, rising above the unstable appearance of daily routine, and giving a new and mysterious meaning to the things and events of this world.

God is unique in the prayer of man, and man is unique in his seeking God. Uniqueness has nothing to do with quantitative relations. "Unique" does not mean "one." All numbers are relative, but the unique is absolute and incomparable. Only the process is unique, because the process defies relation. There is no relation between God and Man, neither difference nor sameness can express the act of prayer. The mystic has described his experience, now and then, as an identification with God. But in doing this he has reduced the metaphorical process of prayer to a sym-

---

When Egyptians pray to Isis as "father, brother, mother Isis," however, these incompatible qualities can scarcely be added together; or when Australians pray to their god and call him "father, grandfather, uncle, elder brother." (Heiler, *Gebet*, p. 143.) A symbolic idolatry, on the other hand, is obvious in the additive character of divinities with ten heads or breasts.

20 See p. 55f.

bolic relation of identity. It is this identification which
has often been called the very nature of mysticism. But, in
fact, this identification is rather a breaking away from
the dynamic and truly mystical process of prayer. It is
a rational endeavor to transform the metaphorical tension
of prayer, which is neither identity nor difference, into
absolute and pure identity. The result of this rational
transformation, therefore, had to be the hypostasis of a
purely abstract concept of reason: "absolute being,"
"essence," "reality" (Plato), "oneness" (Upanishad),
"order" (Lao-tse). India, China, and the rationalism of
Greece are responsible for this transformation of religion
into reason. To be sure, wherever this happened the process of life had somehow to be included into the deification
of a rational concept. In one way or another some kind
of living and loving aspiration was preserved. (Plotinus,
Bhakti, Sufism.) Often a return from pure abstraction to
a living process became necessary (Master Eckhart's
mysticism of birth and will).[21] A wholly rational mysticism
would, indeed, replace life and prayer entirely by an "intuition" of identity between God and man, transforming

[21] St. Augustine expresses this return from "empty" abstraction
to life and love: "We make ourselves empty and see, we see and love,
we love and praise." What Augustine calls here "seeing" is the intuition which is the form of knowledge adequate to the relation of
identity. Intuition has its field wherever the immediacy of an identical
approach is sought for, so in the realm of pure abstraction as well as
in the realm of sensuous factuality. (Aristotle, *Nicomachean Ethics*,
1143a 35ff. and Foss, *The Idea of Perfection in the Western World*,
p. 38.) Here we are faced once more with the astonishing fact that
the extremes of rationalism and sensationalism meet. Intuition, therefore, as a mystical knowledge, appears just as often in the form of
rational and abstract asceticism as in the form of emotional, ecstatic
orgy. In both cases process and consciousness disappear. But in true
prayer no intuition of abstract being or of ecstatic unconsciousness
can substitute for that tension of consciousness between I and Thou
which, as nearness and distance, is known by the name of love.

both into static entities of comparison. The praying man, however, lives the process of transcendence in which there is no one or two, but the incomparable uniqueness of its act.

The uniqueness and indivisibility of the praying process refutes identity as it refutes difference, but it proceeds in the tension which we called "articulation" and which makes consciousness possible in spite of the indivisible character of the process. The praying process reaches upward toward its expression, clarification, and revelation, and in this his striving the praying man is conscious of his mere potentiality. He is conscious, therefore, of a deficiency which keeps him continuously on his way. In keeping him on his way, however, this deficiency becomes the means for his realizations, the revelation of a firm direction. In his awareness of sin and deficiency the praying man receives the blessing of grace. And it is only in the presence of grace that man knows himself as sinner.

The tension of sin and grace, their unity and correlation, repeats the enigmatic union of man and God, and has been since time immemorial the essential character of prayer. This tension is exemplified in the drama of conversion, experienced by prophets and saints, when awareness of sin and despair revolves into an exultant confidence in the divine blessing. This drama of conversion is not only the initiating experience of the prophet, it remains the ground of his whole existence, to which he turns back again and again and out of which he nourishes his faith: for this drama of conversion is essentially beyond time, it is the drama of consciousness as such and plays, as we may say, in eternity rather than in time. But in eternity the praying man carries with him his deficiency as well as his blessing. He can never free himself of his limitation which chains him to the world of objects and mere possibilities. It is his body which makes him a part of the things around him, and "body" indeed has been regarded by religious philosophers as the symbol of sin and the skandalon of human nature. Plato curses the body as the prison of the soul from which only death releases. But the problem of the body is far more complex: it is not only a prison, not merely a hindrance on the way to salvation, it is also the bridge toward blessedness. For only the awareness of our deficiency opens the way to a life of grace.

Therefore the body is not so much an obstacle to life, but an instrument to life, or, as Aristotle rightly put it, a potential for the soul. Only those who have a body, have life and can aspire toward soul or spirit. But, indeed, life and soul are more than the body and its functions. Soul transcends body and makes one even forget the body. It is the meaning of the body to be transcended and forgotten in the life for which it serves. It is the most essential characteristic of the body that it disappears as an independent thing the more it fulfills its service, and that we get aware of the body as such only if something is wrong, if some part does not serve, that is in sickness or tiredness. To cope with sickness makes it necessary to investigate the body as a thing, as this is the necessary task of the scientist. But, on the other hand, to transform the world of mere lifeless things into living bodies, into entities which point beyond themselves toward the process of a unique life, is the equally necessary and noble task of the artist for whom only life counts and whose imagination changes mere things into bodies which become the expression of a dynamic spiritual process.[22] Also the philosopher feels the urge to submerge the manifoldness of lifeless things and their merely symbolic fixation into the simplicity of a life

[22] It is this intensification of mere things to living bodies which is the meaning of still life.

process. He will imbue these things with a world-soul, as the Greek did, or he will speak of the universe as a body, of the "face of the universe," as Spinoza did, and as mythology repeatedly has done.[23]

But more than artist and philosopher it will be the religious man, the saint, who will lift things into the life process and transform them into expressions of a divine grace. When St. Francis calls sun, moon, stars, birds, and trees his brothers and sisters, he carries them beyond their abstract and objective thingness into a living and creative activity driving toward God. He draws them into a process of prayer and makes them part of a universal aspiration for grace. In doing this the saint widens his I, the praying power, so that it embraces the manifoldness of bodies and carries them up to God. Indivisible as the praying movement is, it integrates and unifies life in the face of grace. The praying man stands for all life, he takes all existence into the act of his prayer, he prays for this concentrated union of ever-changing and ever-limited possibilities. But in this way his prayer works not only as an offering and confession of deficiency, but also as an act of overcoming, as a process of growth beyond deficiency. Every prayer is a confession of sin and a purification. And every prayer is an intercession. Intercession is the widening power of personality which stretches beyond the mere I and embraces a world. In the unique process of metaphorical transcendence the praying man is anonymous and prays for the unity of the people of whom he is only an insignificant representative. The symbolic reduction of prayer to a mere ego and

[23] In a certain sense we can regard our modern technique as an endeavor to stretch the instrument of our body throughout the universe; but unfortunately it was not the creative process of the spirit which imbued this ponderous body with life. It became a dead body which did not transcend and express anything beyond.

to the purpose of a finite egoistic fulfillment is a misunderstanding of metaphorical transcendence, just as it is a misunderstanding to reduce God to the "summum bonum," to the object of a finite human purpose. The myth of the praying man who takes upon him the sins of the people and in doing so brings grace, blessedness, and purification to mankind, is a profound expression of the true meaning of prayer as a process of taking the world to heart and transcending it. "People," like "world," are a mythological unity of life, an extension beyond the empirical total quantity of men. People as a living unity come to existence in the metaphorical process by which every one of them grows beyond his ego, expands into the life of others and carries this concentrated and enlarged life towards the judging and redeeming power of God. It is an act of representation, in which man stands for more than his finite existence.

Here we touch on the most crucial problem of the metaphorical sphere: the problem of metaphorical representation, which has often been confused with the very different "symbolic representation." This problem is decisive for the understanding of the following chapters and, therefore, leads here to a more elaborate treatment. The praying man, the man who seeks God, represents the people. The idea of the "People," wherever it comes to life in the history of mankind, is a mythical or religious idea. It was a rationalistic misunderstanding that made the people a product of convention, addition, comparison, or agreement. The greatest political thinkers have understood that the people are united by a responsibility which goes beyond the comfort of the many and which finds expression in the idea of representation. But not just a few represent the many: every one is a representative and, as such, responsible for that greater unity which we call the people. A democratic brotherhood of a high and inalienable responsibility should have been the result of this philosophical insight. Every person, transcending his purposive, reduced, and merely symbolic ego, is a concentrated, purified, and widened unity of life. He is not less, but more than the single men and their aggregate. He is not just a part, but even more than the whole.

This is, however, not so in the sphere of "symbolic representation." Here the representative is a part and signifies only the whole. He is a quantitative part of the sum, but he behaves as if he were the totality. In this way an employee of a shareholder corporation, being a little part of the organization, acts as if he were the organization; the parliamentarian acts as if he were the sum of his constituents. What gives him the right to act, is that he has been selected for this purpose, usually by a more or less arbitrary mechanism, and he has been selected for expediency's sake, to fit in a certain place. The political representation, as it has historically developed, from early Greek times, grew often out of a mere chance-reduction of number brought about by lot. And our political system, born out of the rationalism of the seventeenth century, has adopted much of the practical tendency to reduce quantity and to let the part stand for the whole. "Pars pro toto," this is the expedient simplification in a world in which men have been symbolically reduced to numbers. The representing entity is not weighed but counted. As each one stands for a number, the greater number decides: majority becomes the principle of representation. The element of contingency which is in all symbolic reductions has vitiated also the majority rule, but its practical value has made it unassailable in the political field. Responsibility, the life and soul of all representation, is weakened in this numerical world. The representative is only a number or a part, a mouthpiece, a tool; he reduces his task, as he himself is only a reduced life of bureaucratism. He waits for orders and he blames those who gave the orders when they turn out to be wrong. He is an "executive" and that is all.

The metaphorical representative, however, is no part and no addition of parts; he is no tool and he has nobody to release him from his responsibility. He is alone, he is unique. If he fails, all is lost. He must feel an unbound responsibility for those for whom he stands. He is guilty for them and takes the blame alone. His life is dangerous, but it is not the danger which threatens his own existence; it is the danger of losing the cause for which he stands. He is more powerful and more humble than the symbolic representative. The latter is very little, a mere instrument, but he is proud to take orders from a bigger whole and to fulfill them. The true representative is unrestricted, his responsibility is his order, but his task surpasses the possibility of fulfillment and leaves him to the humility of an infinite service.

The metaphorical representation is essential for that which we call the mythical realm. Myth as well as mysticism are grounded in the unique process of a metaphorical life with its seeming contradictions, tensions, and its transcendence. The most elevated examples of the metaphorical or mystical representation are to be found in those lives which we call legendary. The legendary personality reaches beyond the short time-stretch of his life into the past and into the future. The "time before" becomes a mere preparation to the legendary time; the "time after" will be imbued and sanctified by the preceding legend. Thus Christ's life stands out and cuts into the course of time: we count even our calendar from His birth and we do so because we think that time and world have started on a new way from His life onward. In a similar way the French Revolution started as a legendary phase, a new era with a new calendar.

It is, however, not only in these exceptional legendary lives that the metaphorical process becomes representative. What we call history is the uninterrupted continuity of a process in which all events, even every fact, are transcended by their metaphorical and representative character. This makes history more than a summing up and collection of facts, but rather a creative drive towards future, grown out of the past. The idea of future makes history. The prophets of the future are, indeed, the true creators of history.

Every history, even when limited to the history of a short period or a single life, a biography, is meaningful only in its transcendence beyond a sum of facts into a process of infinity. "World" as a unique and infinite process is not only the background, but enters into every summary of facts if they shall assume the liveliness and wideness of history. There is, precisely speaking, only "world-history," and where the contact with the world-process is missing, we cannot talk of history but only of a purposively and arbitrarily fixed and limited description of an environment, a collection of facts for a specific end. A history with such a distinct purpose, especially all chauvinistic historiography, is only a means for a useful end; it is propaganda and may be perfect propaganda, but never history in the true sense.

Progress carries history because progress is only another word for metaphorical transcendence. We can understand this transcendence as an idea, an "ideal," living in and through all events of history, never exhausted in them, never satisfied and fulfilled, never even fully explained nor interpreted. This ideal destroys just as much as it creates because it is always beyond any achievement of the time. It may be attached to a model, but never as a slavish imitation because imitation again is only a symbolic reduction of similarity, comparison, and repetition. The ideal will always be transformed by its followers, enriched and developed. When people no longer live the ideal they cease to have a history; they stagnate and settle down in the repetition of an organized scheme. They live from their capital and at last deteriorate in the poverty and emptiness of a mere gesture of life.

The history of the individual, equally, carries on in an infinite and unique process. We live neither a beginning nor an end, neither birth nor death. We cannot even conceive the thought of ever not having been or ever falling into the night of nothingness. Immortality is the ground on which we dispose of, organize, and discipline the small amount of years given to us. No life is truly a life which does not permanently live beyond the disciplined and organized stock of limited time and space, in a "world" beyond, in a spiritual process which unites us with all that was and all that will be.

Reflection has tried, however, to transform this metaphorical transcendence of a mythological dynamism into a symbolic interpretation of parts and wholes. And it cannot be said that this endeavor is totally arbitrary and unjustified. The historian has to reflect, interpret, organize, he has to do all this. But he should, in spite of his reflective attitude, never lose sight of the essential metaphorical representation. If he does, he will transform history into a scientific exemplification of a systematic law, and nothing more. This static law will be the meaning and result of his endeavor, and the historical events will merely serve as material of reference for this law. In a reflective theology even God became the law of things, a total, complete necessity. This is what makes Pantheism unsatisfactory; a total necessity receives here the dignity of absoluteness because it is understood as a totality of relative and contingent facts. As if a totality of contingent facts could ever make a necessity, a totality of relations ever make an absolute.[24] In this pantheistic view the whole assumes a holiness which no part as such could ever convey. And although every whole is again only a part of a greater whole, reflection is forced to arrive at a whole which is absolute because it is an object, never to be surpassed by any greater whole. World becomes in this paradoxical reflection an absolute object, rounded out in a "whole space" and a "whole time."

But these ultimate "wholes" are inconceivable. Especially the concept of a "whole time" has caused the most audacious phantasies. The "fulfillment of time" is the messianic idea of a closure of time, a rounding out and systematic ending of the world process. World assumes an end, and consequently also a beginning. World-birth and world-death are the great events in this symbolized mythology, and only in between these limits of a fixed world-era the metaphorical process is still allowed to go on, weakened to a playful, ever repeated change of form.[25] Change as such, transformation as a meaning in itself, a mystery without a secret, becomes the characteristic of a freely invented, arbitrarily constructed mythology. Closed in the "wheel of time," transformation goes on permanently and repeatedly, now as reincarnation or metempsychosis, now in the still more arbitrary and playful way of fairy-tale magic.

[24] See on totality in contradistinction to absoluteness, Foss: *The Idea of Perfection in the Western World*, p. 34ff.

[25] See above, a similar disruption between a fixed necessity and a fleeting, ever-changing chance-world, p. 24.

The theme of all fairy tales is that anything can change into anything, and so the uniqueness of the world-process is broken down into the small coin of manifold repeated processes, one growing out of the other, swallowing the other, hastening after the other. What is left from the primordial uniqueness is merely the paradoxical frame of the one and only world-time, embracing and closing together all the unstable and vanishing changes. But a world-time, as a total time, is never absolute; it is only exclusive to other times of the same kind, and so one total world-time asks for other total times, one following the other.[26] The world-time repeats itself, therefore, in the form of "phases," repeated in a successive series, as they turn up in mythological reflective narratives. Phases follow phases, each of them an image of the whole world-time, each of them a fulfillment of time, entirely rounded out and self-sufficient, but, nevertheless, all of them forming a coherent series of successive phases which, in their togetherness again, make a truly whole world-time.[27] It is the compromise of closing into totality and of acknowledging, nevertheless, that the totality is only a part in the repeated succession of its kind. This compromise of a systematic mythology is at the bottom also of our common-sense distinctions, when we organize in a somewhat arbitrary way the phase of the past, the phase of the present and the equally closed phase of the future. Or when we round out and close up history symbolically and arbitrarily in the phases of the "ancient era," the "medieval age," and the "modern time." Similar are all the cycle-theories of which the

26 See again, *The Idea of Perfection*, on the difference between "absolute" and "exclusive," p. 22.

27 On phases see also Cassirer, *Philosophie der Symbolischen Formen* II, 138. Cassirer emphasizes the division into phases more than the quality of wholeness and seclusion in every single phase which is equally important.

Spenglerian interpretation of history is only one example and one of the most paradoxical compromises of mythological process and symbolic reduction.[28]

This compromise was dismissed, when reflection came fully into its own and erected a clear and expedient system of symbolic organization. The process of creation and life, however, as a metaphorical process, had now to drop into the background, replaced by the balance of a rational system. It is this that we call the "ritualization" of religion. Here is no compromise. The ritual may still feed on symbolically reduced myths, on fairy tales, legends, and other products of a reflective mythology. Its emphasis, however, is on the rational system, on the organization of objective relations, detached from the underlying process, self-sufficient and independent, a sovereign system of a balanced totality.

Ritual and myth belong together, as symbol and metaphorical process do. They should, however, in spite of their close unity, never be confused with each other. In a certain way they even represent opposite tendencies. What makes us confuse the one with the other is the hybrid concept of representation: the widening representation which concentrates a manifold into a qualitative and responsible simplicity is the expression of the metaphorical process and always unique; we find it in the deeply moving stories of the Bible. But the reducing representation is a repeated, expediently selected system, as a means for a definite purpose. Ritual, pure ritual as well as the compromising mix-

[28] Religious men have felt the fallacy of this view. They have broken out of the symbolic totality in a violent "eschatology." Now the divine life had to be found beyond the "fulfillment of time" in a vague eternity which was connected with time in an inconceivable mystery. Mankind has never for long been satisfied by these hazy eschatologies.

ture of a ritualized myth—a constructed mythology, tending toward dogma[29]—stands so hard against myth that
it even fights against the pure religious process and tries
to subdue it in closing it into its fixed system. In the history of religion the ritual fights constantly for domination
and absorption of the mythological process. Although the
ritual receives all its life from the myth, it nevertheless
attempts to strangle the creative life of the myth and to
enclose it in the reduced and fixed symbols of its typical
repetitions.

Ritual is a reduction as all symbolic transformation is.
The holy process, unique, incomparable, and infinite, is
pressed into a part and worshiped in its fixed, exact, and
repeatable limitation. The limit, the frame, the symbolic
order is holy in itself. All emphasis is concentrated on the
limitation, the demarcation or stereotype formula. Out of
the World a small piece of space is cut out ($\tau\acute{\epsilon}\mu\nu\epsilon\iota\nu$) and
sanctified as "templum,"[30] as a holy place and spatial
circumscription, holy because of its symbolic reduction and
closed totality. Time is cut into days and hours, and by
decree one day or one hour is made a holy day or a holy
hour. The infinite process of prayer, carrying the World
in its metaphorical infinity, is banned to a fixed conventional and limited sum of words, filling a fixed and limited
time in a fixed and limited place, patterned as a typical
service to God. The praying man who carried, in a metaphorical representation, mankind in his prayer towards
God, is now restricted to a specific part of mankind, a
quantitative selection: the priests. And the priest, as a
symbolically reduced part, as an organ and instrument of

[29] See above p. 90. Parts of the constructed myth change easily into
dogmatic rule and are used as a justification for repeated liturgical
methods in the daily ritual of the church.
[30] Cassirer, *Philosophie der Symbolischen Formen* II, 127.

the whole body, has not the unique responsibility, but—selected according to the arbitrary scheme of examination or any other contingent scheme of quantitative reduction—administers only an office which deprives him of his responsibility.

The reduction which is characteristic for all symbolization and therefore for all rituals, leaves the greater part of the world, not closed into the symbol, outside of its emphasis. And so this greater part, left out, becomes unimportant and meaningless; it falls into profaneness and indifference. The temple makes everything outside of its doors appear as profane; the holy hour takes from all other hours their blessedness; the liturgy of the church-service relegates every activity besides it and every approach, not closed into its typical formula, to an inferior and inefficient endeavor. The priest cuts himself off from the rest of the people, who as mere laymen are doomed to ignorance and the danger of missing salvation. This is the great bitterness which necessarily accompanies the symbolic reduction: that the greatest part of world and life is thrown into profaneness and indifference. Even worse, the ritual in its sharp and exact demarcation of the symbolic sphere is inclined to emphasize to the utmost the distinction from anything which does not belong to it. And so it has the tendency of changing difference into opposition. What is not holy, and only the ritual is, is unholy. The holy is good; the unholy is evil. A mere indifference with regard to the non-symbolic sphere does not satisfy the rigorous tendency for clear distinction. The line of demarcation would be too vague and too unimportant. What is not brought under the domination of the ritual, must, therefore, be regarded as evil and devilish.

The devil, as a separate power of evil, is the necessary consequence of the ritual-reduction, and he is amply used to strengthen the spirit of submission to the ritual. It may seem an overstatement that the devil belongs to ritual rather than to the sphere of myth and pure religion. To prove this statement by going through the histories of religion, is difficult. The devil, as an invention of the ritual, is often amalgamated with the mythical element of the "demoniac." A distinction, however, should be made between the demoniac, as a necessary element of destruction in all creation and, therefore, a necessary element in all religions of transcendence, and the devil as an instrument of disturbance, uselessness, and arbitrariness. The demoniac element is sublime, holy, the "mysterium fascinans et terribile" of God; the demoniac fear of God lives in the heart of the praying man as the feeling of awe and accompanies the movements even of profoundest confidence, keeping respect and humility awake. The devil, on the contrary, is never sublime, he is just mean, often even stupid, a poor devil; he is not part of the creative process, but a paltry and shabby rebel, working through chance and disorder. As a rebel he does not really stand against God— how could he—but against ritual and order. He personifies the unholy, evil sphere of the world, pushing from outside against the wall of ritual, gnawing at it and undermining it cunningly. The devil as well as the Evil are not so much religious problems, as problems of ritual; and they have occupied an extremely wide space in ritual-discussions, sometimes more so than God. This is understandable: God and the mythical life are more or less absorbed by the ritual, more or less substituted by the system of symbolic rules, by the extraordinarily intelligent network of laws. And it is this system of rules which the community adores, the priest administers, and the temple serves. God himself disappears into the background, while the clear and distinct formula of the ritual satisfies the want for certainty and security of the average man.[31] But the devil remains important for the average man: the devil is everywhere, where the ritual is not. He works in the darkness outside of the lighted realm of the ritual, he works secretly in the heart of weak men, he works against obedience to the ritual, and so the administrators of the ritual—the churches—have to protect their followers against him. For the average man, therefore, protection against the devil is at least as vital as the search for God, and the importance of the devil grows at the expense of the importance of God in the service of the ritual, increasing the fear and driving all folks under the sheltering roof of a powerful church. It may even happen that the devil appears as the only dynamic power, after religious dynamism has become fixed in institutional rigidity. Under such circumstances the devil as the last residue of a dynamic religious life may become a terrific danger to the stabilized and somehow petrified system, and protection against this danger may be forced into hectic, unbalanced, and inhuman practices, devilish themselves, as it happened, indeed, in the times of the inquisition.

Wars and persecution, inquisition and murder were committed, not for the sake of religion, not in order to strengthen the process of prayer, but for the victory and power of the symbolic ritual. Again and again those symbols were confused with religion itself, and so millions of men went to their death in the illusion that they died for the purity of religion, while actually they were sacrificed for the accidental form of a symbolic system. Never could the pure religion of prayer have turned to hatred and extermination: The praying man knows himself as a repre-

[31] The proofs for the existence of God are a symptom for this shift of the Divine position into dependency: God has to justify his existence before the tribunal of a symbolical system, he has to take his place in the clear, distinct and exact totality of conceptual relations.

sentative of the people, united with them in failure, carrying their burden; he could not hate anyone, because he alone is responsible and he alone has to answer for the deeds which are done.[32] But the ritual, on the contrary, takes away the responsibility, piles all sin on the devil or those who are possessed by the devil, and so, in clearing its followers from blame and making them righteous, awakens pride and with it cruelty and hatred of persecution which is a characteristic of the Pharisee and his judgment over the heretic. The symbolic heaping of sin on the scapegoat elucidates, as a primitive ritual, this tendency of the average man, weak as he is, to free himself from his own responsibility and to creep under the protecting shelter of an artificial rite.

Here we have to ask again: Is it justifiable to hypostatize the symbolic sphere? Or have we not to discriminate carefully between the symbolic organization, which is necessary but restricted, and a process which should never be absorbed by the symbolic reduction but should be allowed to carry on, go beyond the symbolic fixation and so preserve understanding and development? Surely it would be foolish to side exclusively with the one and to ask for the elimination of the other: in doing this one would again only adopt the rigid one-sidedness of the ritual, dividing into black and white, holy and devilish. What we defend throughout this work and what we want to confirm here again is the fact that symbol and ritual are indispensable elements, but that they have to be carried by a process, wider than they and powerful enough to transform them. The ritual is a fixation and reduction which has again and again to be thrown out of its narrow boundaries. Therefore prophets had to rise against rituals, saints had to stand up against

[32] See pp. 84, 87.

them, and although persecuted and burnt by the defenders of the ritual, they managed to transform and reform and partly abolish symbols which hindered the creative process of religion. Christ, Paul, the founders of the religious orders and medieval sects, Luther and other prophets of all times went this way: None of them condemned the ritual as such, but every one of them felt that ritual and symbol have meaning only when carried by a movement in the course of which they lose their rigidity and yield to change. In this way the reformer seemed sometimes to take side with the devil, the saint with the heretic.[33]

Neither a devilish power nor an absolute evil has a part in pure religion. The distance to God, the fear of God, living in the process of prayer, is the feeling of sin, and sin grows into hope, confidence, and grace; they are inter-connected in a metaphorical tension. This, however, is only so in the process of prayer; not in the fixation of ritual: sin is here reduced to an independent evil, and evil has only the one rigid meaning that the symbolic reduction allows. Instead of grace which is born out of the heart of the sinner, justice appears as an equally fixed and reduced symbol, with no bridge leading from the evildoer to the righteous. No wonder that the Platonic ritual[34] praises justice as the all-embracing virtue. And it is furthermore obvious that such a ritual of fixed, rigid righteousness has

[33] This may be the rule with all progress: The naught which was the detested sphere in Parmenides' system, became the springboard for Plato and Aristotle; the realm of "confusion" which the Cartesian mathematical symbolism omitted, was the field of investigation for the psychologists and led to the new conception of the unconscious, the imperceptible, and even to the law of continuity in Leibniz' thought.

[34] The Platonic State is nearer to ritual than to our concept of Law; therefore it seemed more appropriate to treat it here than in chapter 8.

its culmination in another strict ritual: the ritual of divine retaliation. It is at the end of his *Republic*[35] that Plato ascends to the grandeur of a ritual of retaliation. When there is retaliation, and not grace, we have the touchstone revealing the true character of this order. Punishment and reward, measured in an exact relation to the evil done, repeated again and again in an endless series of years, is the highest realization of the ritual. Retaliation itself is a repetition of the evil, and in this repetition it confirms the holy order: Confirmation by repetition is what gives necessity to the ritual. Only by repeated confirmation the ritual grows into an absolute and uncontestable law. The more it has been repeated, the older its tradition, the more the accidental and whimsical character of its symbolic reduction is overcome. Priest and judge, therefore, put the greatest emphasis on the exact repetition of the ritual. Salvation is lost and crime revealed in the law court, when the formula has been missed only by a single gesture or word. The repetition of the ritual is the only meaning of the ordeal as it turns up in primitive law. Its accidental and even nonsensical result is sanctified in the minds of men by the fact that it has been ordained and confirmed in its fixed order from time immemorial.

The identification of the "good" and the "lawful" is characteristic for every ritual. The law rises above God, as it started to do in the times of Ezra and Nehemiah, and the development reached its peak in the Maccabean wars. Now only the law was holy, and God's righteousness was the expression of a rigid machinery of law. This had been quite different in the times of the great prophets. God's righteousness had been the lively response of the divine to the changing aspects of human nature (Psalms 18, 25);

[35] Plato, *Republic,* book x.

it had found its most touching expression in God's "repentance," and the prophets do not cease to pray for this merciful and lively response to human repentance. In hellenistic times, however, even prophets do not understand any more the living God of mercy and repentance and try to chain Him to the routine of a law-machinery (Jonah 4). Sin (ἁμαρτία) which had been a process toward grace is now changed into the violation of the formal law (ἀνομία),[36] and so the fixed and static ritual has accomplished its triumphant victory.

"World," being profaned by the ritual, changes its character. It is a finite system of things which in their contingent and isolated nature have the character of "evil things." The evil is now an objective fact, scarcely compatible with God's goodness. Men surrender to its power, which as a cruel and blind destiny makes existence a meaningless contingency. The scientific ritual is foreshadowed in this early rationalism. The scientist, however, supplanted the blind fate by his mechanical order and so he was able to fight the mechanical evil of a contingent nature, sickness, epidemics, famines by his scientific devices, meeting mechanical disorder by an order of a similar mechanical kind.[37]

European history is marked by the repeated endeavor to dominate life and religion by ritual. The abundance of rituals, however, has resulted in a variety of power organ-

[36] *First Epistle of John,* 4, 3.

[37] That the scientific mechanical law presupposes a contingent matter of fact, has already been stated (p. 24). But the mechanical order itself may be regarded as merely contingent, when confronted with a higher necessity. In this way we may understand Aristotle's concept of the "αὐτόματον," the sequence of mere mechanical happenings which are contingent with regard to a final order as a higher necessity because representing the principle of life. (See Aristotle on the contingent nature of the "αὐτόματον" in *Physics,* 197a 34ff. and 197b 19ff.)

izations, fighting against each other and competing for victory. The competition of church and state, especially, has caused misery and death. But it has also brought about a loosening of the ritual fetters. Each of the contesting powers of ritual has limited the scope and weakened the intensity of its opponent, and so room was made for what is beyond all these systems and what had been in danger of being forgotten: the individual and his immediate relation to God. The competition of church and state strengthened the belief in a free brotherhood of men. Most of the ideals of democracy which we cherish today have been born out of this strife, so the lively medieval concept of the unity of the people, the sovereignty of the people, the true principle of representation and parliamentarism. Surely these ideas have not all been kept pure; they have in the course of history yielded to a symbolic reduction: people, to a conventionally united group, parliament to a quantitatively reduced organ with not always adequate responsibility. But the true ideals have been kept alive under the surface and have forced again and again a reformation of democracy. Where the competition and mutual limitation of various rituals were missing—as in Rome and China— the all-embracing one and only ritual has usurped all of life, the state substituting for the divine order, and the state official assuming the charisma of the priest. Here the whole civilization was forced into one imposing but mechanical order.

We live in a highly complex interaction of rituals, and so we have been able to preserve our vitality. We have to cope not only with church and state, but also with the ritual of daily labor, with schedule and timetable. And just as the church fights against the devil, and just as the state fights against disorder and lawlessness, so the daily discipline of labor fights against boredom, threatening at the threshold of its system. Boredom is the threat which drives man into the safety of his daily methodical profession. It creates, however, not only the useful worker-bee, but also the libertine with his lust for pleasure, his frenzy of intoxication. This is the unavoidable consequence of all ritualization: the devil may be responsible for the reliable righteous Pharisee, but also for the revengeful persecutor and destroyer of life outside the order of the ritual. The fear of punishment may contribute to the education of the honorable citizen, but it may also lead to the cruelty of the hangman and the increase of crime; the threat of boredom drives men six days of the week and eight hours a day into the efficient discipline of work, but lures them also on evenings and Sundays to wasting time and to empty orgies of pleasure.[38] The bad is in the track of the good wherever ritual is left to itself and allowed, in spite of its limitations, to signify the whole of man's life.

One of the most powerful rituals is that of exact science, and thus this ritual tries as it did in the Renaissance to absorb the whole of existence and to represent the only and absolute value. Descartes and many after him were inclined to regard the ritual of science as being the whole of reality, and to despise as mere confusion whatever could not be brought down to mathematical formulas. But, on the other hand, modern science has become more humble and has discovered its own relativity. The discovery that the scientific law is a mere hypothesis has given to the sciences of our day their true and even creative place. In consenting to its own restriction, science has assumed an unparalleled buoyancy, an élan, not known to previous times. Instead of perpetuating itself in the boundaries drawn once and for all, science advances, carried by a cre-

[38] Pascal (*Pensées*, chapter 4) foresaw in the early days of the modern ritual of busyness the danger of pleasure-intoxication.

ative wave which permanently expands its volume and changes the system.

Therefore modern science is the most powerful witness to the truth which we defend in this book: the scientific hypothesis makes it definitely clear that we need a system of symbols, that this system is a ground on which we stand and has therefore to be regarded as a highly valuable treasure, but that its true meaning lies beyond its own fixation and that its outlines have again and again to be changed in the growing process of inquiry. It is this destructive, and in its destruction, creative process which we try to grasp in the problem of metaphorical tension.

Science is a ritual and as such a symbolic reduction of truth. The immediate and unlimited search for truth, unbound by systematic symbolism, is philosophy. Philosophy, therefore, is to science what the transcending movement of the searching prayer is to the dogmatic system of theological answers in the religious field. That philosophy and science are different and at the same time serve one and the same truth has been known since time immemorial. Philosophy, however, in its immediate attempt to reach into truth has to remain in the process of searching and has to state its results as problems only, turning every answer into a steppingstone and formulation of a new question. This, its problematic attitude, has enabled philosophy to understand life which can only be "understood" as a problem, as a task to be realized in a future, equally problematic. Aristotle's findings, for instance, his substance, essence, potentiality, and actuality, his concept of the contingent and of the free necessity of the "entelechy" are problems only, stated for those who continue to search, and Aristotle was very much aware of their problematic character. Problematic was the searching will of St. Augustine, so near to faith and love; problematic was Spinoza's substance as a divine power of existence and his interpretation of the intellect as an "infinite mode." Problems are Kant's "apperception," the "thing in itself," the "regulative principle," the free infinite will and the antinomies which as a problematic tension gave rise to the critical philosophy of Idealism.

Science, on the other hand, has its emphasis not so much on problems, but on a closed and fixed system of answers, based on an unquestionable axiomatic ground. To be sure, the sciences will always touch on the problems which philosophy provides; they will even use problematic concepts, as force, substance, process. But they will transform these problematic concepts into exact answers which guarantee and make possible the stable framework and pattern which is necessary in order to master and organize nature. To master nature by fixed patterns is not the task of philosophy, and whenever philosophers have tried it, the result was a utopian scheme and a failure. The task of the sciences, however, is just this kind of mastership, and in order to become masters they have to limit their search for truth, have to resign themselves to a symbolically reduced pattern. This reduction will, as every ritual, be partly arbitrary and contingent. It is arbitrary and motivated by ends beyond the system that science restricts itself to a pattern of quantitative relations. But after having made this expedient reduction, and in the scope of the so reduced pattern, every answer is necessary and of an eminent importance. It is this paradoxical combination of necessity and arbitrariness which makes the sciences efficient, but, on the other hand, forces them for the sake of this efficiency to restrict their search for the ultimate truth, for which philosophy will never stop striving in the humble attitude of a problematic understanding.

Rationalism and empiricism are the two dangers which

lure the philosopher on his strenuous and narrow path into the safer and broader fields of scientific systematization. It was Aristotle's great mission to overcome these dangers which were always present in Greek thought and which were especially present in the character and talents of Aristotle himself. It may be that, in avoiding these two ways of transforming philosophy into science, Aristotle delayed the fixation of truth into exact mathematical systems during the Middle Ages. But in doing this he preserved the lively and even religious character of a searching and problematic philosophy, allowed the dynamic Franciscan schools to become a powerful stronghold of research, and protected philosophy against its annihilation and absorption by the ritualism of the Renaissance systems. Philosophy may tend toward a point where it becomes absorbed by a scientific ritual, just as all religious movements face their crisis in a theological dogmatism. But, on the other hand, it is the awareness of this crisis which has kept philosophy on its guard and enabled it to remain a rejuvenating force.

An estrangement between philosophy and science, therefore, is a disease and a danger to both, to philosophy as well as to science. Science without philosophy would stagnate and hypostatize its symbolic reduction and limitation, and philosophy without the symbolic structure of fixed and finite answers would lose the incentive to ever newly formulate its problems.

6

POETRY AND DRAMA

IT IS the myth which forms the metaphorical process of existence, unique and infinite in its essence. Creation as infinite and unique is what we call "World." World is a process, and its dynamic character is revealed in the element of destruction, contained in all creation and pointing to that which passes away and is overcome: a transitional and hypothetical order. This order detaches itself, appears self-sufficient in its closed totality as an objective continuum and assumes the paradoxical character of an "infinite time" and "infinite space." These continua, however, cannot escape the finiteness of their symbolic origin and so give birth to the antinomies of an infinite space which is essentially closed and an infinite time which is fulfilled, wherever we grasp it. The closed "phases" of time group together in a series which now represents the process of the world and appears in the sequence of past, present and future.

The astonishing element in this development is neither the past nor the future. It is essential for the continuum that its discontinuous moments be knitted closely together, so that each of them is a past for the following moment and a future for the previous one. There can be nothing in between the "continuum." Whatever consideration one has with regard to these moments, every moment passes immediately from a past into a future.

The strange element, therefore, in this sequence is the present. What is the "present"? Does the "present" mean a total detachment from the continuum, from past and future? Does it deny past and future and make time stand still? Can time stand still? Time, standing still, falls out of

time. We came upon the three phases of time when we were
faced with the problem of repetition in the series of phases.
But why is this repetition not limited to the past and the
future: these two correspond to each other as looking
forward and looking back? But the present is different. It
is apart from the two other phases, it even can be stretched
over these other phases, being able to extend, ad libitum,
into past and future. It is, in spite of its symbolic fixation,
mobile and flexible, lifting out of the flux of time whatever
is wanted. To be sure, it cannot extinguish the flux of time
as such: it may trace out its realm ever so far and wide,
somehow the waves of time brush against its wall, and
whoever settles on the isle of the present, knows that he is
only on an island and that the stream of time will over-
flow it. In other words: the contingency and arbitrariness
of its delimination reveal clearly the process of an infinite
movement of which it is only a fragmentary reduction. We
may even turn, like a searchlight, the present now on this,
now on that group of events—St. Augustine already saw
that past and future can be brought into the present: past
in the searchlight of the present and future in the searchlight of the present—but always this lifting and fixing is
done on the ground of an infinite and continuous process.
What we make a present in this way is, to be sure, formed
by our purpose, it is a product of expediency and it is, as
all practical and purposive divisions, a symbol. But as
such it is, in fact, never a true present, but just as well
only a past. For whenever we reflect on a time, we make
this time to a finished, closed, fixed phase and thus to a
past. Even the future became a past, when regarded as an
object of care, modelled according to a purpose which as
a motive belongs to the experiences of yesterday[1] and is

1 See p. 30.

determined and determining, not free, as all past in its fixed setting is unfree and determined. Past and future are thus interchangeable and, therefore, timeless as the static present of reflection is timeless too.

The true past and the true future, however, are never merely reflective. They are grounded in that prereflective process of consciousness[2] which, in the sweep of an indivisible process, reaches forward in the tension of a meaningful direction. Here past facts are imbued with a life toward future and, therefore, never totally gone. The past receives its full meaning of a past only as an element in a process, as a start and steppingstone for a direction. Past is only truly past when carried and evaluated by this process. And, similarly, the future receives its place in the process which is never gone and never merely to come and, therefore, a "present." In this present of process future is the directing element, itself present as a direction, actual in the meaning it conveys to the process. The present stretches, therefore, over past and future, integrating both into a unity: The reflective phases remain, but they have changed into an indivisible process and have lost their isolated character of a factual fixity.

This present of an integrated process, stretching over past and future, is not a mere recollection of a "not any more" nor is it a mere anticipation of a "not yet." It unites metaphorically both into a "being still" and "being already," and thus it assumes a forceful tension which as an infinite present may be called "eternity." The present is eternal, because it has transformed the finite past and the equally finite future into an infinite process. Limits are still there, reflection not being eliminated; but these limits, as birth and death, are means of an inner structure

[2] See p. 73.

only, not of an outward totality and finite completeness. Birth and death are organizing elements in the course of our life, and to that extent we are able to reflect upon them; but they are not experienced as closing our life into a limited whole. They become the object of institutional care and the fixation of rituals, always transcended by the immortality of life and present.

The present, as it is infinite and eternal, is essentially free. The determined structure of reflective pasts and futures—both determined when isolated and both contingent when confronted with the eternal necessity of the present—dissolves in the process of this present. It is only in this process of the present that the structure of past and future receives an aspect of freedom, as an endeavor, as an ought, as a trend toward a higher value and fulfillment.

How do we know about this present? It is the present of the creative process. The religious myths speak of it and name it rightly eternity, but as a dim divination rather than a clear insight. Our thinking too gets hold of it and tries to interpret it symbolically: Now eternity is identified with the symbolic present of reflection,[3] detached from time, a standstill, an abstract entity of systematization, hypostatized by Plato to the eternity of Ideas; now it is interpreted as the sum of all time phases, again only a symbolic, mathematical entity of an additional character: eternity is here equal to "all times," a limited sum of years or millennia. Or reflection takes refuge with the symbol which corresponds, as its opposite, to the "all of times" and

---

[3] It is this symbolic present of reflection which we described above as a searchlight, turned toward various phases of time. It has to be distinguished from the metaphorical and true present of eternity and freedom. This twofold aspect of the present has its parallel in the equally twofold aspect of "rest," as described on pp. 68, 69.

stabilizes the flux not in the greatest thinkable unity, but in the smallest: the moment. Thus the moment, the "now," as a last part of time assumes the character of eternity in the mysticism of Master Eckhart and in the religious philosophy of Kierkegaard. But this "now," even in its sublime hypostasis and in spite of its passionate and decisive character, comes dangerously near to the timeless present of reflection.

The true metaphorical present, however, is not of this kind. Its creative tension, stretching over past and future, was seen in the drama of conversion which, as the drama of consciousness itself, was regarded as beyond time and thus as eternal.[4] It is not an act of a momentary decision, but carries all acts and all decisions, and links our life to other lives in intercession and creative love. It is, however, not only to be found in the devotional process of prayer, but wherever creation is at work. The works of poetry and art express this metaphorical present and make it apparent in the purest and most unmistakable form. Therefore poetry and art are a rich field of investigation with regard to the metaphorical process. The task of this book, however, is to ground the metaphorical process in a broader soil, and to show that what art brings to the surface, is everywhere at work where men think and feel. Every thinking and feeling being is grounded in the present of a creative process. But it is in art and poetry that this truth is lifted into the spotlight of our consciousness. Art is consciousness of the present as of a necessary process of metaphorical tension. Therefore art reaches into depths into which our daily life with its various rituals can scarcely follow. And therefore art is not a whimsical and arbitrary pastime, but a fundamental insight. We grasp

4 See p. 82.

the significance of art best in the truth and destiny of the present.

Wherever art is, the present is. This does not mean that only where art is, the present is to be found. This exaggeration for which some art-enthusiasts are responsible is no true service to art and cuts it off from all other values, especially from religion. But there is, indeed, a difference between art and religion. The praying man lives in the presence of his God; he lives in this presence even when he does not reflect upon it.[5] God as the meaning, expression, and revelation of the creative process remains in a unique and inseparable unity with the seeker and does not become a detached object and content of knowledge. But art as a bridge and mediator between the unique spirit and the manifoldness of things, keeps things in distance to the creative process and thus makes consciousness known as distinct from the things of which it is aware as separate objects. These things stand over against the presence of consciousness, they "object" it, as the word announces. But, on the other hand, the objects of art are deeply embedded in the creative process, remain as objects, nevertheless, an inseparable element of its drive and are submerged into it to such an extent that they seem to lose their independent existence.

It was the body which in the religious and mythical field played a similar role, and equally was submerged into the process of the spirit. The body disappeared as an object and became nothing but the potential of life, expressing and serving this dynamic process. The object of art, like the living body, is an expression of the creative process and has no other reality of existence. It is, like the body, a limitation and materialization of the spirit, it breaks the

[5] See pp. 73, 78.

unique movement of creative communion down into the manifoldness of things; but, at the same time, it becomes the instrument of overcoming this manifoldness, here again resembling the body. The work of art becomes alive, and alive it is, like the body, the vessel of a spiritual revelation.

How can material things become alive? This could, indeed, never happen, if the aesthetic consciousness did nothing but passively receive the object. But, in fact, the object as mere material is transformed by the process of artistic creation. "Creation" is rightly borrowed from the religious realm. The object as material is turned into naught, vanishes, in order to give rise to something entirely new, disappears in the creative process. As a mere "thing" the work of art continues to occupy space and time, can be possessed and can form a part of our environment. But the true reality of the art-work is not in this. Only where the artist failed, the work is nothing but a thing. "Things" fall out of the process of creative life. Whenever we are faced with things and nothing but things, our own consciousness is in danger of being itself turned into an object: the ego. The ego is the counterpart of material things, in relation to these things, in objective causal, mechanical, or final relativity. It is itself merely relative—relative to a totality of objective things which it calls the "exterior world," although the exterior world is no "world" but merely the limited totality of symbolically reduced means, called "environment." The environment only is an exterior world, and it is exterior with regard to the object "ego."[6]

This ego is in permanent danger of being enslaved by the things which it has made its environment. It "possesses"

[6] Descartes's essentially reflective ego, therefore, should have never appeared without an environment. The absolute position which Descartes gives to his ego is borrowed from the very different spiritual I of St. Augustine, which is in a living communion with the divine Thou.

these things, and possession is bought at the price of freedom. What is alive, cannot be possessed, although we speak
of possessing, of having a soul. We *are* a soul, and we
possess even our body only in so far as our body is separate
from life and regarded by reflection as a thing of independent reality. As we saw above, the body becomes a separate
thing when failing, i.e. in sickness, and therefore those
who "possess" their body are usually possessed by it: the
hypochondriac and the hysterical sick. Art works, when
their possession becomes the main interest for the collector,
are mere things and as such they enslave their possessor,
turning the expanding drive of creation into the narrow
prison of a material existence. Money is the thing which
as a mere symbol never comes to life and is therefore the
most dangerous of all possessions. It is rare that the
possessor here escapes the danger of being possessed, of
becoming a slave to his wealth, a lifeless instrument for
the aggrandizement of property.

But even when the ego has hardened in its relations to
things, it scarcely ever loses entirely its contact with life.
This is obvious when we think of the ambiguous role which
the ego plays, being on the one hand a part of the world
of things, in a symbolic relation to them as any object
would be; and on the other hand being an entity of a very
specific weight, growing above the other objects, called even
"subject," and shifted from a mere term in a relation to
the ground of all relations.[7] So the ego assumes the double
role of object and subject, of known and knower, of
thought and thinker. This ambiguity has been overlooked

[7] See p. 17ff., where right at the beginning of this work a similar
shift was stated with regard to the propositional arrangement of
logical thought, where one of the terms of the proposition assumed the
weight of the subject, substituting for the true "subjectum," the
fundamental process which carries the various terms of the proposition.

sometimes by those who either put all emphasis on the objective thought in a world of fixed symbols, or placed all emphasis on the subjective thinker, in order to understand the continuity of process. The greatest philosophers, however, have truly wrestled with this problem, as Heraclitus with his *logos*, Aristotle with his entelechy, Augustine with his process of searching, and Kant with his objective consciousness of apperception and infinite will.[8]

The ambiguity and double role of the ego as an objective fixation as well as a subjective process is responsible for the permanently changing position which the ego takes with regard to its environment. As every fixation is one-sided, limited, and arbitrary when lifted into the subjective process of consciousness, the ego is driven out of every position it takes. Every purpose and its fulfillment becomes a mere means for new and ever new purposes, remodelling incessantly the ego and its environment. A permanent alternation between fulfillment and disappointment characterizes the life of action, of purpose, and realization as long as man does not get his head above this ambiguous realm of oscillation between subject and object and places himself entirely in the *subjectum*, the ground of consciousness as such. He truly lives on this ground whether he knows it or not, and he becomes aware of this ground of his existence whenever he passes beyond the boundaries of his limited purposive self, closed in the walls of environmental

---

8 This "objective consciousness" is no "thing" and in no relation to things, as the body and its organs are considered to be. But even here, between bodily sense organs and the object of the senses no mere relation can explain that which we call perception. Aristotle saw rightly that both, sense organs and their objects, are potentials only with regard to the process of sensation in the course of which they lose their independent character, unified in one and the same act. If sensation had no part in the creative process, then, indeed, sensuous experiences can have no part in art, as they definitely do.

relationship. Driven from past to future and absorbed in every stage of life, he nevertheless has moments, when past and future are seen as mere aspects of a wider consciousness—a present, continuous, infinite, and lasting.

It is art which more than anything else brings this consciousness of the present into the awareness of men. Is art "subjective"? Or is it "objective"? Does it live in an outer world of things or in an inner world? Many religious men may reject art as "worldly," as lured by exterior values, clinging to the manifoldness and variety of objects. And practical men of action may reject art on the opposite ground, as visionary, detached from real life, merely subjective and introvert. Both are right and wrong. Art is neither merely the one nor the other; it is attached to the realm of objects and their variety, but also beyond these objects, surpassing them, negating them in a metaphorical drive which is an inner process, visionary and in so far "unreal."

Art has its own reality, which is not the reality of the object but of the creative process. Reality does not reside in the words, fixed and connected in sentences of a poem; not even in the scenes or acts of a drama as they stand out in detached objectivity. Reality does not reside in the togetherness of colors on the canvas or the multitude of consonant and dissonant sounds of music. All these objective entities are necessary, but they are not real. They have to be known, have to be put into a composition which is made and can be explained. They stand in a symbolic relation of ends to a purposive ego and must, therefore, be interpreted as objects of purposive work in a construction and composition of parts, in a ritualistic repetition of order. As such they occupy a part of space, as the picture, the statue, the building does; or a part of time and may be performed as can a poem, a drama, or a symphony. As such they can be timed, filling a certain part of our daily schedule or of our radio programs. But as such they are not really art. They are regarded as true art only when they express something which is more than an objective piece of time and space, related to other objects in an environment. They represent the infinite present which makes us forget the worthless piece of time, space, and matter together with our own purposive ego. We "forget ourselves" in the great tasks of life: whenever such a task calls upon us, we give ourselves without restraint. Just so, or even in a higher degree we forget our own selves in the process of the present which signifies the metaphorical process of artistic creation.

But "to forget" is not the right expression. Forgetting means losing, dropping. Here, however, an intensive activity takes place; there is gain, not loss, a conquest of a higher realm and reality beyond the finite daily level of a mechanized life. We grow beyond our own ego. Similar to the movement of prayer the artist transcends his I in a living communion with a Thou which is infinite, but which, unlike the religious sphere, holds him in the realm of bodily existence. He may call this Thou an "ideal audience," ideal, because it leads him on in the process of spiritual creation; but not divine, because it represents the needy, failing, and longing life of human existence. What we may call divine here is the process itself, reaching beyond artist and audience, although each of them, artist as well as audience, may take the place of the savior in the life of the other: the audience may look up to the "genius" who creates the work of art as if he be the source of revelation; and the artist, if he is conscious of his high task, will regard his audience as his holy responsibility and he will feel a servant to their needs and longings. The artist who merely expresses his "self" has missed his task and will never reach up into the spiritual communion beyond his little ego. Expression in the field of art is always communication, a communion with a thou, and because of this the work of art will have to express in a metaphorical way infinite possibilities to raise the spirit of an infinite audience. The work of art, although itself a limited expression only, has to stand for all the diverging, contradicting variety of bodily existence, carrying, not unlike the praying man, this integrated variety upwards in an undivided drive, giving to everybody and releasing in everybody the power of a creative spiritual life.[9] The work of art, indeed, is the intercessional factor in this our sensuous world, unifying and transcending the competing and frustrating trends of human desire.

This may happen in an imperfect and less intensive way in early poetry which finds expression in poems of folklore. Here we find an extreme "subjectivity," not much more than mood and atmosphere. The things and events described in such poems are rather insignificant; they are embedded and lost in a tranquillity of the soul. Taken literally they mean nothing, they cannot be interpreted adequately, they only "express." Just this "expression," however, in contradistinction to explanation or reference, is the essential character of poetry, although there are different levels of expression. The subjectivity of the poem is a very special subjectivity, because it reaches beyond the accidental things and events described, beyond the accidental life of the person who experienced them; it claims a general validity which is shared by all other subjects. It unites these subjects in a universal experience, in

[9] So also Kant's definition of the "aesthetic idea" (*Critique of Judgment*, §49).

[117]

a process, surpassing any limited position or character, expressing a world.

That every work of poetry, even a little song, may represent a world, has often been stated, but more as a simile, an emphatic image, than as a truth. But it is a truth, if we think of what "world" really means: the process of creation, enclosing and surpassing a manifoldness of things. "World" is as we saw, a religious concept, and here, indeed, art is interrelated with religion. Not even the smallest poem can come into existence without a religious ground. And from time immemorial religion has expressed itself in the poetical form of hymn and drama. Just because religion is always in danger of limiting itself to an accidental and expedient system of ritual by which world is turned into mere environmental organization, it finds its true life again in the poetic expression of metaphorical transcendence. Therefore the church has rightly taken refuge in poetry and art in order to counterbalance its tendency to fixation and sterility.

For art can do what religion scarcely can try without endangering its holiness: it can descend into the world of things, into the symbolic structure of our sensuous existence. Here in the field of art, therefore, the ritual as a symbolic structure is unavoidable, necessary, an important element for the task of mediation between the two worlds. To be sure, we saw that ritual plays a powerful role also in the religious realm, because religion cannot cut itself entirely off from the material environment. Body and sin belong to the religious experience and open the door for the flight into the security of the ritual. Even the most inward religion of faith, even protestantism, could not do without ritual and without taking in the world of sin. But the religious attitude will, nevertheless, emphasize the negative character of the bodily and material existence; it will take a hostile stand, and its ritual will try to fence this material world off and to make it obnoxious. Art, on the contrary, tries to draw the sensuous sphere into the holy realm of creation, sanctifies and atones the mere profaneness of our daily existence and changes it into an expression of a spiritual aspiration. The ritual, the structure, becomes in this way a positive element of expression. Prayer may be without words, but in poetry speech is necessary and shares in the artistic endeavor. The words and their ritual of structure convey a concreteness, not to be missed in the process of I and Thou which connects the poet and his audience.

Poetry makes use of language. We distinguished between the merely symbolic scaffold of a technical ritual and the metaphorical process of speech itself.[10] Only the process of speech is true language, but this process cannot go on without the use of a technique, a ritual. The more a language grows old, the more the flux of speech is lost. The metaphorical process stagnates and is supplanted by a scaffold of fixed building stones, of words as a technical means for the purpose of expedient understanding. Every language, grown old, will to a high degree develop into a system of exactly defined words with a dictionary meaning, so that anybody can put them together in order to make himself understood. Language as a system of fixed symbols will, indeed, satisfy entirely as long as it is a mere tool for traffic, for expedient intercourse in a mechanized environment of purposive action. Here an artificial language, like Esperanto, will even do a better job. But when it comes to an understanding beyond mere expediency of action: when men seek to understand men, as living persons in the process of life, then the word is only a very fragmentary and insufficient means, and neither the single word nor a mere

10 See p. 61ff.

combination of words conveys what is wanted, but only the process of speech itself. And this process of speech transforms in its dynamic movement every word into an indivisible element in a unique context which has a meaning of its own. It may happen that those who are accustomed to consider the single words in their fixed meaning, will look in vain for the exactitude which scientific discourse asks for, and will reject the ambiguous radiation and manifold refraction which the words seem to show, veiling more than revealing their signification in the expressive process of speech.[11] This may have been the profound experience of Heraclitus who saw contradiction and mutual destruction in the sequence of words. The word as a transitional element may, indeed, be ambiguous and disturbing, when isolated and broken out of the process of speech; but what is not ambiguous and not deficient, is speech itself which conveys a meaning, profounder and even clearer than any detached single word ever could.

The spirit of a language is in the process,[12] not in the word, and just because of that the words must enter into a tension which overcomes their fixation and provides a meaning beyond their symbolic and only apparent sufficiency. The process, therefore, is metaphorical and the metaphor has the task of destroying the rigid reduction and limitation of the word. "Expression" is the characteristic of this process to which the single words and their togetherness are subjected. Who has truly understood that the single word is not a meaning in itself, but that it points metaphorically forward and backward towards the

[11] Signification is distinguished from expressiveness as the symbolic reducing representation is distinguished from the metaphorical representation. (See p. 85ff.)

[12] So Humboldt, *Einleitung Zum Kawi-Werk, Gesammelte Schriften,* vii, i, 46. Compare also above pp. 59, 61.

process into which it vanishes, will ask for another and more adequate articulation of the process than words can ever provide: an articulation not of words, but of meaning, an articulation, the caesurae of which rise out of the natural flow of the thinking- and speaking-process.

Here, however, a serious misunderstanding should be avoided. It is not so that words are first conceived, as building stones of language, and that the articulation of meaning is added afterwards in a synthesis of fixed symbols. On the contrary, language is first of all a living communication of thought which finds "embodiment" in concepts, and every concept, as the body did, points beyond itself and vanishes as a fixed entity the more lively the process of conceptual communion develops. This is what Hegel's dialectic rhythm meant to show, the "self-movement" of concepts in the process of the spirit. But reflection transforms the living bodies of thought into fixed objects, into signs or symbols which now have to be put together in an outward synthesis. It is because of this mechanical atomization that a new force of unification is needed in order to draw the atoms into the vortex of a living process of meaning. This unification or articulation may seem arbitrary or artificial, but it is so only when judged by the equally artificial standard of word-atoms against which it works as a technical antidote, a ritual, mastering the dead material and bringing it back to life again.

This articulation of the thinking-process, expressing "meaning" intensively and lifting above a mere summing up of words, will introduce a caesura, a breathing-interval, wherever the process of meaning comes naturally to a halt. This caesura, however, like the time-caesurae of Aristotle,[13]

---

[13] Aristotle, *Physics*, 222a; see also on articulation pp. 37 and 155f.

should be not so much an element of division as of unification. For it will gather up and concentrate the flux of words for the sake of transmitting them to the following: Metre or rhyme, or whatever artificial device the poet may use, will serve as a natural intensification of meaning. But it will do this only when the master makes us forget the device, when the caesurae fall in naturally with the articulation of thought and, therefore, do not hinder but heighten the dynamic process of meaning. Meaning lives beyond the words, the one as well as the combination of the many. It grows out of the communion of concepts, uses and disposes of the words according to its own insight, in a tension of the present in which no single word as such stands out, but is lost in the process and its structure of articulation. Therefore also these structures, the articulation of rhyme and metre, have to serve, and if they degenerate to self-important rituals, when forms like the sonnet become as such a goal for skillful production, then play is the result, not poetry. In true poetry the complex rituals are turned into simplicity of meaning, for meaning is simple, when expressive, and poetry has to achieve this simplicity[14] in overcoming the complex mechanism of its artificial structure. So it may be that art is a forceful striving though the result is peaceful simplicity. Simplicity is always a negation,[15] the negation and overcoming of the complex. This negating simplicity is the infinity and absoluteness, the indivisible present of the process.

This present is not a phase in time. It is, as we saw,[16] the tension by which past and future are metaphorically

[14] The more childlike simplicity of folk songs is due to the fact that they have not gone through the complexity of the ritual. What they convey is a simple mood.

[15] On simplicity, see Foss, *The Idea of Perfection in the Western World*, p. 49ff.

[16] See p. 108ff.

united and overcome. In this togetherness of tension temporal succession has vanished; but this togetherness should
neither be confused with temporal simultaneity nor with
the togetherness of space. Time and space, as "continua,"[17]
are not the pure expression of the infinite process; they
are both enclosed in the process of the present and are
both transcended. Art, therefore, is neither merely temporal nor spatial, but has its sphere beyond these forms.
This is why the work of art can and must "play" with
times, spaces, and things. The play-theory of art which,
taken seriously, would make of art an hedonistic device of
self-enjoyment, receives a limited justification when restricted to the spatio-temporal material. Every great work
of art plays with events and things, that is, it shows their
frailty and limitation. But the limitation of things and
events, their playful and futile character, will be the true
theme of great art only if it awakens in us the consciousness of a present which is eternal and which endures beyond
the futility of time and space.

The eternity of the poem is the eternal present of the
creative process.[18] The necessity and "general validity" of
the poem is this its tendency. Tendency or process was
what we found as the essence of law and as the "intentio"
of the lawful universal. Every work of art as a process is
general and claims validity, although it is unique and individual. As the expression of an infinite present and process it is a world, individual and unique. Nothing but the
transcendence of process bestows uniqueness and individu-
ality.[19]

17 See p. 39.
18 We will return to the problem of the present, when treating the
element of rhythm in music and fine arts (chapter 7).
19 Who sees in Law merely the comprehension of a multitude of
cases will never acknowledge the existence of an "individual law" in-

The difficulty, however, which the artist has to face is the danger of losing the grace of an infinite vision by lowering himself unto the sensuous order of a finite ritual. In the fight for a sensuous expression, linking his vision to the life of the average man by rules and techniques, the artist faces the same tragic experience which the prophet undergoes when trying to make his vision understood by the people around him. The artist, however, faces an even greater difficulty. The praying man lives the life of the people, it is their and his own sinful deficiency, out of which he is lifted into grace. He is one of the people and is embedded in their life, never quite losing contact with his surroundings. But the artist is alone with his vision, he is the one who gives, and the giver is always alone. His loneliness may become unbearable if he does not ground the grace of his creativity in the grace of a higher power, knowing himself a mere instrument, not a giver only, but one who receives and as a receiving vessel near to those who are destined to receive from him. In this way only will the creating artist be able to understand the barriers of reception which separate him from his audience, and in understanding he will be able to remove them. He will, in humbleness, take sides with his audience, seek an expression adapted to their power of understanding; he will be critical to his own work and will learn to give only what can be received. The technique of expression will become an essential part of his endeavor. Inspiration must carry him, but the critical knowledge of expression will tie him to the limited world of his audience. Only the genius can be both, inspired and critical, a visionary and a technical scholar. But only the genius who combines both will be able to

herent in the unique art-work. But see on the different interpretations of "law," p. 162ff.

present to mankind the concrete and integrated life of a world-process.

The vague and sketchy character of the poem, its short and somewhat abbreviated nature, the glance of a limited perspective may make it appear inadequate to the sublime task of representing a world. Even when developed to the length and consistency of an epic, it still has only a limited perspective, and further: its long-drawn stories burden it with so much material that some kind of purpose will have to reduce the rankly growing details. It may happen that such a purpose becomes even the main interest, as for instance, the glorification of a people, national pride, historical self-consciousness. The more this is the case, the more the matter of fact, the things and events in their historical reality, in their symbolic reference and relative significance will become important. A one-sided perspective will be brought to our attention, not the present as such, not the world as an infinite and transcending process. Only very rarely, as the work of a genius, such a poem may become the true realization of that which poetry claims to be.

There is, however, one form of poetry which leads more than any other to the realization of a world. The tension of an indivisible present stretches here over things and happenings and unites them in a process of universal validity: the Drama, and its most representative form, the Tragedy. The drama is, as its name tells, action, process. Aristotle,[20] therefore, lays the greatest emphasis on the action as such, on the plot, and declares the plot to be the most important element in the tragedy. The reasons, however, which he gives are not convincing and they are rooted deeply in the symbolic, scientific, and rational attitude of

[20] Aristotle, *Poetics,* chapter 6.

Greek thinking. Because our life generally serves a goal, and because we regard a goal as extremely valuable, the purposive action, explicable by expedient motives, is the main feature of the drama. So Aristotle not only states very exact rules for the characters as being means of motivation for purposive actions and, so to speak points of intersection for conflicting events, but he also stresses the importance of a realistic treatment of time. The continuum of time is the natural framework, the technical element of unity which binds the people and events together in a consistent whole.

There are, certainly, very useful hints in this Aristotelian aesthetics. Aristotle scarcely says anything which is not of importance and bears some valuable truth. Even in his limitations he is still extremely helpful. His aesthetic theory shows, indeed, quite clearly, how far the school rules are able to lead. They can only explain some minima of technical achievement, they can only prepare the material in reducing it into a simplified order which makes it easy to enter into its limited structure. It is unquestionably true that the poet has to be accurate in showing the motives of his heroes and in placing these heroes in a clear relationship to their environment so that the mutual dependence of man and environment can easily be grasped by the spectator. It is furthermore true that the environment, with all its events and personages, has to be worked into a clear pattern of time and space in order to give a natural consistency and continuity, unity, and balance to the manifold happenings of the plot.

But although this may be very useful, what, after all, is achieved by following these rules? The poet leads us on the way from cause to effect, from means to end; he makes it easy to follow the hero's purpose, the practical stages with which he approaches his goal; he imitates[21] the natural and rational process with that kind of intensified imitation which corrects nature's accidental deviations and distractions; he imitates so well that we have no trouble in penetrating into the lawful and typical course of events. When it comes to the "Peripeteia,"[22] however, the whole nicely constructed building breaks down; everything turns out to be at the end very different and by no means as clear-cut and expedient as the logical structure made us expect. With our systematic understanding, built according to scientific methods, we can just reach the Peripeteia —and here Aristotle leaves us alone. Something very inexpedient and unfitting, not included in the pattern, suddenly smashes down upon the hero: fate, the "deus ex machina," arbitrary, discontinuous, inconsistent. The rules Aristotle tries to state for the Peripeteia, are all more or less centered around accidents, hence the importance of sudden recognition,[23] unexpected revelation. This makes it clear that chance has entered the field and has become the mainspring and ruling power of Greek tragedy. Here may be a certain weakness, not only in Aristotelian aesthetics, but even in the structure of some Greek tragedies. Necessary and meaningful is here only the purposive action of the hero—the breakdown is only outwardly connected to it, as an intrusion from the outside, mostly from the divine sphere, working through accidents, unforeseeable and in no relation to the intrinsic course of events.

This is the point, however, where modern tragedy enters and transforms considerably the Aristotelian laws. To be sure, the process of action remains very important; but the process of action is not to be understood as a limited

21 Ibid., chapter 4.   22 The sudden reverse of events in a drama.
23 Aristotle, *Poetics*, chapter 11, where he tries in vain to combine Peripeteia and necessity.

happening, closed in motive and end and typically related to a purposive agent, the hero. The dramatic process cannot be entirely derived from the causal intercourse between a purposive subject and an environment, exhibiting the hero only in so far as he is a center of active or passive motivation. The hero is a hero only if he grows beyond the typical, merely symbolical simplification of action and reaction. In other words, the hero is a hero if he is an individual, a personality, and he is this only if his deeds are not merely traceable back to certain motivating influences and not merely absorbed in a definite fulfillment of a premeditated end. He extends, so to speak, backwards and forwards indefinitely; he represents more than his little self, he represents—as in the religious sphere—mankind in a metaphorical[24] way with all its conflicting motives, with its limitations and its longing beyond. What we call the hero's motive and end, is only one thin thread of thought and action, detached and abstracted for the sake of explanation out of the abundance of life, out of the complex tissues with its crossing, interwoven strings. The hero knows more than this end, he carries himself towards it, not only in order to fulfill it, but to transcend it and to "fulfill" a fate which is far beyond the limited end of his limited action. For this Beyond no satisfaction of fulfillment exists: a hero like Macbeth or Hamlet goes from the beginning not only the way of fulfillment and success, but also of failure and destruction, and the stronger his force, and the greater his intelligence and foresight, the more inflexible is the necessity which leads him "into the sear, the yellow leaf." One could say—although not quite correctly—that heroes such as Macbeth and Hamlet from the very first "intend" also their own ruin; but the word "in-

[24] On metaphorical representation see chapter 5, p. 85ff.

tention" or purpose would be too restricted and too much
tied to the relation between man and environment, while
the hero, on his way to destruction, reaches far beyond
any environment. This Beyond must not always be physical
death, although the purposive ego, having its most comprehensive realization in its body, will in failing be struck
foremost in this its body: the hero can reach his Beyond
also by a spiritual growth which makes him surpass his
previous goals and all limited goals whatsoever. In this
way tragedy passes beyond Peripeteia and leads in one
indivisible process necessarily over death and destruction
into a higher life of resurrection.

This shift from outward events to an inner development
is also reflected in the role which "evil" plays in Greek and
modern tragedy. In Greece the evil is mostly met in the
world of outward events, even chance-events which because
of their chance-character assume the nature of fate
(tyche), or when personified appear as the working of a
cruel demon. In modern tragedy no fate, no chance, no
demon have their place. Destruction is rooted in the very
heart of the hero whose own self is the source of failure,
sin, or guilt, and it needs only the awareness of this his
inner failure to reveal in him the transcending movement
of grace, his resurrection beyond the finite level of his
purposive and failing nature. The parallel to the religious
realm is obvious.[25]

If this is so, then the plot, indeed, fuses into one unity
with the life and character of the hero. The plot becomes
the mere manifestation and realization of the hero's life.
But this can only be done, if the hero's character is "representative," if he represents in metaphorical extension more
than himself and turns out to be the destiny of his fellow-

[25] See p. 82.

men, assuming, in spite of his individual concreteness, the
general validity of a law which makes a whole world trans-
parent for our understanding. In this way it happens that
the other personages of the drama appear not as exterior instruments of fate, thrown into the way of the hero in order
to lead him to his destiny, but more as the outgrowths of his
own inner life, personifying his secret wishes, as Lady
Macbeth, or as phantoms of his imagination, as the
witches and Banquo's ghost in *Macbeth* and the father's
visionary appearance in *Hamlet*. Shakespeare is great in
blurring the line between the hero's phantasy and the ex-
isting objects of his environment.

Under such circumstances, obviously, Aristotle's law of
temporal unity cannot remain unchanged. Unity must be;
this unity, however, is not the product of an outward
framework of space and time. It is the unity of the hero's
life-process which has the tension of an infinite present.
What achieves continuity is not the natural continuum of
the setting, but the inner necessity of destiny, revealed in
the life and character of the hero, and wherever this destiny manifests itself, continuity is felt, as the tension of
a representative life, indivisible, simple and reaching in a
lasting present over spaces and times. Whether the tragedy
plays in one act at a stretch and in one place, or whether
it plays in five acts and fifty scenes, all in different places
and times, as so often in Shakespeare's plays, the unity
is a unity of tension, residing in the hero's metaphorical
transcendence which transforms times and spaces into an
indivisible unity of the present. In the face of this heroic
life, men and things lose their self-importance and independent existence and point beyond themselves to a sphere
with regard to which they are only transitional stages of
one and the same world-process.

Tragedy, therefore, is the most mature form of drama:

failure and destruction are necessary elements of the metaphorical process, and that which perishes and, in passing
away, reveals a higher world, is the symbolic, purposive,
constructed environment of the ego with all its deeds and
fulfillments. It is not to be wondered that tragedy grew out
of the service to a god, out of a religious process, and that
it transcended the mere ritual as which, after all, it was
invented and from which it preserved some symbolic construction and content. Divine sacrifice, life, death, and resurrection was its original theme as it sprang out of the
Osiris-Dionysos myth, and immortality remained from
then on to our time the leading idea of great art and
poetry, from Egypt's grave-statues to the Holy Mass and
the Greek and Christian tragedies.

That tragedy crushes us and lifts us up at the same
time—that we feel sorrow and joy in one—has its reason in
the paradox of the metaphorical process which overcomes
and in overcoming transcends. This is the secret of the "sublime," raised by Burke and Kant to a fundamental problem.
The sublime is not a quality of the things, of the environment, depicted and described, it resides in the process by
which things and environment are surpassed. It may be
called a feeling, even the most essential feeling in poetry and
art. And so it may be necessary to broach the problem of
"feeling" in poetry and art, as Aristotle did. According to
him the tragedy should generate the feeling of pity and fear,
and should in doing so, either purify these feelings or
liberate us from them. Here Aristotle's statement lends
itself to different interpretations: is it the meaning of
tragedy that emotions are raised? Or, on the contrary,
should tragedy free the audience from them? Both interpretations, followed to the extreme, have unsatisfactory
results: Is tragedy a means to generate sensation, to bring

orgy into play and so to compete with certain drugs? Or shall tragedy eliminate sensation, empty us and so again compete with chemistry in providing a kind of spiritual laxative? Both solutions of the problem are similar: sensationalism and rationalism touch each other, as they so often do.[26] Therefore we should be equally suspicious with regard to both solutions. The metaphorical process alone provides the ground for an adequate treatment of the problem.

Feelings, Plato says,[27] are most often a mixture: pleasure alone is seldom to be found, displeasure equally seldom; the one is mixed with the other. The concept of "mixture" is, as we saw above, the outcome of a symbolic fixation and depicts an outward synthesis of fixed entities. It seems to say that there is on the one hand pleasure, clearly defined and demarcated, and on the other hand displeasure, equally fixed in its boundaries, and that these two feelings "mix." Also Aristotle's "golden mean" is a kind of mixture of extreme entities, the two of which exist separately, before they are shaken up into a mixture in order to produce life. Aristotle's true thought, surely, does not stop here,[28] but the wish for a clear line of demarcation, as it is at the bottom of all symbolic thinking, may have led him and Plato to the stating of opposites and then to their combination in "mixture" or "mean." In acknowledging these combinations Plato and Aristotle advance, certainly beyond the symbolic exactitude of abstraction, but this advance results again in a construction of mere togetherness in a synthetic way.

[26] See pp. 11, 81 footnote.

[27] Plato, *Philebus*, 36ff., especially 46ff. On the deficiency of the concept "mixture," see above p. 61.

[28] Aristotle, *Physics*, 188b and 189b, 190b. Aristotle acknowledges an underlying substance, mediating between the opposites (compare 1069b 8 and 1075a 32).

The truth, however, may be found on a different plane: pleasure, as such, and displeasure, as such, are limited to practical expediency, and they belong entirely to the realm of the purposive ego which has reduced itself to a definite end and its fulfillment in an environment of suitable and unsuitable means. Pleasure is the reaction of this ego to suitable means and the easy fulfillment of the goal; displeasure is the reaction to unsuitable means and inexpediency of the environment. In a world of limited symbols, pleasure is synonymous with useful and useful with good, and pleasure and usefulness will foremost concern the body as the organization of expediency, as the immediate environment of our purposive ego. In the body-sphere, indeed, the "summum bonum" is greatest expediency and satisfaction of ends. The hedonists, from the Cyrenaics and Epicureans unto the utilitarians, have considered foremost the bodily sphere of human existence, i.e. that which man and animal have in common. And they were scarcely able to conceive that man, properly understood, begins where the bodily mechanism of ends with its reduction to pleasure and displeasure is left behind.

The man who truly "feels" will not just feel pleasure or displeasure, he will feel a tension, because true feeling is a tension. And this tension will contain inseparably and even indistinguishably pleasure as well as displeasure, both being transcended in this tension. The truly "good" and "holy," therefore, will not be felt as pleasing or as displeasing, also not as a mixture, in the Platonic sense. It will be felt as a metaphorical process of transcendence in which the contradicting and conflicting feelings are overcome and survive in a way which can neither be called pleasure nor displeasure. Neither pleasure nor displeasure give their mark to the creative process of the present which is beyond the sphere of ends and the satisfaction of their fulfillment.

Between the two poles, however, between the symbolic fixation in its rigidity and between the pure metaphorical transcendence, many intermediate stages may be found—the Platonic-Aristotelian "mixture" and "mean" was already one of them. If we want to characterize the development from the one pole to the other in its intermediate stages of feelings, we can say that the more a feeling corresponds to a finite want and a definite fulfillment of an end, the more will it be one-sided, symbolical, and the more be labelled either as pleasure or as displeasure. The less this is the case, the less it will be possible to classify our feeling as pleasant or unpleasant. This feeling will simply express the tension of the metaphorical process. Or, in other words, the easier it is to interpret an event as a definite fulfillment of a limited purpose, dictated by the environment, the clearer it will be connected to a feeling of bodily reaction. This is what we call "sensuous feelings." And these feelings will be the more sensuous, the more immediate and close the relation between want and fulfillment is. The needs we can fully satisfy are always material, bodily needs, and the feelings, attached to them, are bodily feelings of pleasure and displeasure. If we are thirsty, drink gives the sensuous pleasure of satisfaction. If we are tired and bored, sensuous entertainment, in killing time, will bring a momentary satisfaction and pleasure. Pleasure is short, for it is born and dies in the passing moment of fulfillment, leaving emptiness behind. The wider, on the other hand, the tension between want and fulfillment stretches, the more we rest in the present of the process: Our feeling, here, nourished by memory of the past and imagination of the future, will develop into a metaphorical integration, transcending the bodily restrictions of symbolically reduced means. Such a feeling, the feeling not of satisfaction but of process, tension, and the present, is what we are used to call a "spiritual emotion." Hope, faith, and love are spiritual tensions, spiritual emotions. Joy is an emotion which surpasses the moment and connects our past with our future. Joy lives, therefore, mostly in anticipation, happiness too; and it is just this wide stretch of joy and happiness which makes us prefer the joy of anticipation to the momentary and transient pleasure of satisfaction.

It is common to sensualism and rationalism that they consider only the pleasures of the body, and thus either glorify lust and orgy, or preach asceticism. Also asceticism emphasizes the sharp distinction between pleasure and displeasure, and therefore, after having isolated them, guards against pleasure as a necessary source of displeasure. This rational calculation in the field of sensuality finds its parallel in Hedonism, where discrete pleasure and pain are weighed and the latter counterbalanced by the first. So rationalists and sensualists, especially in the time of the Stoics and the Epicureans, meet in the endeavor, to flee pleasure and displeasure alike, a fact which shatters the ground of every utilitarian philosophy.

The ethics of Empiricism, regarding pleasure and displeasure as the mainspring of action, reduces man to the sensuous realm of the body. This ethical system lacks the insight that man lives more than a mere animal life with its relation between body and environment. The most essential decisions of our life are not necessitated by pleasure and displeasure. On the contrary, we "forget ourselves," we sacrifice the body, as the symbol of expediency, and with it renounce all small satisfactions, comforts, and pleasures in order to live for a task, an ideal beyond the possibility of a finite fulfillment. The martyr of whom we say that he is joyful in his suffering, is far beyond the naive distinction between pleasure and displeasure, and every person, living for something greater than his own little ego, feels a similar spiritual emotion.

Hedonism was the black side of Greek rationalism; feeling will always have the stigma of sensuous feeling for those who emphasize the symbols of a finite order. This is the paradox of Platonic love that it means to be a spiritual emotion, but that it dies away in satisfaction and so reveals its finite, expedient character as a means for a definite purpose. It is Aristotle[29] who discovers the spiritual character of "Eudaimonia" and anticipates the wisdom of future times. Although his statements with regard to this fundamental concept allow very different interpretations, one thing stands out clearly: Eudaimonia is not the pleasure which accompanies the fulfillment and dies away with the achievement of a definite goal. Eudaimonia expresses the tension which arises out of the process of activity. It has no goal besides its own life of tension. It is an infinite present embracing past and future and representing in this its infinite present the blessedness of the Divine.

Not sensuality alone, but also finiteness, limitation, reduction, the fixation of intellectual order have their share in the emotional sphere. For it is the end, the fixed goal which throws life into the adventure of success or failure, possession or loss, satisfaction or despair—or better, delivers life to both of these stages. For success is partly failure, possession never without loss, and satisfaction a short illusion which carries over into distress. Thus man is shaken by fear and hope, and the shorter the course of time is which runs toward the goal, the more this emotion is heated to a flame which consumes his existence. So the end spurs on and may be responsible for the achievements and the activity of life, but it would make life a meaningless up and down of emotional excitement if man had not

[29] Aristotle, *Nicomachean Ethics*, 1176b 1ff.

the spiritual power to regard beginning and end, birth and death, plan and fulfillment as a mere scaffold over which life, undivided and immortal, stretches,[30] raising us not to a state of indifference, but to an integrated and enduring emotion of a creative present.

The present of the spirit is not detached from senses and intellect. Soul is not an entity, fenced off from body and mind. Body and soul belong together as symbol and metaphorical process. We live our purposive bodily existence in a sensuous environment with its short satisfactions, its empty and full times, its empty and full spaces. But this whole sensuous construction and symbolic order is carried by a tension of the present which we call spirit or soul, transcending the reductions of our fixed relationships. Spirit overcomes sensuality, soul overcomes body. But, on the other hand, it is this sensuality, this body over which alone spirit and soul can expand and proceed.

The soul-body problem has been obscured by confusing it with the mind-body problem. Mind and body, the objects of rationalism and sensationalism, are both symbolic systems when abstracted and cut off from the underlying soul-process. They are similar to each other in their relationship of parts and wholes, and are similar in their failures. Spinoza was not altogether wrong in treating mind and body as finite perspectives of a similar order. The division of the body into parts, in contrast to its living function, the body as an organized system has to be understood similarly to the organized system of the symbolic mind. No wonder that these organizations correspond, and that even the laws of mechanical causation can be adapted to the understanding of relations between body and mind. The doubt of some thinkers whether the mind is to be regarded as a reality in itself. or whether

30 See p. 109.

there are merely independent and isolated thoughts, has
its ground in the fact that mind, indeed, like body, can
be considered in its parts separately. But just as body
becomes alive in the unity of these parts and vanishes as a
mere potential in the process of the soul, transcending its
character as body, so the reality of the mind is not in mind
itself which may be only a summing up of interrelated
thoughts, but vanishes in the necessity of a process, called
soul, spirit, or will, for which mind or intellect is only a
potential. Therefore beyond the system of mind and body,
as a whole of related parts, stretches a process of a questioning, willing, loving infinity which cannot be explained
by mind or by the physiological body-organization. It
manifests itself in both, although never exhausted by any
of them, because it transcends them in the consciousness
and communion of I and Thou, and this, indeed, is what we
call soul or spirit.

And now, at last, we are able to answer the question:
What is the role that feelings play in poetry and art? Does
art serve the emotional life and does the artist as well as
the spectator, have to go through all these emotions? Yes
and no. The poet and the spectator feel the exultation and
distress of the hero; they feel, as Aristotle says, pity and
fear. But the action of the drama entangles in the maze
of happenings, draws into the network of a narrow environment with all its pleasure and pain, success and failure
only in order to lift beyond into a tension in which these
things lose their singular importance and grow into a unity
of life, representative, indivisible, and simple. In this infinite process of the present the various changing, conflicting, and exciting feelings are transformed into the
spiritual emotion which is neither pleasant nor painful
and which may be understood as confidence, faith, or love.

This is the purification of which Aristotle speaks, purification being the transcendence into a spiritual process of tension and extension, beyond the stage, the hero, and our own little self.[31] Therefore the tragedy has to crush as well as to lift up. But that which is crushed is finite and transient and that which is strengthened is infinite and lasting.

It may happen that the poet does not succeed in carrying us beyond the little world of ends, fulfillment, lust, and pain; then the work of art lacks "distance." For this is the very essence of poetic or artistic distance. Wherever we are stuck in the shallow water of lust and pain, in the fussy happenings of success and failure, there we may feel pity for the poor fellow or fear for the weakling and his personal troubles. But the whole affair remains too much of a singular event, and confessions, made by a stranger, have, because of this their fragmentary character, a painful effect. Only where we love, are we able to widen the narrow facts into an integrated present of a whole life. Great art makes us love and thus transforms what would be a singular confession into a unity of life in which we share and by which we extend even beyond our own narrowness and lack of distance with its self-pity and fear for self-preservation which would chain us to a limited and sterile shelter.

Where spiritual transcendence is lacking, we are caught in the typical actions and reactions of environment. This "realism" arouses pleasures and pains, none of which go beneath the surface. But it may happen that the lack of distance, the narrowness of a strange environment closes

[31] Self-enjoyment means play. Play is that kind of activity which has self-enjoyment as its immediate goal. The famous play theory of art has here its root: whether one calls it self-expression or self-realization or self-enjoyment, it is all mere play, mere entertainment, but never art.

too tightly around us, so that we are forced to break out, to repel and push away in an instinctive reaction of flight. Tragedy has here its counterpart and caricature: it is the "comical," and its bodily reaction is laughter.

Comedy needs just that which tragedy avoids, the lack of distance. In its extreme form, as farce, it should not be regarded as poetry at all. Its object is the narrow environment, symbolically reduced, the expedient, useful relation of means and end, clear and exact like a mechanism.[32] Action becomes typical, persons change into types, reducing the metaphorical abundance of life to a fixed formula. This formula is repulsive, and we condemn a person whose typical fixation we criticize as lifeless and unhuman: we call him a "pedant." The pedant, indeed, is one of the most important personages in comedies. Whether the pedant puts on the air of a learned woman or of a misanthrope or of an hypochondriac, to mention some of Molière's famous fools, it is always a person who is simplified, cut and dried to a formula, using his environment as means for his one and only purpose. The pedant is, so to speak, nothing but one single attribute, he lives the proposition of identity where the subject is symbolized by itself as a predicate; he lives this predicate as the only motive of his life and finds nothing in his environment but that which corresponds as a means to this one and only motive.[33]

[32] This point is excellently stressed by Bergson in his book on laughter.

[33] The comedy is a symbolic simplification of the world to a narrow environment. Who does not belong to the specific environment will never understand the comical element. The comical is, therefore, not only narrow in its content, but also in its unifying effect on mankind. Every nation, every community, even every family has its own jokes, where others cannot join in laughter. Not so with tragedy. If we, however, follow Aristotle's advice too strictly, to choose the hero's character according to the motivation of the plot and make him nothing but a causal factor in the mechanism, then tragedy comes danger-

What the plain comedy needs, are typical people, typical events, a systematic subordination of the whole under one main idea and purpose which may even be propagandistic. All detail, not serving the symbolic tendency, has to be left out, it would only divert from the one track and spoil the effect. Effect is what is wanted, and the comic effect will be typical too, often repeated with slight modifications. The arsenal of comic tricks is limited, the rules, the ritual, the routine are fixed. Writers of comedies, i.e. of plays which are nothing but funny, are rather technicians, skillful virtuosi, than poets. The true poet will not be satisfied with such a limited bit of life, he will, wherever he touches this field, instinctively draw away from the mere farce.

Here, however, an objection may be raised: if the narrow and pedantic reduction of life is nothing but repulsive, how can we feel anything but displeasure when faced with comical experiences? In fact, the comical effect is in the beginning displeasing, but it changes into something like pleasure. Plato,[34] therefore, uses his concept of "mixture" just with regard to the comical. But here the inadequacy of the vague idea of "mixture" is apparent: mixture should be understood as tension, and tension, indeed, was what characterized "feeling" and leads in its wider expansion from sensuous to spiritual emotion. In the comical, however, no true tension is to be found. There is a mere alternation and succession of dissatisfaction and satisfaction,

---

ously near to comedy, is reduced to the typical, and will only find an echo in those who belong to the same typical environment. Such tragedies grow obsolete very quickly, just as the average comedy does.

Aristotle, however, does not quite overlook the difference between the tragic hero and the typically reduced comical personage. He states that comedies use three definite types of persons and show the typification already in the symbolic names of these personages. (*Poetics*, chapter 9.)

[34] Plato, *Philebus*, 48.

and because both are entirely separated, detached and unmixed, the succession of the one after the other appears as a sudden and surprising revulsion. The unexpected element in all comical events is, in fact, based on the lack of continuity and tension; and so the suddenness of this revulsion can manifest itself in the bodily eruption of laughter.[35]

Discontinuity, in its extreme, is the principle of all comical events, and—as an extreme—it caricatures the symbolic detachment and fixation. There is no joke without the breach of continuity which surprises; we do not expect it, living a life of continuity. The comical, here, appears as the opponent to life; and as such it proclaims the principle of chance, of accident, or coincidence. That chance rules over our life, that nothing really is necessary, that we are faced every moment with a surprising adventure which turns meaning into nonsense—this is the philosophy of farce. This philosophy is a distortion of life, to be sure, and the satisfaction which this distortion gives is only a pseudo-satisfaction. The liberation which fun provides is the insight that life, tension, continuity should not be taken too seriously: chance is adopted, discontinuity is justified as a liberation from the lawful and burdensome necessity of a responsible life, and so a shallow pleasure of satisfaction is provided. Therefore laughter leaves emptiness behind, indifference and fatigue. Laughter will seldom spread where real deep interest is at stake.

Here, however, another, more serious variation of farce may be mentioned: the grotesque. If it is true that great

[35] Laughter has often been explained as a release from tension. This may happen; but it is not so much tension, as displeasure, from which laughter releases; and this displeasure may sometimes have its reason just in a lack of tension which depresses us as unhuman and lifeless. Therefore people who are "loosened up" by alcohol or tiredness are more ready for laughter than intensive and concentrated persons. Boredom asks for amusement.

art, just as great religion, expresses confidence and raises from death and destruction,[36] then we have to distinguish it from a pre-artistic or magic sphere, where fear and suspicion make man build fences of protection and invent means of liberation from the dismal forces of life. Discontinuity, chance, surprise are here too, but not as symptoms of a funny world; they are symptoms of a sinister world of chaos which the suffering individual is eager to shake off. In times of chaos men return to a magic form of art, using the demoniac aspects of life for their stories and plays: sickness, insanity, death; but they turn them into grotesque means for laughter in order to regain their inner balance. This is done in the novels by Thomas Mann (*Magic Mountain* and *Tristan*, etc.), where sickness and death, or in comedies as *Arsenic and Old Lace*, where corpses and insanity, are used for comic effects. The grotesque will always appear and take hold of those ages which are under the strain of disaster, feeling the sinister and chaotic aspects of life, but advanced enough to appease the mind by laughter.

The funny and the grotesque are both inefficient and futile means to cover up, rather than to heal, the diseases and deficiences of our existence. The truly great comedy is neither only funny nor grotesque, but has a more creative attitude to life. It is the continuity and meaningfulness of our existence which it cherishes, and because of that it turns accusingly against those distortions which the vulgar farce enjoys. What it wants, is to make us see the true values behind the masquerade of selfishness and stupidity. It depicts accidents and pedantic fools in order to raise our disgust. But if it is real poetry, it will not do it by showing us the exaggerations of caricature. It will be

[36] See pp. 84, 131.

true to life and give us the complexity of human characters, where the good is close to the bad; it will not make us laugh, but smile at the weakness of man. It will not be funny but humorous; for humor has a serious element, it does not simplify and reduce life, but tries to understand life in its contradictions. Humor may be critical, but just. It faces the weakness and failure of man, but it never loses faith, and it measures the deficiency by the infinite resources of betterment. Humor sees men as shallow and profound, as vicious and virtuous, and it puts emphasis on the dark sides of life only in order to strengthen the belief in the light ones. Farce debases, but humor lifts up. The beautiful creations of humor, therefore—some of Dickens' men and women, Cervantes' Don Quixote—may make us smile but not laugh. Shakespeare, in his great tragedies, feels from time to time the urge to strew pearls of humor in the profound sadness of his stories and gives us in his humorous scenes moments of rest and thoughtfulness, as stations on the way of his tragic genius, beyond which the tension of the dramatic process stretches with renewed intensity.

That farce and caricature are distortions of nature, nobody will deny. It is the exaggeration of a pedantry which grows out of the symbolic ritual. But tragedy, in its way, is an exaggeration of nature too. Surely, comedy as well as tragedy move away from the "normal." But this similarity is only a seeming one. Comedy builds on the symbolic reduction: the reduction cannot be stressed too much; if it is, the result is caricature and nonsense. But the sphere of tragedy is that of the metaphorical process, infinite in its present. It can never be exaggerated: the more it widens, the more it is adequate to its essential idea. It cannot be distorted, being itself the judge and standard of that which is distorted. Symbolic representation can lead to misuse and stagnation; the metaphorical representation, as a growing responsibility and unity of life, never does. The symbolic representation may reduce man to a mere organ, to a snout or a belly; the metaphorical representation may be stretched, yet it will only the more fulfill its task of embracing the world in its abundance, mankind in its conflicts of joy and suffering.

This extension beyond the normal is, therefore, no distortion in the field of great poetry and art: it is stylization. The normal, nature as such, in its purposive and expedient structure, man in his environment, is the material of poetry. But the poet who is satisfied to depict it as it is, will never create a work of art. He imitates, and imitation is not art. It was the fallacy of Greek aesthetics to found art on imitation. Surely, Plato[37] and Aristotle[38] saw that it is not just the superficial and accidental appearance of nature which the artist has to "copy," but the law in nature. This law, however, was nothing but the typical generalization of the symbolic system and by concentrating on this typical aspect of life, the poet easily confounded the tragic and the comic hero.

The aesthetics of imitation forgets that the poet may use the normal, typical, expedient nature, but that he has to enhance this nature and to transcend it in a drive which we call stylization, transforming nature into the simplicity of metaphorical representation. Here things stand for more than they are, environment grows to a world, man to an expression of humanity. Happenings assume the necessity and infallibility of fate. Stylization ennobles every object, carries it into a concentrated life of service. Metaphorical representation expressed responsibility in

---

[37] Plato, *Symposium*, 211.   [38] Aristotle, *Poetics*, chapters 2 and 9.

the religious process of prayer. And as prayer confesses the sinfulness of man and in confessing atones, so tragedy expresses conflict and failure, and in expressing, transcends and purifies. This can only be done by stylization which creates distance and detaches man from his bodily sensual, expedient sphere of pleasure and pain. Distance by stylization is the mark of great poetry which carries us beyond the environment into a world. It is *Imagination*, as the power of the poetic genius, which extends environment to world, uses the things of nature, but widens them so that they lose their narrow appearance and grow into the distance of universal greatness. Imagination is not an arbitrary capacity of invention, it is more a power of discovery: discovery of greatness in small things, discovery of distance in nearness and narrowness, discovery of the infinite metaphorical Present in the fragmentary symbols of transitional things and events.

Imagination and the distance it creates detach us from our narrow environment and lift us into a world of intensive reality. This reality has often been misunderstood as an "artistic appearance," as a "make believe," and people have been led to the assumption that the satisfaction which tragedy conveys is the awakening from the dreamworld of the stage and its horrors to a true and more balanced reality of everyday life. But just the opposite is true: the reality of the tragedy is so strong that it shakes the foundations of our empirical existence and makes us see its vain superficiality. A new standard of values arises, linking our little life, walled up in its accidental environment, to a wider process of service. New tasks impose themselves on us, strengthen our sense of responsibility and make us humble. Humility is a mark of true greatness, while bumptiousness shows deficiency and ridiculous limitation. Conscience grows when men are thrown upon their own inner resources, in the distance of their individual and responsible self—distant to the narrow pressure of things, possessions and environmental happenings—and here, in the responsibility of a conscience, tragedy touches at the problem of personality. Personality is the great unknown for which we search in transcendence, in the metaphorical abundance and infinite present. Here we are led to the simple fact that men, beyond their purposive actions and beyond the fixation of their character, know a higher unity of life: personality. Art as well as Ethics and Religion meet in this sanctuary. Great art has always served the ethical and religious drive towards this center. The contribution of tragedy is the strengthening of a conscientious and responsible personality.

7

MUSIC AND FINE ARTS

In the course of this work one main distinction struck us again and again as extremely important: the distinction between the metaphorical process and the symbolic reduction. We met it in the logical field when we considered the function of the proposition, the *subjectum*, and apart from it the fixed conceptual terms. On mythical ground we found the split again, now as the creative process of prayer, and, in distinction to it, the ritual, a symbolic pattern which reduces the religious life but has permanently to draw strength out of the creative process. World-process and environment were two other names for the same bifurcation. And as we proceeded further and descended from the world into human life and its spiritual expression in poetry and drama, we had to face a similar distinction: the heroic destiny, representing an infinite world, spreading beyond and absorbing its limited environment; and besides the flexible "here and now" added up into a series, a spatial and temporal continuum, forming an outward pattern of unity. Artistic distance, at last, was once more the expression of a spiritual tension and integrated present, overarching the particular objects and events and drawing them into a background where the sensuous momentary fulfillments of lust and pain fade away; and in distinction to this distance of stylization we found mere imitation, always in danger of degenerating into technical dexterity or into the belittlement of a comical reduction as a flight from life and responsibility.

It is this twofold attitude which is necessary for the full understanding of life: the metaphorical spiritual process carries and transcends the reduced and expedient ritual in its imitative, symbolic order.

When we now try to apply this knowledge to the realm of Music, it is as if here more than anywhere these distinctions held true. The problematic sphere of music, secluded from the rest of the world, closed to all explanations, opens up to those who understand the interconnection of symbolic reduction and metaphorical process. It is first of all the measure, the beat which represents the symbolic fixation in music. Measure is the repeated and in its repetition, the organizing pattern of music. The measure is the scaffold, the exact ritual, guaranteeing a minimum of technical balance, and the conductor has to watch over its punctual observation by his beat in order to secure the continuum of repetition. The division into 6/8 or 3/4 measure, as an arithmetical pattern, a ritual—confirmed in its imitative repetition—is a necessary and extremely useful means for an expedient construction. The student has to learn when the one and when the other measure is expedient, and sometimes it may be useful to transform and rewrite a piece of music in a different measure. Here we have, indeed, a general technical knowledge, a purely rational and symbolic pattern. And, in a similar way, this holds true with regard to the finer and more complicated techniques which the student learns as "technique of composition," or as the "doctrine of form." As the dramatist organizes his work skillfully into acts, the acts into scenes which build the structure of the play, so too the musical dramatist has to organize, to "compose," which means he has to put his material together according to rules, and the rules have to be learned by technical training. He has to know the importance of repetition when done in certain patterns; repetition, variation and imitation confirming and enhancing the effect, the summing up of parts to a whole. It is a technical device which aids in clear grouping and repeating of the same or similar formulae. Unquestionably this is a highly intellectual technique. The aesthetics of music will be able to ground it in an exact scientific system, teachable and learnable. The student will have to train himself in these aesthetic rules, and the school to which he belongs will sanction this system as a ritual. Fights between rituals will blaze up because each school will declare its own ritual as exclusive and absolute, confusing, as in the religious field, the mere ritual with the true spiritual process of creation.

The astonishing fact, however, is that this abstract, symbolical element draws extremely near to the sensuous element in music. It has often been stated—and naturalism has built its aesthetics on this idea—that measure and beat resemble closely the bodily pulsation of our blood. Some aestheticians, faithful to the theory that art is imitation of nature, have taken the musical beat for an imitation of the heartbeat. They have elaborated this theory and have explained the Song as an expedient accompaniment for bodily work, regulating by beat and measure the combined efforts of a laboring group: fishermen towing ropes through the water, or lumberjacks lifting and letting fall their axes in measured time. These theories are not only right, in a limited way, but they are enlightening. They reveal the close connection between the rational, symbolic sphere of purposive expediency and the sensuous sphere of our bodily organization.[1]

This connection has an even more striking consequence, the phenomenon we call "orgy." The repetition and speed of beats makes the tempo in music. A quick tempo influences the pulsation; an increase in tempo may cause a sensuous

[1] See pp. 81 footnote and 137.

excitement, bodily lust, and in its extreme, the trance of orgies, as has often been done in religious rituals. The same effect can be achieved by chemicals and, indeed, since time immemorial both means have been used—the quick repetition of beats and the administering of drugs. Drum-beats, repeated endlessly, together with the repetition of the same body movements have resulted in the trance of orgies which often end in bloody self-mutilation and torture. Crowds play an important role in these orgies, and here again the beat of marching feet together with the quantity of the whole, has served the intensive pattern of purposive action where each single individual, reduced to an equal part—exchangeable, replaceable—became a cog in the machinery of the ritual. Every soldier knows of the importance of the beat in order to raise mass-orgy and mass-action, and only where this device does not suffice, is it supplemented by the administering of alcohol. Here again the affinity can be seen between an abstract mental organization and the abstraction which makes the body into an unconscious object of a merely mechanical nature. It is life as consciousness which has been eliminated by the lifeless scheme of the beat as well as by drugs, and it is because of this that the body as a rigid object now functions merely according to mechanical and physiological rules.

The sensuous and rational pattern of measure and beat, however, is by no means the essence of music. It is a technique, a ritual, and as all ritual important and vital only, when overcome. The powerful element which overcomes measure, is the *rhythm*. Only with rhythm we enter into the true realm of music. But symbols have an inclination to dominate: the ritual tries to set itself up above the mythical process, to absorb the metaphorical drive. So also here measure and beat have usurped the place of the rhythm and have often been regarded in aesthetical systems as the general term under which rhythm was only granted a specific and minor role. But rhythm is not a mode of measure; rhythm, on the contrary, is the force which breaks the domination of the measure, violently changes and transforms it, stylizes and overcomes. Rhythm is the metaphorical process of music, and as all metaphorical process it transcends and transforms the symbolic fixation and reduction, destroying the self-sure and complacent order of the measured pattern. Valued by the standard of this pattern, rhythm may appear as a chaotic power of destruction and disorder; but it is, in fact, a higher order, and in its tension and conflict it realizes something which measure never could achieve. The uniform and regular measure is stretched here, condensed there in the tension of rhythmical power; but the irregularity of this chaos is held together by the necessity of a continuous indivisible process, changing the mere repetition of succeeding beats into an infinite, because simple and indivisible, present of tension. From the first beat till the last we are bound by a breathless spell, the heart, as we may say, seems to stand still, expressing the extreme opposite to the repeated pulsation.

Rhythm is the power which transcends, uses, and makes valuable the devices of repetition and order. Rhythm is the unifying process, intensifying the tension of the present which is an eternity, very different from the eternal nothingness of orgies. Here is no mere quantity or multitude, but an indivisible simple unity. Rhythm as such does not bring a fulfillment or solution; these belong to the realm of ends, terminations, and after the end a new beginning would have to start. To be sure, there is always again some new beginning, the rhythm—irregular in itself—may be repeated in its irregularity and tension all over again, and the aesthete may place great emphasis on this repetition.

He may point to the kind of music where such permanent repetitions are most obvious, dance rhythms, march rhythms and the like. But first of all, it should be remembered indeed that the repeated measure will always remain the technique, the closed pattern, the underlying scaffold of the piece; the "composition" as a whole will ask for certain repetitions of parts. And furthermore, wherever repetition is felt as a main feature and gives, as such, full satisfaction, we are indeed on the boundary line between art and a mere bodily activity: in marching rhythm we enjoy our body, and equally in waltz rhythm and other dances. They may result in lust and excitement, but the more this happens, the less will such music rank among the works of true art. The truly artistic works of this kind may modify the mere repetition by always new variations, harmonies, instrumentations; an abundance of surprising deviations will cover up the dull repetition of the mere beat.

Those who regard the generation of bodily feelings as the meaning of music and who consider that besides the measure only the tempo is essential, misunderstand thoroughly the proper essence of music: neither tragedy nor great music are created in order to raise ecstasy; such bodily self-enjoyment is a childish immaturity of primitive people or a second childhood of senility. Orgies are only narcotics and leave us more helpless and empty than before.

There is, however, a reason for the overemphasis of measure, beat, tempo, excitement in music. This reason is the abstract limitation of rhythm to the temporal sphere exclusively. Here again we have a symbolic reduction which falsifies our understanding. Rhythm is by no means only temporal rhythm. As merely temporal the rhythm, indeed, may become very similar to the beat and may be confounded with measure. But true rhythm is just as much spatial as temporal. The tension of the present is the ground of all art, and the present is a metaphorical integration of space and time.[2] The present stretches over the flux of temporal succession and holds it in a continuous togetherness where no sound is forgotten and no tone is sunk into the past. Who truly experiences the beauty of a piece of music, does not forget the first bar, when the second begins, and has not in mind at the end only the last bar, while all the previous have sunk into oblivion; he holds in the tension of the rhythmical present all the bars, preserved as a continuous and indivisible unity.[3] Only where this is felt, is music understood, and only for those who understand in this way, the piece does not end with the last tone, but keeps on singing, just as the tragedy lives on in us, and the more so after the curtain falls. Certainly, an enormous effort of concentration is needed in order to preserve this tension of the present. No drifting along in sweet sounds, no forgetfulness in the trance of orgy; what is needed, is a sincere struggle, a fight for the present, aided by the rhythmical power which again and again welds together the discontinuous little measures of repetition, transcending them in an indivisible metaphorical process.

This present of tension in which everything is preserved and nothing drowned in the oblivion of the past, can rightly be called a creative memory, a power of remembering. But remembrance presupposes forgetfulness. Only

2 See chapter VI, p. 123.

3 Mozart writes in a famous letter: "Das Ding wird im Kopfe fertig, wenn es auch lang ist, sodass ichs hernach mit einem Blick gleichsam wie ein schoenes Bild im Geiste uebersehe, und es auch garnicht nacheinander wie es hernach kommen muss, in der Einbildung hoere, sondern wie gleich alles zusammen." ("The thing becomes finished in the head, although it may be long, so that I can afterwards embrace it in the mind, so to speak, with one look, like a beautiful picture; and I hear it in my imagination not successively as it must be heard later on, but somehow all together.")

that which has been forgotten can be remembered. Therefore the present of rhythm as a creative process of remembrance, needs the forgetfulness, out of which it rises, and this forgetfulness is provided by the discontinuous measure and beat. All discontinuity means oblivion. Discontinuity restricts, limits, shuts off, atomizes. The repetition, therefore, of beat and measure enhances oblivion as a breaking of continuity, as an atomization into detached moments. Oblivion surrounds the single beat which again and again starts anew.[4] But just this breaking asunder and oblivion is the necessary condition for the remembering process. In this process the fixation of forgetfulness has its positive share: it works as a resisting force and so intensifies the unifying creativity of the rhythmical process. In this way every detached entity is separately regained by remembrance and, therefore, achieves an importance of place which makes it reach from this place as a distant entity across the stretch of the memory. Without this fixation of oblivion we would only experience an indivisible tension of the present, no articulation of a structural order. So, although rhythm is the vital element of remembrance, the remembered content in the order of a differentiated distance asks for the fixation of forgetfulness.

This creative fixation of forgetfulness, although an obstacle in the process of remembrance, stimulates the process and provides articulation in the stretch of its tension, as measure, metre, repetition of the theme, variation do.[5] The repetition of the discontinuous series is

[4] When beats follow in quick succession, something like a quasi-duration may result out of the blurring of one into the other. This may have the exciting effect of a perpetuation of discontinuity and may lead to drowning of memory and surrender to the perpetuated now of the orgy.

[5] Quite a different fixation of forgetfulness, which has to be carefully distinguished from the creative fixation mentioned above, is the

fruitful, its regularity is, to be sure, only a mechanical, a technical device, taught as a regulation or rule, and, like all rules, it is merely invented as techniques are, not discovered as an inner law. Regulation and inner law differ as symbol and metaphorical process do.

But here again we may stress the importance of the compromise between metaphorical process and symbolic fixation which we found frequently in the course of this work and which was most clearly embodied in the "continuum" and the "organism."[6] Rhythm expresses continuity of process, but the repetition of discontinuous elements introduces the continuum, the objective whole, the fixed structure. It is here, now, that we can discriminate clearly between beat and measure which we have used synonymously until now. While beat emphasizes mere discontinuity, measure and metre[7] are the expression of the continuum, that is, they are discontinuous and continuous at the same time; they have variety and unity, but they stress more than these the repetition of the same, and so they stabilize the continuous process. Measure and metre, therefore, mediate between beat and rhythm and have been largely emphasized in civilizations which, like the Greek, are highly organic

---

fixation in writing or in learning by heart. Both of these, writing and learning by heart, have no vital share in the process of remembrance or any living tension whatsoever. They simply store away, and what is stored away in this manner is not remembered, but "recalled," i.e. it is brought to attention, when needed, and stored away again, when not needed any more. The fixation of structure as a necessary part of the remembering process prepared and enhanced the power of remembrance; the fixation in writing and in learning by heart, however, simply substitutes for remembrance, replaces remembrance, makes it unnecessary by providing instead the mechanical device of the written note or the equally mechanical habit of the brain-trace. Our habit of keeping things in writing or in learning them by heart, therefore, has largely destroyed our capacity of an active and creative remembrance.

6 See p. 39.   7 See p. 122.

and show the transition from a static to a dynamic era. Metre in poetry and measure in music will be important in times of technical perfection when rules and regulations have been fixed as having universal validity. But these devices will never quite get away from the element of arbitrariness which characterizes their mechanical order[8] and distinguishes them from the inner law, the inner form of the work of art. This arbitrariness has, therefore, to be overcome by the necessity of a lawful process. As letters and words are transcended by the lawful process of language, so beat and measure are transcended by the lawful process of rhythm by which they are "remembered."

The rhythm, in transcending all these devices of forgetfulness and welding the process into a memory of togetherness, has surpassed the merely temporal succession of tones which beat and measure emphasized. In doing this rhythm confirms the truth that art is never merely temporal or merely spatial. Art is art, because it is aware of the inseparable unity of space and time, a unity which is stressed in the rhythmical process of the present. And this present is still more intensively expressed by another element which emphasizes to the highest degree the spatial character in music, adding to the temporal rhythm a spatial rhythm: the rhythm of pitch, of distances between high and low tones. What we call *harmony* is a spatial rhythm of pitch. Harmony is a tension, and it is a tension which stretches over a variety of distances in tones, of spatial distances from high to low.[9] Musical rhythm, therefore, is fully understood only when temporal rhythm of short and

[8] Aristotle (*Rhetoric*, 1408b) distinguishes between rhythm and metre and calls metre artificial because of the repetition involved.

[9] On the metaphorical truth of high and low tones as spatial differences see p. 59.

long intervals is combined with the spatial rhythm of various distances between high and low pitch. Wherever one and the same tone is repeated in a temporal rhythm, we are led instinctively to the abstraction of a mere temporal series, of mere tempo, to bodily feeling and excitement. But when the differences of pitch are combined with the differences of intervals, the rhythm of spatial distance with the rhythm of temporal duration, then only an indivisible unity of a spatio-temporal rhythm arises, a purely spiritual tension of the highest concentration. And it is this full rhythmical process which we call *melody*.

Rhythm in its purity and concreteness is melody. Melody is that which cannot be taught nor learned, which makes the rituals of the schools break down. Melody is the life of the spirit, it comes as a grace or it does not come at all. No rules can force it because it is the metaphorical process which transcends rules.

Melody is never sensuous or orgiastic, and never merely an intellectual pattern. It uses both, intellect and senses, but it purifies them and leaves them behind. No melody, therefore, can be interpreted as an expression of pleasure or displeasure.[10] Often the same melodies have been used for very different texts, gay and serious, tragic and exultant. Handel and Bach, especially, knew that the metaphoric nature of melodies transcends every particular interpretation. This infinite width and transcendence beyond any fixed interpretation gives distance and an unparalleled representative power to music and melody.

Melody is the essence of music. But melody does not only comprise that which goes under the name of "melodious." Certain aesthetics have restricted the artistic value, called

10 This is different with tone-systems, major and minor. They correspond to certain interpretations, and are therefore a much beloved object of psychology and a psychological aesthetics.

beauty, to that which represents an expedient, organic
balance, the rounding out and closing off into a satisfying
fulfillment of a finite purpose. This very rational and symbolic reduction has a typical form, easy to grasp with a
minimum of tension; it is what we call amiable, agreeable,
sweet, lovely, charming. It works more on our bodily feelings, as a sensuous satisfaction, and it is not lasting, but
momentary and frail. Great music has to break the egg-
shell of this frail sweetness, it has to distort even the organic balance and contentment, it has to stylize, and in
doing this, it is "expressive." To be "expressive" is more
than to be agreeable or sweet. This is a beauty which lasts,
because it is the spiritual beauty of tension.

Rhythm is tension, melody is tension. There will certainly also be release and relaxation, but only as transitional phases in the great process of rhythmical melody.
The vague differences of consonance and dissonance play
much too great a role in musical discussions. A rational
aesthetics will always show preference for the well-rounded
and satisfactory consonance which is pleasing, organic, expedient. Its rituals will put fences up against the destructive power of dissonances, and the common sense of the
masses will stoutly refuse any innovation in this respect,
just as the bulk of the people wish that tragedies should
have a happy end. Relaxation is, according to Burke, the
meaning of beauty. But this kind of beauty turns easily
into boredom. Certainly, the dissonance of the tragedy
does not perpetuate the cry of death or the crushing down
of a world, but carries us beyond and has its kind of
"solution" in another sphere. And so has the tension of the
melody, even if felt as dissonant, its own solution beyond
the sensuous sphere.[11] Every tone of the scale has in itself

11 As we distinguished between two aspects of rest (p. 67f.) and
two aspects of the present (p. 109), a finite one and an infinite one,

[159]

a tension to its overtones and is more or less dissonant, not to speak of the tension between the tones of the scale as such. Even the octave has a minimum of tension, but so little that it sounds empty and boring, it is nearly perfectly consonant. Absolute resolution into consonance does not exist, there are only grades of dissonance. Tension is the essence of music, and the whole historical development of our western music has been stimulated and guided by new discoveries of dissonant tensions. Every new musical style is "awfully dissonant," the music of the mature Mozart not less than that of Beethoven. Mozart's music seemed to contemporaries an "outburst of violent passion" an expression "of hard fight, bitter and biting pains."[12] Our body has the inclination to assimilate every disturbing dissonance as much as possible, just as our language tries to appease every metaphorical tension to a fixed concept, with the result that our languages are built out of dead metaphors, our music out of original dissonances which habit has transformed into consonances. That to which we are accustomed, is always consonant; it is the instinctive goal of our bodily constitution to smooth down the strenuous tension into a comfortable customary ease. Therefore every creative effort has to break the indolence of this ease in conquering a new field of tension, in widening the volume of the new, the unaccustomed, the metaphorical, and the dissonant.

Melodies, therefore, are never quite closed, but are open: they are a beginning, a question asked, a listening into a distance. Because they are open they can be developed be-

---

so we may distinguish here between two kinds of musical solution: the finite and sensuous relaxation of a consonance, on the one hand, and the infinite spiritual process of integration, on the other hand, to which both consonances and dissonances lead.

[12] Hanslick, in *Vom Musikalisch Schoenen* (p. 16) quotes this and other astonishing criticisms.

yond the little number of sounds of which they consist. The melody itself forces to this development, it is itself the movement of its own transcendence and results necessarily in a musical development. Only when melody is developed, can it become truly representative, as all metaphorical processes are representative in their drive for transcendence. We mentioned above the representative quality of the faithful who in concentrated tension of prayer responds for mankind; we mentioned the tragic hero who in the tension of destiny absorbs his environment and represents a world. In the same way the melody represents in its concentrated tension more than a series of tones, and manifests in its development the march of a fateful necessity, drawing us into the infinite process of a world. All symphonies, especially those of Beethoven, lift us into the spiritual tension of an infinite present.

Melodies have a lawful necessity of their own. But this lawful necessity should not be confounded with rules and methods, applicable to the temporal and spatial continuum,[13] with measure, repetition and the construction of chords. There is a definite distinction between law and rule, between form and technique. Many people, even artists, may confuse art and technique, form and rule. But while rules and techniques can be learned and applied with virtuosity, they, nevertheless, do not enable the creation of a masterwork.

To be sure, rule and regulation are indispensable, they have an important, though negative value. They are there in order to be overcome, as beat and measure are overcome by rhythm.[14] The ritual has to be learned, but only in order to be transcended by the genius of the master.

[13] The word "continuum" is here used in the same way as on p. 39ff.
[14] See pp. 151, 157.

Great art begins where ritual leaves off. Whenever the ritual remains self-important, we are still in a pre-artistic era of magic. In the magic era the ritual is most essential; it is all-powerful because it has to protect men by its rigid order against a world of chaos and thus replaces this dismal world by its own reality of order. Order is here salvation, it is a fence built against an hostile world, hiding and replacing this world.[15] But when superstition changes into religion, magic into art, not fear but confidence becomes the reaction toward the infinite world; the ritual has now to lead toward this world instead of fencing it off. The ritual has from now on meaning only, if it carries beyond itself and extinguishes itself in the movement of a creative process. Therefore the student who has learned the rules and rituals and has become their slave, is more estranged from art than the layman or the amateur who at least has not got stuck in the machinery of technique. Therefore all those aesthetic theories were sterile which placed emphasis on that which exists only in order to be overcome: the ritual, the mathematical order, symmetry, proportion, balance, etc.

The lawful necessity or inner form of a work of art, however, in contradistinction to rules and regulations, expresses the creative process in its transcendence. Although it cannot be learned by general rules, it carries a universal claim. The uniqueness of the work is at the same time its general and universal validity and forces the understanding and appraisal of everyone. Everyone should and can enter into the tendency of this process. It was the tendency that gave validity to the "universal" of conceptual thought;[16] it is here the tendency again. But the universal of conceptual thought was, as we tried to explain, a compromise

15 On the pre-artistic era of magic, see also pp. 142, 143.
16 See p. 19ff.

between tendency and object, between the process and a predicative fixation. Because of this, its compromising character, it remained a mere program, an empty anticipation and outline to be filled by a totality of cases and a totality of predicates. It was applicable to these its realizations and remained, apart from them, a mere framework. Just so, rules of technique are a framework, an empty program, to be filled.

In the work of art, however, there is no compromising universal which can be abstracted and which anticipates its cases of reference. Here the universal character lies in the individual work itself; it is the lawful necessity of its process. The work is unique, not typical, and whoever abstracts a program or rule out of its concrete existence, should be aware of its very limited validity.

Whenever music deserts its core—the full metaphorical integration of melody—and deviates into partial realizations, putting emphasis either on temporal rhythm or on harmony alone, then it draws nearer to a scientific systematization. This one-sided emphasis is, indeed, an abstraction, and therefore necessarily leads to a program: schools will be set up to fight for this program, rules and techniques will come to the foreground and take the lead, and the composer will consciously and intentionally follow a preconceived pattern.

It was the spatial rhythm of harmony which conquered the musical field during the Middle Ages and Renaissance, when the Cantus Firmus of Gregorian Chant was used as a scaffold for harmonious constructions: tone lines, accompanying each other mutually in an ever-increasing number, as a polyphony of voices, emphasized the spatial continuum and did so at first in a calculating and ritualistic manner. Composing was, indeed, what the word literally means, a putting-together according to a fixed pattern and fixed rules, and these rules of harmony were built on a spatial continuum of small and equal distances, small and equal tone-steps, stable, quasi-tenseless, a scale which allowed the construction of chords in conformity with it. These rules of harmony, like those of repetition and variation, however—useful as they may be for the student and even for the master, serving as a scaffold for his work[17]—will in all their efficiency never suffice for the creation or even the explanation of a great work. They will, moreover, be inadequate, when the period of one-sided emphasis on harmony or rhythm gives way again to a period of melodious creation, when out of the abstract ritual an inspired polyphony rises and when melody reappears under the colorful drapery of an harmonious tissue. A relapse into an overemphasis of spatial subtlety may occur: French impressionism may be regarded as such, highly intellectual and sensuous, ornamental, a program-music, illustrative and imitative, a recitation without words, a background and stage, where somebody has to act, at least in our imagination.

This emphasis on a spatial continuum, however—one-sided as it is—will always be overcome in order to restore the full metaphorical unity of melody. The first reaction, in our time, was an equally one-sided emphasis on temporal

[17] As the ritual of measure, beat, and repetition tried to swallow up the true metaphorical tension of rhythm in the temporal field (p. 151), so also this ritual of constructed harmonies, built on the pattern of the scale, usurps the field of spatial rhythm, and makes believe that harmonies are only built according to rational, abstract and at the same time organic and physiological rules. These rules, indeed, can be explained by mathematics and physiology—ratio and senses supplementing each other here again—and are very useful for the construction of student fugues, school variations and even school songs, resembling simple folk and popular songs. They are, however, only a very inadequate scaffold for the master, and can never fully explain the true metaphorical tension of rhythm and inspired harmony, and still less that miraculous creation which we call melody.

rhythm, and so it was possible for jazz and similar rhythmical forms to conquer the field for a certain time. Out of this feverish transitional period melody begins to rise again and to take its legitimate place, as it had in classical times. Harmony and rhythm are drawn into the present of a significant theme which tears up the background-curtain of an accompanying continuum, develops in tension to this accompaniment and gains strength and beauty in this fight. The ritual of a spatial and temporal continuum becomes a mere environment, and the theme, battling against it, matures, grows and emerges triumphantly out of the concert of forces.

We observed a similar development in the dramatic realm: the Greek tragedy emphasizes the unity of the background, the natural continuum of time and assigns to the hero his place in this continuum. The modern tragedy, however, changes the emphasis: it is the process of the heroic life which in its tension carries the drama, represents continuity and uses places and times as it needs them. Just so the late medieval and again the impressionistic music emphasized the continuum of a tissue, expressed in the interwovenness of flux and chords, making little allowance for the adventure of melody—while the great masters emphasize the melodic power and let the "Melodia triumphans" absorb the harmonious tissue.

The enormous structure of harmonious rules assumes a new and very different task: it is not background any more, but it adds body and breadth, a certain spatial volume to the thematic drama. Our giant orchestras serve this bodily breadth, and so, indeed, become a danger because of their technical complication. Our music is an image of our time: the technical complexity of our life is mirrored in the virtuosity, in the technical structure, in the bodily mass of our musical creation. A superhuman effort in melody and rhythm is needed to animate these ponderous bodies and to draw them into the transcending spiritual process of metaphorical tension. No wonder that from time to time the desire arises to throw overboard this burden of technique and ponderous physical volume, and to return to the simplicity of the song, to vocal music, to chorus, and their melody. At the end of Beethoven's ninth symphony this longing finds its first and deeply moving expression. Strong forces drive today back to choral music, as to a fountain of youth.

The same principles which music teaches, Fine Arts will have to confirm. This must be so if really no essential difference prevails between the so-called temporal and spatial arts. Art is one great sphere, and its fundamental truth is the metaphorical unity of space and time. That the organs of our body serve more the one or the other, that our ear is more directed toward temporal flux, our eye more towards spatial togetherness, is unimportant: the spiritual experience is neither located in the ear nor in the eye; it uses all organs of the body, but it transcends the information they give.

In the field of music our attention was attracted first by the temporal rhythm; in the field of fine arts it is first attracted by the spatial rhythm, by high and low, bright and dark. Color, light and shadow are the main elements of a tension which generates a concentrated unity of the present. This tension of color-distance and light-difference, however, is not a merely static coexistence, it is movement too and therefore also temporal. We speak of light as "flowing in," "breaking through" darkness, and this is not just a playful way of diction; we speak of radiating, flashing colors, of the power with which they burst forth. The spatial rhythm of color- and light-differences forces us to follow them in a temporal rhythm, and this is very different from the arbitrary way with which we take in the parts of a space for the sake of mere orientation. Whoever has entered a church-nave and has immediately been drawn into the rhythm of light and colors, reflected by the windows and spread through the darkness, dancing over walls, columns, arches and vaults, knows the rhythmical power and dynamic pull which light and color have.

The temporal element which is a part of the spatial rhythm of color and light, is enhanced by the still more effectively temporal rhythm of design. The contour, the way a line is drawn, smooth or jagged, flowing or abrupt, gives rise to another rhythm, and this rhythm is essentially temporal, forcing us to follow in a specific variation of tempo. Just as we could abstract the temporal rhythm in music, so we can in Fine Arts, and here as well as there this abstraction may appeal to people, but it does not provide the full artistic beauty. There are times which concentrate on the drawing and neglect color and light, but even the most beautiful drawings of great masters— Michelangelo, Holbein, Ingres—can only be regarded as preparations, as fragmentary endeavors, sketches, studies; they may give a certain satisfaction, but more by that which they leave us to guess, than by that which they actually show. The color-rhythm has to supplement the contour-rhythm, and only the indivisible unity of both, their metaphorical tension, creates the mature rhythm which we called "melody" in the field of music. The painter's melody is this unified rhythm of design and color, and it is greatest where we cannot abstract the one from the other, as in the sublime works of Rembrandt or Titian.

The melody of line and color cannot be learned. What can be learned, is the "measure," not the rhythm. The distribution of the objects, the "composition" as a balance and symmetry, can be learned. Here we can use fixed rules, the rule of symmetry, proportion, regularity, correspondence, imitation. The foundation of measure, its most important device is here the frame; it is the pattern and ritual to which every painting has to submit. And as in all rituals, there is an element of arbitrariness in the choice of the frame, its geometrical form. Custom will play a great role, bodily habit will: the European Art has chosen a different ritual than the Far East.

The student will be asked to take the frame very seriously, and to repeat its form in dividing the picture up like a chessboard. And so the principle of repetition, the principle of the beat will transform the picture for technical reasons into a system of bars, of little fields, as a scaffold which facilitates the filling in of contour and color. The student will furthermore learn to distribute equally and symmetrically the weight of his figures, nowhere too light, nowhere too heavy; color and light have also to be spread uniformly, not too dark here, not too bright there. A certain correspondence will be taught as a device of balance: a bright spot in one place should correspond and balance another one in a certain different place. Symmetry, measure is essential as a teaching of the schools and should, indeed, never be neglected. But, on the other hand, all this does not yet make a work of art, neither does the conscientious observation of the rules concerning complementary colors, their physiological supplementation, the "cold" and the "warm" colors; all these rules which are abstracted from our body-constitution and merely provide a satisfaction of sensuous pleasure. The student will have to learn all that and he will use it in order to imitate nature in its organic and expedient form, especially the human body which more than any other object represents a purposive expedient environment, a system of

organization, provided by nature.[18] What the student accomplishes in this way will give the satisfaction which a
well-done imitation and clear organization of purpose can
give: it will be pleasant and may even, in a limited way, be
called beautiful. But this kind of beauty[19] should not be
confounded with the true artistic beauty. The beauty of
art is "expressiveness," and expressiveness transcends the
merely pleasant, regular, expedient technical balance and
organization. It asks for stylization, and stylization surpasses, sometimes violently, the mere imitation of natural
proportion and symmetry. Stylization breaks and distorts
the organic, purposive form of things, in order to knock
them out of their self-important seclusion and to turn them
into a humble expression of an infinite life. Irregularity of
form, a very definite accentuation, catching the eye here by
a strong patch of color, there by a flash of light, contours
which seem to press things or to make them grow—all this
will shake the balance of the composition and will weld
things into a unity of rhythm which seems to neglect the
frame and its pedantic measure. Not this outward pattern,
but an inward life, concentrated, stressed to the utmost,
guarantees the unity of the work which is not the unity of
an object, but the unity of process, transcending the symbolic ritual of the constructed thing.

The constructed thing is necessary, as the body is neces-

[18] Kant, *Critique of Judgment*, §65, 66.

[19] The "beauty of nature" is generally understood as organic and
emphasizes the adequacy of means to end or of the sample to its type:
regularity, health, expediency, efficiency, strength, skill, suppleness,
etc. But, to be sure, an artistic vision may often creep into our ad-
miration of nature, and then a certain stylization will unconsciously
be imposed upon the natural object, and a different standard will be
adopted; so when we call nature "picturesque" or sublime. Here the
crumbling of organic or expedient things and their disintegration by
the process of life may give an inkling of some power beyond plain
expedient realism.

sary for the soul, a structure beyond which the movement of life transcends, fixed in a measurable form, intelligible in its relations to other things of a similar fixation. These things, however, are fixed only in order to intensify the transcending rhythm which leaves on them the mark of stylization. While in everyday life the "thing" appears to be the resting element, present in its quiet isolation, it is here forced to renounce its self-sufficiency and to become a mere means for the significant tension of rhythm which now alone represents the stability of the present. Although the intellectual order of the organized thing is preserved and although, therefore, the subject matter as tree, animal, man must be understood by typical concepts of universal thought, this conceptual order is integrated into a unique and dynamic unity which is not less but more than the universal concept. The unique should not be confused with the particular which is nothing but a case under the comprehensive whole of a lawful universal. The unique is a process of an infinite representative power, inexhaustible by the particulars of mere thought.[20] When Plato and Aristotle emphasize rightly that reflection can only grasp the "essence," the universal, not the individual concreteness, they do not consider that understanding which is beyond reflection, although not deprived of thought, the understanding of the unique. In the realm of life, universal interpretation is a mere steppingstone to the understanding of the individual in its unique and incomparable lawfulness.

The understanding of the unique is not "subjective." It has an objective claim, is communicable and open to everybody who can rise above the symbolically reduced facts of everyday life. That this experience does not close man into the shell of his ego, but, on the contrary, opens his soul to

20 See p. 117, 85.

other souls, is obvious to those who know that the presence of the unique implies a communion of consciousness between I and Thou.[21]

For it is this living communion into which the subject matter enters and which deepens its typical and general character, so that it becomes a truly metaphorical representation. The things depicted stand for more than their fixed and objective meaning, they are not only the object, the material, but also the challenge for the artist who reaches through them and beyond them into the process of a creative communion. "Expression" means an overcoming which is at the same time a negation and an intensification. The particular thing or story is lifted out of its place, out of its relations of spatio-temporal objectivity into a present which does away with its self-importance, but, on the other hand, enables it to reach beyond into the wider sphere of imagination.[22] We understand this thing or story by transcending it, as all profound understanding is a transcendence and overcoming of its particularity. In this way any object can become a challenge and provide the incentive of reaching beyond, although the intensity of this drive depends on the intensity of the challenge which the subject matter is able to procure. Human life will present a greater challenge than inorganic things because human life will resist more, but finally lend itself with greater immediacy to the uniqueness of the creative process.

The unique is never a thing, but a process which stretches forward and backward beyond the typical and closed fixation of the object into a development for which the universal concept serves only as a structure and scaffold.[23]

[21] See p. 116.   [22] See on imagination p. 146.
[23] The conceptual universal will lend itself the more easily to the aid of the creative process, as it is itself an intention, an anticipation of the thought process, not entirely deprived of a dynamic character (p. 19).

What the portrait, for instance, presents, is an object, a body, fixed and limited. But this fixed and limited object, if created by the genius of the artist, forces the spectator to draw it into an evolving process in which it expands to an all-embracing life.

This process of development will be actually performed in all its phases and stages wherever the so-called temporal art, drama, novel, or music, is experienced. This, however, is not so with "spatial art," painting and sculpture. Here the spectator has to unfold this development by his own creative understanding. He can do this only when allowed to remain a considerable time in the presence of the work of art and to concentrate on the fullness of its content, a procedure not to be confused with reflective analysis or literary interpretation.[24] And here it is again the metaphorical unity of time and space which defies the rigid classification into temporal and spatial art: As all temporal art is experienced in a rhythmical present which seems to transform the successive phases into a unity of togetherness, not unlike the present of space,[25] so all spatial art has, in the mind of the spectator, to unfold in a successive development, introducing a temporal element, not to be missed for the full understanding of its dynamic function.

Where the work of painting or sculpture does not lead to this dynamic extension, where the process of understanding is unable to transcend the fixed structure, because abstract schemata are presented, the spectator is arrested in

[24] The reflective analysis concentrates on some definite relations which are considered in their isolation, are compared, distinguished and kept apart. Because of this reduction, the reflecting mind will have some difficulty to change into the all-comprehensive consciousness and integrated memory which alone is fully aware of the unique tension of process.

[25] See p. 154.

the contemplation of the undeveloped form and can do nothing but repeat the theme or figure. Here a mere ornamental repetition, a ritual will be all he achieves, but such a ritual may satisfy him if he is content to substitute an intellectual order for the expression of life.

Early painting and early sculpture emphasize strongly the ritual of an intellectual order. They begin with the frame: the wall is given for the mural, the gable or niche for the statue, similar to the objective framework of time, provided for the drama by the Aristotelian aesthetics. This frame will be repeated in the equally clear-cut, geometrically constructed objects of subject matter. These objects will be "framed" by a sharp contour, and even the color will add to the intensification of the isolated form. In order to convey to these fixed and framed objects a still greater importance, the background will serve as a detached foil, it will in its turn become a ritual, not only as a frame, but as a stage upon which the objects act, and it will, as any ritual, be sanctioned by tradition and by the rules of the schools. Thus the gold-ground played the role of a ritual in Byzantine art, and the so-called Rembrandt-brown in the seventeenth and nineteenth centuries. It may even happen that the background assumes an importance which not only detaches it from the foreground, but makes it the main feature of the work of art. This will be done in times of a sophisticated and sensuous style, as for instance in the times of French impressionism. With excellent taste as well as with great knowledge of physiological laws, these impressionists manage to cover their canvas with a colored carpet. The things of the foreground are one with the background. But this is not done in a rhythmical tension. There is little of tension in an art which indulges in an ornamental pattern, harmonious and pleasing.

Thus in the field of Fine Arts, not less than in the field of music, melody as an integrated rhythm is in danger of getting lost in methods which preserve only a part of its inherent richness. The emphasis in such periods is either on the geometrically fixed and static objects of the foreground, or exclusively on a background tissue, woven with infinite taste and sensuous pleasure. Reason and senses replace here again the metaphorical uniqueness of the rhythmical process. They are both abstractions from the living unity of rhythm. Abstraction, however, will lead necessarily to an ornamental ritual. Art has withdrawn from the world. "L'art pour l'art" is the slogan which goes with this work, secluded in its own balance, shut up in the rituals of its rules. The doctrine of symmetry and balance, of tone and color harmony prevails, will be taught and learned, self-sufficient in its own perfection.

Whenever "art for art's sake" is preached, we are faced with the danger of a ritual which has lost contact with life. It is the abstraction of mathematics or physiology which here substitutes for stylization, a quasi-scientific method of technique which replaces the abundance of imagination. To be sure, early primitive men have expressed their experience in abstract patterns of an ornamental ritual. Primitive man, indeed, has a strong inclination toward abstraction, for magic needs the symbolic fence of an abstract order against the overpowering force of life. Ritual keeps primitive man from being drowned in the abundance of experiences which he feels too weak yet to master and which seems to threaten his existence.[26] It is fear which makes people tend toward schematism and pedantry in order to compensate for their lack of inner substance and strength.

In classical times of maturity, however, the indivisible

[26] See p. 143.

process of rhythm and melody will restore the lost unity of foreground and background, of things and process. The student may still learn to lay out first a uniform background as a grounding, and then to draw neatly the contours of his figures and to illuminate them by coloring— the great masters make with the ritual whatever they want: the background grows into the figures which either seem to rise out of it or to submerge into its infinity. Color and light do not merely clarify and enhance the drawing, but often cover it and blur the contour. So a rhythm of color, lines, figures, background evolves, an indivisible process of tension, a simple and infinite melody.[27] And this melody maintains itself in and against the background, develops in a dynamic rhythm and represents a destiny, a world.

Great art will need the living process of rhythm and melody, the dramatic, even tragic stylization which expresses the things and events of this world in their frailty and futility, in joy and sorrow, passion and death, shows things as alive and reveals in living things, in human lives that transcendent process which we call personality.

[27] In a similar way the statue detaches itself from the background of the wall or niche and expresses space itself in the rhythm of its contours, broken in light and shadow.

8

LAW AND ETHICS

THE idea of personality touches on one of the most dis-
puted problems of philosophy. Every age has to cope
with it, and every age has its answer. No wonder that the
endeavor to simplify, to reduce, to symbolize was nowhere
greater than here. It is no mere accident that the word
"persona" which we use for personality has been adopted
from the language of the theatre: it is the role of the actor,
the mask he wears, the typical task he has to fulfill in the
purposive action of the plot. The mask, the typical symbol
of a role was used for comedies as well as for tragedies;
but it is the comedy in which the type, the role as a fixed
mask, as a limited reduction to a formula is an essential
feature.[1] Here the caricature, the exaggerated masklike
reduction to a typical symbol was most necessary. It is a
diminution which makes the comical person into a type, a
role, a fixed mask. And everywhere the comical symbolization will result in such a diminution of life—or better,
in a humiliation. This humiliation will be carried like a
mask: the animals of Walt Disney are human beings with
animal masks; it is human life, humiliated and ridiculed
which amuses in these animal roles. One has only to compare any of these creations of Walt Disney's sarcasm with
the Egyptian animal statues, a cat or a falcon, and the
difference will be clear: in these statues is true art because
here is not humiliation, but elevation, a representation
which embraces a greater and richer life, not a representation by reducing to a mask. We may call these animals
demoniac because by demoniac power we understand something which elevates the realm of nature, just as we call

[1] See chapter 6, p. 139ff.

"holy" that which lifts beyond the human level. Great art as a representation of metaphorical extension, points in animals toward the demoniac, and in humans toward the Divine.

"Persona" as reduction and role will always be in danger of slipping down into the sphere of comedy and caricature. This is even so with the kind of reduced person which we call "persona iuris" and which turns into a nonsensical abstraction, when its self-sufficiency with regard to life is too rigidly stressed: "Fiat Justitia, pereat mundus."

We have touched the field of law before: as a ritual in the mythical religious sphere. There it was the legal system of the church, and, although the kinship between the church law and the secular law is great—so great that we observed a strong competition between both rituals—there is nevertheless a considerable difference. Every ritual, to be sure, strives for domination and exclusive authority, and so does the church-ritual. But in spite of this the church never quite forgets that it serves something beyond its own order, with regard to which it is a symbolic reduction. God may be absorbed ever so much by the ritual: yet He is alive beyond the system of rules. Even in the ritual of the Platonic State some divine and unfathomable power has to be considered beyond the system of rules.

Not so with secular law: Here the symbolism is consistent and uncompromising. The symbolic system is essentially a reduction, but a reduction which stands for the whole.[2] There is nothing above or beyond this whole; on the contrary, whatever is not included in the system, is beneath its level, and has either to be omitted as unimportant, or has to be adapted to the pattern. These two possibilities result in two different schools of law and politics: the rational "law of nature," eternal, unchangeable, dis-

2 See chapter 2, p. 13ff.

regarding the concrete variety of social circumstances; and the realistic law of power, an organization of facts, a statement and fixation of the momentary balance, changing with the circumstances, but always molding them into an order which uses them and turns them into means for its stability.

In both cases law is free. It is free because it does not acknowledge anything which limits it or transcends it. It is a totality, detached and fixed, as all symbols and symbolic systems are. The center of this free law, the kernel of the symbolic crystallization is that queer unity which we call the legal person: free, detached, fixed, and total, as the law itself.

The first of these two systems, the law of nature, conceived by the Stoics and powerful until to our time, regards the freedom of the person as entirely rational, even mathematical: Every person is a number, a "whole number," and as such is a symbol of totality, of the whole world. The Stoic sage is a legal person, because he is nothing but the unchangeable symbol, the part which signifies the whole, the microcosm which symbolizes the macrocosm. But in spite of representing thus the principle of total discontinuity, the detached and lonely entity called the free person enters in a mathematical equation with other equal persons. They form a series and add up to a sum. This sum, again, is a sum of equal entities, it is the State which in a loose way connects the entirely autonomous persons of law.

Relation, therefore, just as in the mathematical realm, comes into the spotlight: What, after all, is a number but that which it signifies in the calculus. Number has to take its place in equations, and arithmetic is the ingenious system in which number becomes representative. The legal person, likewise, takes its place in the calculus of relations and becomes the crossing-point of those legal relations which the law calls obligations. It is no accident that the "law of obligations" became the central chapter of the Stoic-Roman code of abstract law, and that this Roman law of obligations grew in influence in a time when human relationship came more and more under the spell of mathematics through the commercial and monetary development. Obligation or contract is the essential principle of this law, and the true significance of the legal person is derived from its contracts and obligations. "Person" is here a party in contracts, and nothing more. A sophisticated book-keeping is invented in order to regulate and make evident the legal life of the person who appears in these books as an "account." The account is the person, as the result of addition and subtraction, a number, representing the economic capacity of relations. With regard to this total system of economic capacity the individual person assumes the role of a dependent entity, a mere administrator; and property with regard to things turns out to be not more than an occasion for obligational relations between the administrating persons. The legal person in this order is indeed tied to all others. The principle of symbolism which made him a whole makes him also a part, representing a bigger whole. The person is free only as an administrating entity, as a symbolic representative, as an official in the service of an all-embracing organization. In Rome this philosophy resulted in a glorification of state service, but its more consistent development led to a socialistic system. In Socialism the mathematical symbolism finds its true fulfillment; Saint-Simon, the founder of modern Socialism, was a mathematician, a student of D'Alembert. Socialism has the fanaticism of number and equation and, proud of its rational foundation and its eternal validity, disregards the realism of circumstances and the inequality of men.[3]

The state, according to this Law of Nature, is the total addition of obligational relations, and therefore not only the guarantor of contracts, but itself a huge contractual entity. The Stoic doctrine of the detached legal person finds here its supplement in the Epicurean[4] doctrine of the "Social Contract," revealing once more the brotherly relation between rationalism and sensationalism, Stoa and Epicurus. Later this alliance has its renewed confirmation when Hobbes adopts the Social Contract and builds on it a mathematical state-theory of calculation, and equally in Locke's famous *Treatise on Government*, where the Stoic law of nature is welded together with the contract-theory and with other clearly sensualistic views which belong to the second order of law, and will now be the object of our attention.

This second ritual of law, as mentioned above, does not consider a total sum of equal and therefore addible persons; it hypostatizes the particular, actual bodily existence in its momentary and changing constellation and makes it a symbol of the whole, a microcosm. It has contempt for the abstract, mathematical symbolism of the series, for

[3] Socialism in our time has developed as a counter-movement against capitalism. But this does not mean that they have nothing in common. On the contrary, they fight each other because of their similarities. The administrative character of the legal person, his shrinking into a mere representative of an objective entity is clearly seen in the capitalistic enterprise, where the owner is the administrator, and where the property which he administrates is symbolized in an account or a number on a balance-sheet which is dependent on the numbers of other sheets. Enterprises, therefore, were forced into trusts, where their merely administrative and dependent character became obvious.

[4] The Epicureans regarded contract and convention as an expedient means to protect the individual happiness against intrusion.

equality and the sum. It substitutes for all this an immediate and even more rigid symbolism: the part assumes
here the role of the whole without the mediation of relationship, and it does this in a somewhat irrational way
which at times took on an orgiastic flavor. Orgy and ritual
are not entirely strange to each other.[5] The freedom of
this legal person is not the freedom of the calculus, not the
freedom of the flexible number, free in entering equations. It
is the freedom to throw off all relationship of equation. It is
the freedom of total difference, not only to other persons,
but even to every moment of its own existence. Identical with
itself and emphasizing this symbolic identity, the person
is an extreme expression of discontinuity, asking for free
realization of a full life, where every moment of existence
has its own justification in itself. The slogan of this ritual
is: free power, free action, entirely unbound and unrestricted.

For this person, in contradistinction to the one discussed
above, there are things—there are, even, only things:
While the abstract person of equation knew only persons
and was to things merely in a mediate relation—this person of free power has no immediate relation to persons,
but only to things and treats other persons as if they were
mere things.[6] In other words, Property begins here, property as a power of self-confirmation, private property as
a means of self-preservation and self-aggrandizement.

That these two types of legal symbolization not only
supplement each other, but are even scarcely ever entirely
separated, is obvious. Compromise between the rational-

[5] See p. 150.

[6] Kant, therefore, rightly emphasized in his categorical imperative
that men should not treat men as means; this precisely was what the
philosophy of the time following Hobbes and Gassendi did, regarding
man as a product of egoistic impulses: La Rochefoucauld, Saint-
Évremond, Mandeville, La Mettrie, Holbach, Chamfort, and others.

[181]

istic and the sensualistic version is what history usually provides, but with a definite inclination of the balance either to the one or to the other side. Compromise is the more necessary as none of these systems can even be realized in its pure extreme. And so it happens that the detachment of the free person of power cannot be preserved more efficiently than the detachment of the stoic person. Here too the free person in all its difference to other persons has to come to grips with these others. This is not done in a relation of equality, to be sure, but in a relation of difference, of mutual exclusion. Property, therefore, as private property, is generally defined in law books by such a relationship of exclusion: a person has private property with regard to an object, if he has the right to exclude all other persons from the object. So "all the other persons" slip through a back door into this ritual. Totality is the backbone of ritual. In one way or another the "all" have to play their role. If the free person of power cannot treat others as mere things, as he is inclined to do, then he has to enter with all others into a relation of mutual exclusion, of mutual measuring of strength, of competition. And here a minimum of equality enters—no symbolism can omit equality entirely. It is the equality of the ground on which competition can be had: equality of opportunity for competition. Freedom now becomes "freedom of competition." The paradox of this freedom, however, is that the result of this freedom can only be the loss of freedom as the submission of the loser to the winner. It is the "survival of the fittest" to which this system tends; and to make the paradox still more complex, competition involves the loss of freedom not only for the loser in the fight, but also for the winner. For it is the prize of the fight which grows in importance beyond the fighter: the "things" for which the person of power was ready to sacrifice all others, make him sacrifice himself too; property, wealth become more important than the person. The sum, the totality, not of obligations but of material objects enslaves the free person, makes him not dependent in a network of administration for all, but dependent on conquest, on acquisition. Connected with all through the idea of potential acquisition, the free person is reduced to a mere instrument for the aggrandizement of property which grows beyond the limited self of its "owner," and which, in fact, is not enjoyed by him nor by anybody else, but, on the contrary, sucks blood and health out of the body of its slaving owner.[7]

Not always are these extreme consequences to be found: the fact that both hostile brothers, Socialism and Liberalism, in fighting had to adapt themselves to each other and to adopt some of their opponent's ideas, has taken the edge off both of them. Socialism has lost some of its abstract rigidity by adopting sensualistic ideals in Bentham's school of Utilitarianism, where pleasure became the object of a mathematical calculation and bookkeeping, a very paradoxical combination. On the other hand, Liberalism blended its ideal of individual power and its unrestricted realization with the—not less paradoxical—creed that competition and the fight for victory would turn out as a benefit for everyone and thus result in an equal satisfaction and happiness for the whole of society, an extremely strange and socialistic drop in the liberal cup.

All this shows that Socialism and Liberalism are only two abstractions, two extreme positions of one and the same ritual, the ritual of freedom as symbolic reduction. As extremes they separate and unite alternatingly and

[7] Without putting too much emphasis on the distinction of words, it is interesting to observe that Locke in his *Treatise on Government* comprises life and liberty under the all-embracing, all-powerful concept of property.

[183]

sometimes look very much alike: their worship of capital is alike, the position which they give finally to the state as a police-force, regulating the free intercourse and fading away to a mere instrument of expediency, is alike too. Freedom, at last, the great ideal of law, is equally claimed by the one and the other system, and lost equally by the one and the other. How could it be otherwise considering the nature of all symbolic reduction:[8] it is the part which feigns to be the whole. The "free" person is symbolically free because it assumes the role of a whole and therefore seems independent. But a "whole" is a construction, life enters into this whole of a symbolic abstraction and confuses its order. How many contradicting definitions of legal freedom have been taught in the course of history? The simple meaning of the word has been turned around, so it became its opposite. Freedom as "limited license" is a cautious paradox; this paradox becomes more audacious, when freedom is defined as obedience to law, and it develops into self-destruction in the famous dictum of Robespierre: the despotism of freedom. The symbol of the free legal person is a sublime idea and will always remain an ideal to be striven for. But its inconsistency and deficiency shows that, in spite of its necessity as a ritual, it needs justification and correction from another and higher sphere.

It can scarcely be questioned that man is not merely a legal person, that his meaning is not exhausted by his place in an organized society. Man is not merely a citizen of a state. Aristotle faces this question and sees its importance more than any one of his predecessors.[9] The totalitarian ritual of the Greek city-state crumbles under his scrutiny.

8 On reflective freedom and contingency see p. 50.
9 Aristotle, *Politics*, book III, chapter 4 and *Nicomachean Ethics*, 1130b 28.

[184]

Man is not a citizen only, not free merely in equality or competition, he is more: he is an individual, and as such he transcends the position into which the ritual places him. Whether the ritual is socialist or liberalist, each one can be good, or bad, in as much as it enables a man to transcend his legal position and to reach his true destiny. At times the one ritual may be more expedient, at times the other. Aristotle was no "empiricist" who merely observed actual facts; on the contrary, he believed in a very definite ideal, transcending mere facts, and these facts were of a relative value to him because under different circumstances they served the absolute ideal in a different degree. He believed in a development towards a goal, and the rigid ritual of law had—as everything else—to yield to this development. He called the process which changes, transforms, and permanently rejuvenates law the process of Equity.[10] Equity, indeed, is the metaphorical process which brings the right and the wrong so near together in the tension of life that they sometimes change their place and substitute for each other. Without the correcting power of equity, law would become nonsense. "Pereat mundus" would indeed be the result, if law as a fixed ritual became self-sufficient and exclusive.

Times may come, when the symbolic reduction has so stiffened that even equity cannot dissolve its rigidity. Then a stronger power of disruption has to step in, and this dynamic power is the power of revolution.

Is there a "right to revolution"? Is there a right to break right? This paradoxical formulation points to the true character of the problem as a metaphorical one. The problem of the "right to revolution" dominated the political discussion throughout the Medieval era and the

---

[10] Aristotle, *Nicomachean Ethics*, 1137a 31ff.

Renaissance.[11] First it was acknowledged only in a shy and reserved way, but then it took on vigor, and at last it was stated not only as a right, but as a duty to God. The *Vindicia contra Tyrannos* of 1579 makes revolution a supra-legal, international command, and it was this new spirit and passionate belief in revolution which gave the impetus to the great revolutions of the seventeenth and eighteenth centuries.

All reformers were revolutionaries: the prophets, Christ, Paul, and St. Augustine. "Law works death," "law raises sin," says St. Paul. The aim of the revolutionary, however, is not destruction for destruction's sake, but destruction in view of the fact that the ritual is deficient, that in assuming exclusiveness and self-sufficiency it fills its members with empty pride of perfection and separates man from man. Not always can the reformer give a clear interpretation of his vision: the inadequacy of the present order imposes itself so vigorously upon his mind that he often cannot see beyond its destruction. But, in fact, it is a positive new ideal which works in him, in spite of his incapacity of explaining it, and this ideal resumes form and clarity in the fight for its realization. The curse which prophets fulminated and always will fulminate against the tyranny of a deficient ritual, rises out of a blessing which lives in them, and this blessing pours out of their message, when anathema changes into sanctification, hatred into love.

It has been said that love does not want to destroy, but to preserve. Quietistic love has been praised, a love which is satisfied with comtemplating the beloved object and lost in this blessed contemplation. But this is not even true

11 John of Salisbury, *Policraticus* III c. 15; VI, 24-28: Marsilius of Padua, *Defensor Pacis*, I, c. 7-8; 12-13; 15, 18; Cusanus, *De Catholica Concordantia* III, c. 4.

with regard to the love of God which in praying seeks and
strives, shaken by fear and trembling and is kept up by
confidence. Mere passivity is surely no true love. The process of love is a creative drive, a force which, in spite of its
tranquillity of the present, lives a life of active realization.
What ritual separates, love has to pull together. It is the
subjectum, the ground of consciousness which extends beyond the products of symbolic reduction, until they meet,
driven out of their seclusion. The separation was necessary,
the I and the Thou are needed, walled up in their environmental limitation for which the ritual of the law and its
freedom are a condition, not to be missed; order is needed
as a fixation of estrangement, social ritual is needed and
so is the tragedy of its inadequacy and failure. All these
are needed, but they are needed in order to be overcome—
for it is only in their transcendence that they receive their
true meaning. The true meaning of ritual, of all the systems
of law and forms of the state and society, is that they
break down in the face of love—that they turn out as
empty vessels, to be filled by love. Social organizations and
legal systems must be inadequate because they are essentially reductions and cannot live up to the demands of
love. This is rooted in human nature and cannot be
changed. The orders and systems, however, receive meaning
through their advance towards the demands of love. The
relative value of social systems in the course of history is
measured against the absolute standard of an unchanging
love.

This infinite process of love is the true essence of "personality," and its sphere is ethics. The so-called ethical or
moral *systems* are rituals which try to usurp the field
of ethics, but are ethical only in so far as they foster love
and make its expansion possible. Taken by themselves they
are neither ethical nor unethical, but simply indifferent,

not less than the school rules of artistic creation are indifferent to beauty and receive meaning only in the mind of the master who carries them beyond themselves. The abstract school quarrel about socialism and liberalism is just as meaningless as the quarrel about impressionism and expressionism. A system, handled by creative and loving men, will be a good system, and it will depend on the historical tact of the leading men to choose the system which according to situation and people is best fitted to spread love and to realize its demands. That there are systems which under no circumstances whatsoever and among no people could lead to a creative life, is obvious: not every symbol has meaning. The fact that there are and have always been errors and monstrosities, is not to be doubted, and therefore a sincere criticism with regard to ethical and social systems is extremely important in order to examine their capacity for educating the people and their adequacy with regard to time and circumstances.

The relativity of ethical systems does not refute, but confirms the absolute character of ethics. It is just this relativity which makes the creative process of transformation and education necessary. Love builds on relativity, deficiency, and limitation. Love sees in failure the ground for its necessary work. Therefore it is distracted neither by painful nor by joyful experiences. Disappointments do not reach into the depth of love—on the contrary, they stimulate love to stronger efforts. Problem children are those which mothers love most. The eyes of love are not fixed on the moment, not on the social position, not on the habitual character, not on the narrow status of profession, not on the achievement and success which are important for those only who are indifferent to higher values. Love sees the future which it anticipates, and in the scope of this, its wider vision, failure and success look very much

alike.[12] Love lives the infinite life of the Present which in
an indivisible tension holds past and anticipates future.
Love believes in this future, it does not attempt to change
arbitrarily the beloved object, but tries to bring the potential qualities into action, liberating them from the dross
with which a life of reduction and fixation has covered
them. Every true education is like that: it takes into account what nature and environment have furnished, talents,
knowledge, skills, virtues and vices, but it does so only in
order to strive for something which is never totally given
in the account. Love as belief in personality is, therefore,
ready to sacrifice the accidental achievements of a purposive existence; the true personality can often only be
realized in this way. To realize a personality, however,
means not more than to free the creative process. Personality is not a reality in the way in which any object is
real: personality is never finished, never perfect, never at
the goal, but always only on its way. This way will lead
to stations, to hypothetical achievements—and these are
the fixations which ritual demands, the ends which mo-
rality and law command—duties and works to be done.
But as important as these works and achievements may
be, love itself is beyond works and achievements. An ethics
of purposes will, as Kant saw, result in utilitarianism and
hedonism. The inner disposition, the will, as an integrated
process of love, is beyond these things. Work is necessary,
work is good, but work is good only as the manifestation
of a will, and it can never quite satisfy this will, because it
has to compromise and resign in a reduction of the in-
tended. Repentance and shame are the feelings with which

[12] Lao-tze says: "Great success may appear like failure . . . , great
fullness may appear like emptiness. The way of the holy man is to
serve and not to contend." (Quoted by Yang, *China's Religious Heritage,* p. 165.)

love looks back on the failure of its work. A fully satisfying work is not to be found in the realm of ethics, if not in the false ethics of the Pharisee.

Here again the reducing character of the symbolic sphere becomes evident: Whoever concentrates on the work alone, omits the inner disposition, the drive which gives meaning to the work. It is a fallacy to call disposition, character, drive, something less than the deed which is done. Disposition will necessarily drive toward deeds, toward the actualization of itself. But every such actualization is only a reduction, a part fulfillment and is surpassed by the disposition which always carries beyond. The sphere of symbolic law, the judge, has to reduce action to its mere result, to the work, depriving it of its intrinsic meaning and substituting for this intrinsic meaning some outward systematic coherence of expediency, as all symbolism is compelled to do.[13]

To cut the potential rigorously off from the actual was the fallacy of Greek rationalism, and it was in Aristotle's metaphysics that this problem was for the first time seriously broached, although not solved.[14] In physics, biology, psychology, everywhere the paradoxical nature of the potential obsessed Aristotle's mind, the potential in its relation to actuality. But in the last culmination of his system, in God, he seems to lose sight of this problem and to resign in an actuality, walled up in the identity of an empty circle. In the human realm, however, in the ethical realm, potentiality could not be dismissed, and so the highest human achievement, man's Eudaimonia, found its realization not only in meditation, but in love, mutual love which Aristotle calls friendship. But love, although a process—not separated from its end, a potentiality which is its own actualization and therefore a true expression of

[13] See p. 9.   [14] See p. 37.

Eudaimonia—has to stand its test in free, contingent, and finite works which never can exhaust the infinite potentiality of love's aspiration. Love as a necessary process of the will transcends the sphere of a free but contingent action which is doomed to fall short. Love has the tragic fate of being always ahead of its actions, its environment, its successes, living a life of future or better: of an infinite present. This infinite present of love carries a general validity, a lawful necessity, as Kant rightly saw; but it is not the validity and lawfulness of a system of regulations. It is the law of a process which reaches beyond any reflective and contingent system. It is free because it builds on free choice, but it transforms this free choice into a necessity[15] which knowingly condemns its contingent choices and preferences as guilty limitations of the mind.

Even science yields to the vision of an infinite drive for truth and regards its achievements henceforth as mere hypotheses, as working-grounds, as formulations of the searching process, as springboards for always new results. In this way the scholar becomes a creative personality, and scientific truth an expression of the creative process, carrying infinitely beyond any symbol of fixation. It is this insight into the interconnection of science and ethics that made Kant recognize the primacy of ethics over theoretical reason.

Personality is transcendence. It lives in the various stages as well as beyond them. When Buddhistic schools denied the unity of the self, they failed to recognize, beyond the many disconnected phases, the process of transcendence which is in itself the strongest unity and reality. But it is not only that every self lives, with regard to his own limited ego, the various stages of his life and at the

[15] See p. 51.

same time beyond them: the loving personality lives the difference of I and Thou, and at the same time beyond this difference. There is no identity in the process of love, identity being a relation of fixed symbols. The Upanishad and other mystical teachings yield here to the fallacy of symbolic reduction, confusing symbolic identity and metaphorical process. Neither love nor compassion identifies the ego and the thou; on the contrary, such a symbolic reduction makes the process of love impossible. Whoever sees in the beloved nothing but his own self, is without love. Self-love, as defended by Aristotle and hypostatized to a divine life, is not love. Here the Greek ethics and metaphysics have their limitation. The process of personality does not close up in the circle of identity, nor in the objective, fixed and perfected ego, identical with itself. Love is never, as Plato thought, a mere detour, a means for a purpose and therefore superfluous when the purpose, the perfect end and order has been reached.[16] In the light of this ethics, friends and neighbors are only instruments for the sake of finding oneself—a higher, maturer self, to be sure, but nevertheless only a limited, total, and "perfect" self. Whoever defends self-love and measures the love of the neighbor by the standard of a love to himself,[17] fails to understand the

[16] There is no need to enter into the discussion about Eros and Agape, raised by Nygren (*Agape and Eros*) and de Rougemont (*Love in the Western World*). As Greek thought wavers between rationalism and sensualism, the Greek Eros will appear: now as a way to rational knowledge, now as a way to sensuous ecstasy. True love, however, as a process which transcends the rational and the sensuous—including and overcoming both—may be akin to what is called Agape. See also above pp. 137, 138.

[17] The Biblical dictum: "Love thy neighbour as thyself" (Leviticus 19, 18) is, according to modern scholars an indequate translation from the Hebrew, and should be worded correctly: "Love thy neighbour, he is like you." In this wording the dictum comes near to the many Biblical commands to be good to the stranger, "for you know the heart of the stranger, as you have yourself been a stranger in

metaphorical tension of love which presupposes and unifies difference in men. Even about ourselves we gain knowledge only when we understand others and are at least as far away from the ego and strangers to ourselves as we are to others. There is a secret of distance and difference in love which keeps respect awake and perpetuates the tension of a creative process between men.

The philosophers of self-love have built on a half truth. If they have not simply used the word self-love for the relation of identity, then they have cut man into a multitude of successive lives, everyone in love with the next, and all of them in a developing, movement of the self. Thus self realization became the essence of a Narcissus-like ethics. It cannot be denied that this kind of ethics may provide for self-education, and that man can converse with himself and can draw himself upwards into a future. But this philosophy of phases[18] constructs life out of parts which represent wholes. It is a systematic mythology, it symbolizes and ritualizes. In the true and undivided history of the individual the unity of bodily existence can fully mature and transcend its fixation only in a metaphorical process with another, separate life. Love, therefore, presupposes the difference of fixed lives, the difference of characters, reaching into the process of love from the distance of their enclosure.[19]

The difficulty which destroys here again every possibility

Egypt." It is compassion, not self-love which is here the foundation of neighborly love.

[18] On the dissection in phases see p. 91f.

[19] Another endeavor to escape the ethical conflicts is the unification of bodies into an enlarged body. Here is not a successive part-whole order of phases, but a simultaneous part-whole relation of a symbolic giant-body, comprising in it the bodies of individual men. This kind of ritual is to be found in the Stoic and medieval Corpus mysticum of mankind and in the "body politics" of the secular law.

of a rational understanding is the metaphorical tension and split of life in the loving process of I and Thou. Are there here, we are tempted to ask, two souls united into one? But, in fact, there are not two and there is not one. Multitude, the one and the many, are here just as much discarded, as in the religious sphere where we rejected the fallacy of an arithmetical treatment.[20] The one and the many have meaning only in the empirical realm of things. We may speak of a number of souls in order to satisfy the common-sense attitude of daily life. We may even speak of a relation of difference or identity in order to explain the issue in a reflective way. We will and may use these categories in our daily language, but we should be aware that it is the fundamental problem of life and consciousness which as a metaphorical tension unfolds here, in an infinite and unique communion of process. As the paradox of I and Thou, of praying man and of God, became a problem in the religious sphere, and as this same paradox of I and Thou, now as the paradox of the artist and his audience, became essential in the sphere of human creation—so again in the field of ethics it is this distinction between I and Thou which keeps us in the tension of a never-ending search. Here no work can mediate as it did in the realm of art. Body and bodily fulfillments are bridges as well as barriers of separation and, beyond work and body, I and Thou face each other in the spiritual tension of love. The failure of work and of all bodily achievements draws love near to religion, and this may be the reason why in the face of love art loses its power, while religion remains alive.

[20] See on monotheism and polytheism p. 78. Leibniz says: "Many years ago, when my philosophy was not yet mature, I attributed a place in space to the souls. . . . But after better consideration I saw that this did not only involve countless difficulties, but was even a μετάβασις εἰς ἄλλο γένος. If we speak of one or many souls, we should never mean quantity. . . ." (ed. Gerhardt, ii, 372)

But the tragedy of love means a more lasting trial than the tragedy of art and even of religion, where salvation is found either in work or in faith. While the religious man carries the failures and unsolved problems of his and his people's life upward into the grace of God, and while the artist, a blessed creator himself, spends the fullness of his grace among the needing people who long for it, here in the field of love, creator and creature hold each other in the tension of a mutual service which, although carrying grace, never fully atones. Nowhere the flow of creativity, therefore, is as enduring as in love, nowhere so steadily increasing by the mutual service of lover and beloved which are to each other both creator and creature. But nowhere the way is as infinite and the process as unfulfilled, because here man, bound to body and work, feels more than ever the failure of his limited existence. Because of this tragic enigma man has tried to escape into a compromise: he has hypostatized his bodily seclusion and, isolating it, has worshiped his holy self.

The differentiation of life, its seclusion in body and character has caused tragedy in the sphere of love. The finiteness of our existence is felt as a deficiency with regard to the infinite demands of love. Guilt, conflict, and sacrifice grow out of this unavoidable seclusion. No compromise, no solution of expediency can mitigate this tragedy. Even the most concentrated life, in the integration of its conscience, cannot overcome the bodily enclosure, the character-seclusion, and in shame and repentance it confesses its inadequacy of service. The doctrine of self-realization may avoid much tragedy and provide for a stable, smooth, and complacent approach to the goal. The true service of love, however, has to start where self-realization leaves off: It starts beyond the self by sacrificing the self for the sake of a transcending service, seeking in unification with an-

other self to break the bodily seclusion. In this togetherness both lovers reach beyond, but with them remains the
feeling of deficiency and guilt which is rooted in the finiteness of their existence. Devoting themselves unconditionally
to the service of the beloved, they, nevertheless, fall short
in their duties, denying themselves to thousandfold needs,
because their limited capacity makes them break down before the infinite demand of love. To be sure, the lovers
will, similar to the intercession of prayer, close a world of
human suffering into their love for each other, and they
will not remain untouched by the needs and longings of a
world beyond their own existence. But because of their insufficiency, failure will fall as a shadow upon their love and
provide them with the sad wisdom of resignation. Dostoyevsky was haunted by the feeling of guilt, of denying himself to those who needed him, and so his heroes are torn in
their love to persons whom they are unable to serve.

In moments of such a failure hatred may rise out of love,
self-hatred; for hatred is the passion with which man turns
against and tries to destroy a being which endangers the
beloved Thou. Here we clearly perceive, how strongly the
human soul is directed in humility and service toward the
Thou, and how little man is aware of his own self. There
is no self-love, except as perversion, but there is self-hatred,
because it is our love and awareness of the *other* which
makes our failure of service a source of hatred, turned
against our own self. Self-hatred is despair to fulfill the
duties of love, and this feeling is by no means rare: we find
it in men like St. Augustine, Dostoyevsky, and many others.
Although a dangerous and destructive attitude, it may
become fruitful and creative if it enhances the endeavor to
serve and strengthens the force to fulfill our duties toward
the beloved life.

Struggle remains the fundamental attitude of a sincere

love; struggle, not fulfillment and rest. Freedom in the field of ethics, therefore, can only be linked to struggle as a process of liberation, expressed in service and sacrifice. The illusion of an accomplished freedom in the realm of state and law cannot blind us against the insight that our struggle with contingency and insufficiency is everlasting. It is not only the contingency of environment, of place and time, which stands in the way of an accomplished freedom. As far as circumstances are in conflict with the necessity and uniqueness of personality, love—similar to art, playing with times, spaces and events[21]—will have to gamble, to risk: it will have to leave the consequences, even the preservation of our bodily existence, to a more or less accidental working of events and to obey the demands of personality alone. But the problem reaches into far deeper grounds. It is the essential split in life itself, it is the breach of consciousness in I and Thou which holds us in an everlasting distance. And although the illusion of self-realization, with its false pretension of self-love, smoothes down the struggle, and although self-preservation and detachment from others, in contract and competition, procure a shallow innocence, indifference, and good conscience —guilt and the feeling of responsibility keep the struggle alive.

It is not to be wondered that men have abandoned a life as severe and exacting as the life of ethics is, and that they have found contentment and refuge in the rational organization of a collective ritual of law, as discussed above. Responsibility, this heavy burden, was here lifted from them or at least shared with a multitude of others, so that the individual could breath easier. But it should not be forgotten, that the law-ritual will never do without the ethics of service in which it has to find its true life and

21 See p. 123.

source of revival, as all rituals build on a dynamic ground. The communion of I and Thou in love and sacrifice will have to remain the inexhaustible source out of which the collective body draws strength. The I may here, in metaphorical representation,[22] assume an extended responsibility, carrying the people toward a Thou which, as an equally extended and infinite power, appears as a "volonté générale." Rousseau's mythical interpretation is a profound truth and is at the bottom of all historical and social understanding,[23] although he himself mistook communion for contract, lowering his sublime insight to the fashion of the day. The time was no longer ready for true communion. It had shaken off the last fetters of a loving service and had replaced them by that loose contact which it called "society." But society, as it has been glorified since the eighteenth century, is not a fountainhead of ethical values; it is rather a phenomenon of disintegration and it preserves only small remains of its unified past. Its essential feature is the full detachment and free play of its members which are the atoms into which the collective body dissolved. These atoms are by no means "personalities," they are interchangeable, not unique; typical and not individual. The Renaissance and the following centuries have confused these typical products of disintegration with the true dynamic personality. But it is not love which unites these typical entities; it is suspicion, mitigated by contract, and competition, mitigated by the ethical minimum of honesty and fairness. As they are typical products of an atomization and abstraction, science has built its knowledge of the human species very largely—and rightly—on these members of society. But even "man," the universal, is not fully represented by these social atoms. Universals are a framework, to be filled by concrete life, and concrete life resides

22 See p. 85.   23 See p. 88.

in the communion of I and Thou, in personalities which are the true meaning of "man," because they alone are alive. "Sub specie aeternitatis," to use Spinoza's words, only these dynamic personalities count, because they are the expression of a drive beyond, a drive imbued with freedom and sacrificing love.

This love sheds its light on the struggle. It lifts man beyond himself and his success. It fosters a belief, a future, it strengthens something which is beyond any stage of the way, beyond any particular accomplishment. Through service all works, all fulfillments of duty receive a transcendent value of blessedness and even of joy. It is the living process of personality, out of which new duties arise, infinite and inexhaustible. Service in its true meaning is service to personality: it is followership, and for the follower the model is a living law, never reduced to a fixed formula, and therefore a responsibility greater than any symbol could be. God is an expression of and a belief in personality, a living law, abundant in its duties and transcending any fulfillment.

It is in this way that the metaphorical process of personality becomes the drive for reform and progress. Personality is the "Good" itself and it makes good whatever is deficient: the empty structures of organizing rituals and social orders. As a force of reform, of conversion and progress, this process creates and destroys orders and in doing so protects against the threatening stagnation of a symbolic fixation.

Our age is a creative age, rich in crises, responsibilities, decisions, and therefore in danger of going astray. Old orders are torn down, new ones have not had time yet to grow. It is easy to understand that in a time like this, voices of warning are heard, warning against the flood which threatens to break all the dams of order and ritual.

Men stand up to preach and glorify symbolic fixation. This is understandable as a political reaction of caution. But it is nevertheless dangerous to emphasize a part-truth. Philosophy, as an impartial judge, has to fight, wherever it finds a one-sided and partial view substituting for truth. The symbolic view is a one-sided view, it becomes an untruth when not placed in a wider setting. Therefore it seemed necessary to emphasize the metaphorical process and its widening power, and to envisage the symbolic organization as a reduction, useful and indispensable, but meaningful only on the ground of the other. The metaphorical process carries life and history, and it carries them in transforming and, if necessary, destroying the symbolic order.

INDEX

INDEX

[203]

KJV DEVOTIONAL

for Men

NICK HARRISON

HARVEST HOUSE PUBLISHERS
EUGENE, OREGON

All Scripture quotations are taken from the King James Version of the Bible.

Cover design by Dugan Design Group
Cover photo © Eberhard Grossgasteiger / Unsplash
Interior design by KUHN Design Group

For bulk, special sales, or ministry purchases, please call 1 (800) 547-8979. Email: Customerservice@hhpbooks.com

KJV Devotional for Men
Copyright © 2022 by Harvest House Publishers
Published by Harvest House Publishers
Eugene, Oregon 97408
www.harvesthousepublishers.com

ISBN 978-0-7369-8487-4 (hardcover)
ISBN 978-0-7369-8489-8 (eBook)

Printed in China

22 23 24 25 26 27 28 29 30 / RDS / 10 9 8 7 6 5 4 3 2 1

INTRODUCTION

You've probably picked up this book of devotions for men because you were drawn to the fact that it features the King James Version of the Bible. If so, you're one of the millions of Bible lovers who still prefer the beauty and classic rhythms of this four-hundred-year-old translation of the Bible to the many new translations or paraphrases of God's Word.

The "Authorized" King James Version of the Bible was the result of King James I of England's direction that a translation of the Bible be readied for the Church of England. Seven years later, after the painstaking work of more than fifty qualified men, the new Bible was published—not as the King James Version or Authorized Version (that designation would come two centuries later) but as the more cumbersome *The Holy Bible, Conteyning the Old Testament, and the New: Newly Translated Out of the Originall Tongues: & with the Former Translations Diligently Compared and Revised by His Majesties Speciall Comandement.*

It should be noted that all the translators were well aware of the gravity of their task. All were university graduates—many from Oxford and Cambridge. With precision, they diligently crafted the monumental book that has served generation after generation of Christian believers.

3

Some of the fans of the KJV include Pulitzer Prize–winning author Eudora Welty, who has written, "How many of us, the South's writers-to-be of my generation, were blessed in one way or another, if not blessed alike, in not having gone deprived of the King James Version of the Bible. Its cadence entered into our ears and our memories for good." Indeed, she speaks not just for those from the American South but for fans of the KJV here and abroad, not all of whom were religious people.

Even skeptic and Nobel Prize winner George Bernard Shaw sang its praises.

> The translation was extraordinarily well done because to the translators what they were translating was not merely a curious collection of ancient books written by different authors in different stages of culture, but the word of God divinely revealed through His chosen and expressly inspired scribes. In this conviction they carried out their work with boundless reverence and care and achieved a beautifully artistic result…they made a translation so magnificent that to this day the common human Britisher or citizen of the United States of North America accepts and worships it as a single book by a single author, the book being the Book of Books and the author being God.

The great British statesman Winston Churchill opined, "The scholars who produced this masterpiece [the King James Bible] are mostly unknown and unremembered. But they forged an enduring link, literary and religious, between the English-speaking people of the world."

Today, the King James Version of the Bible remains extremely popular, standing firm against the plethora of additional translations. In fact, it is still the second-best-selling version, after the New International Version.

If you still remember the Scriptures you memorized from the KJV in your youth and can't quite see the advantage of the sometimes awkward phrasing of newer versions, I think you'll find solace, support, and guidance as you enjoy time with the Lord and with His Word, the King James Version of the Bible.

A MAN'S EYES

I will set no wicked thing before mine eyes (PSALM 101:3).

The light of the body is the eye: if therefore thine eye be single, thy whole body shall be full of light. But if thine eye be evil, thy whole body shall be full of darkness (MATTHEW 6:22-23).

A man's eyes take in many sights on any given day. But some of those sights can lead a man into sin if he doesn't police his vision. An envious eye may reveal a covetous heart. A critical eye may indicate prejudice. A roving eye may harbor adulterous desires. Every Christian man must determine that he will "set no wicked thing" before his eyes. Rather, he must affirm that his eyes be singularly focused on light, not the darkness of sin.

"Our eyes, when gazing on sinful objects, are out of their calling, and out of God's keeping." —THOMAS FULLER

Learning to Enjoy Silence

Be still, and know that I am God (Psalm 46:10).

The presence of the Lord is everywhere but is better perceived in stillness. The world around us is geared toward noise, activity, and ambition. To be still and know that He is God requires that we make time for stillness.

Perhaps in prayer we have told God we want to hear His voice; we want to know how to make wise decisions, but we sense no reply. Is it because we find listening to God in silence uncomfortable? We reason that we should be up and about *doing* rather than sitting still in silence.

All the while God has answers to our every question, but He wants us to seek the answers in communion with Him—often *silent* communion. The riches from God's treasury are often mined from silent canyons, not amid the clamor of busyness.

Be assured, if we will not search out stillness, neither will it search us out.

"There is hardly ever a complete silence in our soul. God is whispering to us well-nigh incessantly. Whenever the sounds of the world die out in the soul, or sink low, then we hear these whisperings of God." —Frederick W. Faber

LOVE ONE ANOTHER

This is my commandment, That ye love one another, as I have loved you (JOHN 15:12).

How do we love others? Basically, we're *there* for them. We learn to know them as we would like to be known by them. We engage them by drawing out their history. We open a line of communication that allows them to trust us as friends, not just acquaintances.

Jesus was with His disciples for a good three years. Daily they saw His love toward others as He healed the sick, fed the multitudes, and in the grandest display of love, died on the cross for the sins of all. This tells us that love, above all, is sacrificially giving to others freely.

Love, then, isn't hard. It's thinking of others in the way Jesus thinks of us.

"If we do not love one another, we certainly shall not have much power with God in prayer." —D.L. MOODY

Forgiven and Forgiving

Be ye kind one to another, tenderhearted, forgiving one another, even as God for Christ's sake hath forgiven you (EPHESIANS 4:32).

The man who thinks he has no need for forgiveness is a lost man. The Christian man is one who has seen the true depth of his sin toward God and toward others. Forgiveness is a primary need if he is ever to experience God and restore fellowship with a person who needs his forgiveness.

A regular inventory of our relationships should reveal if there's an offense toward God or others that we must make right. When we see an offense either against us or toward another, it's time to allow our hearts to become tender and exercise forgiveness, confession, and even restitution, if necessary. A forgiven Christian man has removed a heavy burden indeed.

"To be a Christian means to forgive the inexcusable, because God has forgiven the inexcusable in you." —C.S. LEWIS

The Thoughts of a Godly Man

For as he thinketh in his heart, so is he (Proverbs 23:7).

For most men, our thoughts are often random, wandering here and there based on external circumstances. We sometimes forget that our thoughts are the sum total of who we are. Take away our thought life and we are just an empty shell.

God cares about our thoughts. He would have us daily submit our minds to Him and center our thoughts on His will. Far too often the thoughts of an undisciplined mind take us in directions we don't want to go. Every man must identify the recurring thoughts that turn into temptations and reroute them to the mind's recycle bin. Evil or negative thoughts must be replaced by creative thoughts that are positive and God-affirming. For most men, this involves retraining our brains, and with the Holy Spirit as our Helper, we can learn to think rightly.

"Imagination is the hotbed where this sin is too often hatched. Guard your thoughts, and there will be little fear about your actions." —J.C. Ryle

11

NATURAL EVANGELISM

Though I preach the gospel, I have nothing to glory of: for necessity is laid upon me; yea, woe is unto me, if I preach not the gospel! (1 CORINTHIANS 9:16).

God calls every man to share the good news of the gospel in whatever way he is gifted to do so. For many, some ways of evangelism seem forced and unnatural, but a gifted man will find creative and effective ways to simply share with others. The problem many men have is they don't look expectantly for God to open the door of opportunity to share the gospel.

Ask God to bring the right person who needs to hear about Christ your way and respond naturally as to how God has worked with you. Let nothing feel forced; simply share and follow up with private prayer for the person in need.

"The question of speaking to souls is a question of personal love to the Lord Jesus Christ. Do not say you have no gift for it. Do you love Christ? If so, you will never lose an opportunity of speaking a word for Him." —G.V. WIGRAM

Edifying the Church

Even so ye, forasmuch as ye are zealous of spiritual gifts, seek that ye may excel to the edifying of the church (1 Corinthians 14:12).

The word we translate as "church" literally means "called out" ones. And within the church of God's "called out" ones is a love every Christian man must have. For to love Christ must also mean to love His bride. And every man has some gift to bring to edify his fellow believers. The work may be small or large, but whatever the task, God has appointed it to be accomplished.

Have you discovered how God wants to use you and your spiritual gifts to edify your fellow believers? Be zealous of spiritual gifts and pray for an understanding of the way God plans to use you. Don't shrink back from giving to the church, for in giving, you will also receive.

"A spiritual gift is a supernaturally designed ability granted to every believer by which the Holy Spirit ministers to the body of Christ. A spiritual gift cannot be earned, pursued or worked up. It is merely 'received' through the grace of God." —John MacArthur

RESISTING THE ENEMY

Submit yourselves therefore to God. Resist the devil, and he will flee from you (JAMES 4:7).

Every Christian man is Satan's target. This brutal enemy has plans to render men ineffective in their personal life—and in their spiritual life. However, no man is left unguarded by God in the battle. Safety is found in submitting entirely to God and resisting the specific influences Satan has devised to take you down.

Resisting must begin with the very first hint of temptation. If we don't resist early, we're more likely to fall into Satan's trap. The best warriors have learned how to identify their enemy and defeat him. So must every man. Be strong in the Lord. Submit to God. Resist the enemy at every turn—and watch him flee.

"Many men have no heart to resist a temptation. No sooner does Satan come with his solicitations—but they yield...He is a valorous Christian who brandishes the sword against Satan, and will rather die than yield. The heroic spirit of a saint is never more seen than in a battlefield, when he is fighting with the red dragon—and by the power of faith puts the devil to flight!" —THOMAS WATSON

FRIENDSHIP

A friend loveth at all times, and a brother is born for adversity (PROVERBS 17:17).

Many Christian men lament their lack of deep friendships with other men. They read of the closeness of David and Jonathan and wish for something like that in their own lives. Friendship, like so much else, is a gift of God. A man with no friends misses out on a key relationship in spiritual growth. For the love of a friend reveals the love of God, and during times of adversity, a true friend becomes God with skin. To have friends, one must show himself friendly. To enlarge one's circle of friends begins with asking God for the gift of friends. It then requires us to move out of our comfort zones and reach out, perhaps to those we sense are in need of friends too.

The strength of a church is largely determined by the extent of the friendships within the fellowship of the church.

"There is a brotherhood within the body of believers, and the Lord Jesus Christ is the common denominator. Friendship and fellowship are the legal tender among believers."
—J. VERNON MCGEE

SERVANTHOOD

Whosoever of you will be the chiefest, shall be servant of all (MARK 10:44).

By love serve one another (GALATIANS 5:13).

In God's upside-down economy, the way up is down. The way to be a "chief" is to become a servant. Laying down one's life for others is inherent in the Christian life, and the most spiritual men are those who serve others.

How can one serve? By noticing and meeting needs that are within your ability to meet. A servant's eyes are always alert for the needs of the one served. And because such alertness isn't natural, we must train ourselves to be servants. One way to become better servants is to consider Christ, who, though Lord of all, reduced Himself to become a servant of all. In His humility, He was exalted. Serve others and the reward will be yours.

"The secret of abundant helpfulness, is found in the desire to be a help, a blessing, to all we meet. We begin to be like Christ only when we begin to wish to be helpful. Where this desire is ever dominant, the life is an unceasing benediction. Rivers of water are pouring out from it continually to bless the world."
—J. R. MILLER

THE SECURE MAN

Watch ye, stand fast in the faith, quit you like men, be strong (1 CORINTHIANS 16:13).

Our source of strength as men is from the God who first created us, now empowers us, and will eventually welcome us to a heavenly home in His presence. While we're here in this earthen body, let's be not just men but *strong* men. Men of true faith; virtuous men who stand up for right and object when we see wrong. Let us be men who are possessed by the Spirit of God.

Let us be active men. Passivity in Christian men is a shame. And sadly, it can be contagious. But so can strength become contagious when true men are willing to be counted as righteous, denying evil and promoting good.

Be strong in the day at hand. Be a man.

"Christianity makes men, not babes. Adorn the doctrine of Christ by your manliness. In the Church, in the world, in business, in conversation, in prosperity, and adversity, [act] like men! Let no man despise you; and let no man despise the Gospel because of you." —HORATIUS BONAR

17

Role Models

Be ye followers of me, even as I also am of Christ (1 Corinthians 11:1).

Ye are our epistle written in our hearts, known and read of all men (2 Corinthians 3:2).

We never know who's watching us. As Paul notes, we are all epistles, read by those we meet along the way. Even this very day, someone may be influenced by observing how we react to an unexpected circumstance. Paul could encourage the recipients of his letters to follow his example. Why? Because he followed Christ.

For each of us, following Christ *must* lead to the kind of life others can likewise follow. We must each make sure the "epistle" of our lives, read by all men, is one worth reading.

"The example of the godly man is a living, standing memento to all around him of Christ, death and eternity."
—Cornelius Tyree

TAKE NO THOUGHT

Take therefore no thought for the morrow: for the morrow shall take thought for the things of itself. Sufficient unto the day is the evil thereof (MATTHEW 6:34).

One of the clearest indications the enemy of our souls is at work is when we're thinking of the future and we hear the enemy whisper *What if…* followed by worry-inducing scenarios that shake our faith. Such scenarios as, *What if* there's a food shortage? *What if* there's another pandemic? *What if* there's an atomic war? *What if* Christians are sent to jail? *What if* I lose my job? *What if* my wife leaves? *What if* my child turns away from the Lord?

The list is endless. *Endless!*

But the good news is that our resources in God are also endless. Beyond endless. There is simply no way God's going to run low on anything we need. As for what happens in the future, God is already there. He will not be surprised at world events or at the events that will shape our individual futures.

So as Christian men, we must stand firm against every whispered "What if" and answer it with "God's got this!"

"Worry is the cross which we make for ourselves by over-anxiety." —FRANÇOIS FÉNELON

OVERCOMING THE PAST

Remember ye not the former things, neither consider the things of old. Behold, I will do a new thing; now it shall spring forth; shall ye not know it? I will even make a way in the wilderness, and rivers in the desert (ISAIAH 43:18-19).

What man does not have events in his past he regrets? However, if a man is remembering past sins that God has Himself forgotten because of the forgiveness we find in Christ, those memories are at best wasteful and at worst destructive.

Many a man has labored for years without success to overcome memories of a sinful past. And needlessly so. Every man must acknowledge his past failures and then *move on*. In so doing, God is enabled to open a way through that past wilderness and bring forth rivers in that forsaken desert.

What events of your past still haunt you? Confess them, acknowledge God's forgiveness, and then forevermore, let those memories become monuments to God's mercy and grace.

"Being in Christ, it is safe to forget the past; it is possible to be sure of the future; it is possible to be diligent in the present."
—ALEXANDER MACLAREN

THE COMPLETE MAN

Ye are complete in him, which is the head of all principality and power (COLOSSIANS 2:10).

A man is incomplete without Christ, but when that man is born again and has become a new creation in Christ, he is reckoned by God as "complete in him."

The full import of that truth may take years to fully appreciate. In fact, many Christian men wander through life for years still feeling incomplete. Recognizing the many benefits of Christ's redemption will clearly continue for as long as a man lives and is worth a lifetime of pondering and appreciating. While many men may strive for a sense of completeness, from God's point of view, a man is already complete when he is "in Christ." What many men assume as a goal, God sees as a starting point.

"Let us understand, that all who have really fled for mercy to the Lord Jesus Christ are, as Paul assures the Colossians, complete in Him! In themselves they may be poor shortcoming sinners—but seeing they have laid hold on Christ, God looks upon them as complete—completely pardoned, completely righteous, completely pure—no jot or tittle of condemnation can be laid to their charge." —J.C. RYLE

WE ARE WARRIORS

Though we walk in the flesh, we do not war after the flesh: (For the weapons of our warfare are not carnal, but mighty through God to the pulling down of strong holds) (2 CORINTHIANS 10:3-4).

Many men, when they were boys, often pretended to be great warriors, fighting for the triumph of good over evil. Now as men, that game of pretense has become reality in that we are all called to be spiritual warriors, not wielding "carnal" weapons, but pulling down satanic strongholds wielding "mighty" spiritual weapons. Praying men are in the front lines of battle today. But they must not battle alone. Every Christian man must join them, equipped for spiritual battle. Passive warriors are an oxymoron.

Today God is calling for men to see the battles for their families, their countries, and their faith for what it is—a tremendous assault from a ruthless enemy. The spiritual army God is assembling is not a volunteer army, it's an army of conscripted men. To be saved is to be enlisted.

"You must watch, pray, and fight. Expect your last battle to be the most difficult, for the enemy's fiercest charge is reserved for the end of the day." —CHARLES SPURGEON

SEASONS

To every thing there is a season, and a time to every purpose under the heaven: A time to be born, and a time to die (ECCLESIASTES 3:1-2).

What season of life are you in now? Every man goes through changes as he ages that are, for the most part, God-ordained. Young men are called to bear yokes older men can no longer support. Older men bring wisdom to the table many young men lack.

Happy is the man who is content with whatever season of life he's in. Bitter is the man who laments the passing of one season to the next. God has called us to live the allotted years He's assigned us. We must never look back to a previous season with regret, nor should we look ahead to the next season with presumption. While we are alive today, let's love this present season and fully embrace the gift of life while we can.

"God's purposes have all their seasons of fulfillment. His judgments each have their time of visitation. Mapped out in clear perspective, your every dispensation was fixed from everlasting in the eternal mind of God." —GEORGE MYLNE

A MAN WHO WILL NOT FEAR

God is our refuge and strength, a very present help in trouble. Therefore will not we fear, though the earth be removed, and though the mountains be carried into the midst of the sea; though the waters thereof roar and be troubled, though the mountains shake with the swelling thereof. Selah (PSALM 46:1-3).

Every man is prone to some sort of fear. He may fear financial lack, relationship failure, vocational loss, health decline, and more. But every one of those fears and all others are vanquished when God is our very present help in trouble. Nothing can shake the man whose life is rooted in the providence of God.

When a man is easily shaken, it's time to become *un*shakeable. It's time to shift our burden from our shoulders to God's strong back.

A man's fears may be few or many, but every one of them is conquerable through Christ. The very purpose of trouble in our lives may be God's way of proving Himself as trustworthy while also making us unshakeable.

"God incarnate is the end of fear; and the heart that realizes that He is in the midst...will be quiet in the middle of alarm."
—F.B. MEYER

The Gift of Sex

Flee fornication. Every sin that a man doeth is without the body; but he that committeth fornication sinneth against his own body (1 CORINTHIANS 6:18).

We live in an age when sex as God meant it to be has been greatly diminished. Sexual pleasure is a gift of God to be treasured between a man and his lifetime mate. And yet this gift has been corrupted by Satan to the extent that sexual immorality has been normalized to a staggering degree. Even Christian men are taken in by the promises of porn or the acceptance of sexual sins that were once easily understood as not allowable for men who claim Christ as Lord.

Today, men must flee fornication—in practice and also as entertainment fare in the form of movies and television where sexual permissiveness is routine.

God can restore the rightful place of sexuality in a man's life—if he will renounce any known sexual sin.

The irony is that the gift of sex is enhanced by submitting our desires to God's provision instead of taking the shortcut of sexual sin.

"All sin, particularly the habitual practice of sexual sin, is an unholy boldness in evil!" —CHARLES SPURGEON

HEROES

And what shall I more say? for the time would fail me to tell of Gedeon, and of Barak, and of Samson, and of Jephthae; of David also, and Samuel, and of the prophets: Who through faith subdued kingdoms, wrought righteousness, obtained promises, stopped the mouths of lions. Quenched the violence of fire, escaped the edge of the sword, out of weakness were made strong, waxed valiant in fight, turned to flight the armies of the aliens (HEBREWS 11:32-34).

Every man needs heroes. Even as boys we looked up to certain men as those we would like to emulate. Heroes abound in the Bible, but who are our heroes of the faith beyond the covers of our Bibles? Have we read the lives of stalwart men like Jim Elliot, Oswald Chambers, Watchman Nee, Ben Carson, and others? Do our children or grandchildren know these men?

May God let us be the best version of the heroes God sees in us. May the heroics of past men of faith show us the way.

"God is preparing His heroes. And when the opportunity comes, He can fit them into their places in a moment. And the world will wonder where they came from." —A.B. SIMPSON

God's Word

The word of God is quick, and powerful, and sharper than any twoedged sword, piercing even to the dividing asunder of soul and spirit, and of the joints and marrow, and is a discerner of the thoughts and intents of the heart (HEBREWS 4:12).

All scripture is given by inspiration of God, and is profitable for doctrine, for reproof, for correction, for instruction in righteousness (2 TIMOTHY 3:16).

The grass withereth, the flower fadeth: but the word of our God shall stand for ever (ISAIAH 40:8).

When walking in the dark—in our case a dark world—a light is necessary, not optional. Our light is the Word of God. The Word directs us and it corrects us.

Frequent are the temptations to decide for ourselves the right path to take, but without the light of Scripture shining on the path ahead, we're prone to straying from God's will for us. Never make a decision in opposition to God's Word, realizing that such tempting "opportunities" will surely come. Knowing God's Word will save us from many a fall.

"The vigor of our spiritual life will be in exact proportion to the place held by the Bible in our life and thoughts." —GEORGE MÜLLER

Riches in Heaven

Lay not up for yourselves treasures upon earth, where moth and rust doth corrupt, and where thieves break through and steal: But lay up for yourselves treasures in heaven, where neither moth nor rust doth corrupt, and where thieves do not break through nor steal: For where your treasure is, there will your heart be also (Matthew 6:19-21).

Every man must know where his true treasure is…for that's where his heart will follow. The call of God is to reject this earth's riches in favor of incorruptible heavenly treasures.

We work for monetary wages, but the treasures awaiting us in heaven are those we give freely to others in the way of time, love, affirmations, and yes, finances. There is no wiser financial investment than that of giving to others who need what we have. In giving, we find a curious freedom that releases us from the need to gather more into larger barns.

"God's purpose in promising to reward with heavenly and eternal honors the faithful service of His saints is to win them from the pursuit of earthly riches and pleasures, to sustain them in the fires of persecution, and to encourage them in the exercise of Christian virtues." —C.I. Scofield

The Integrity of a Christian Man

The integrity of the upright shall guide them: but the perverseness of transgressors shall destroy them (PROVERBS 11:3).

There is a reward to the man of integrity that money can't buy. Likewise, there is a perversity to dishonest men that will soon destroy them. A Christian man knows by God's Word and by experience that in the long run (and often in the short run), honesty and integrity pay good dividends.

Integrity can be learned in the same way anything can be learned—and that's by experience. Hang with other men of integrity and follow their example. Remember to always choose the right thing, even when it's hard to do so. Eventually, choosing the right thing will become your default action.

"Be satisfied and thankful, you who are taught by the Spirit of God, to walk in integrity. You are rich in faith, and heirs of the kingdom—and in this world you have and shall have everything that infinite wisdom and divine love sees fit for you!" —GEORGE LAWSON

Working as unto God

Whatsoever ye do, do it heartily, as to the Lord, and not unto men; knowing that of the Lord ye shall receive the reward of the inheritance: for ye serve the Lord Christ (Colossians 3:23-24).

Every man has a calling. For some, it's a calling based on a secular career. Others may have a calling based on talent. For others, the calling is based on a learned ability. Yet others may work in full-time ministry. But no matter what our calling—from plumber to salesman to executive to pastor—we are not working for another person. Our work is first, last, and always unto God.

Excellence in our calling is mandatory. And though we may fail many times, we still pursue the goal of the "reward of the inheritance" reserved for those who have worked "as to the Lord."

"No duty should be done with half a heart, or half a hand. Let not the heart be absent while the hand is at work...Seek the way of working quietly with sober diligence and peaceful energy; and thus whatever you do, you will do it with all your might." —George Mylne

GOD'S SOVEREIGNTY

Declaring the end from the beginning, and from ancient times the things that are not yet done, saying, My counsel shall stand, and I will do all my pleasure (ISAIAH 46:10).

During the course of a lifetime, a man enjoys much and suffers much. During the former, we rejoice at the graciousness of God, but do we also trust in God during the latter times?

Yes, we do, if we understand that the purposes of God shall always stand, regardless of man's opinion—and that those purposes always work toward a goal God has in mind.

Trust in God's sovereignty lifts a huge burden from our backs. And instead of paralyzing our prayer life ("Why pray if God has predetermined the outcome?"), it invigorates our prayers. In praying, we participate in God bringing about His sovereignty.

Prayer has been likened to laying down the railroad tracks where the locomotive of God's will wants to go. Pray then with confidence and expectation.

"Divine sovereignty is not the sovereignty of a tyrannical Despot, but the exercised pleasure of One who is infinitely wise and good! Because God is infinitely wise He cannot err, and because He is infinitely righteous He will not do wrong."
—A.W. PINK

The Joy of the Lord

O come, let us sing unto the Lord: let us make a joyful noise to the rock of our salvation. Let us come before his presence with thanksgiving, and make a joyful noise unto him with psalms. For the Lord is a great God, and a great King above all gods (Psalm 95:1-3).

A joyless Christian is an oxymoron. There's no lack of joy to be found in Christianity. As we learn to live in the joy of the Lord, we find renewed strength during hard times. We find happiness during blessed times.

Christian joy is not a worked-up emotion. It comes as a gift from the Lord Himself. In *Him* is fullness of joy. The package deal of salvation contains more than enough joy to meet life's demands. Therefore, come before His presence with thanksgiving, and make a joyful noise with psalms.

Why? Because He "is a great God and a great King above all gods."

"There exists a delight that is not given to the wicked, but to those honoring Thee, O God, without desiring recompense, the joy of whom Thou art Thyself! And this is the blessed life, to rejoice towards Thee, about Thee, for Thy sake."
—Augustine

A Man's Body

Know ye not that your body is the temple of the Holy Ghost which is in you, which ye have of God, and ye are not your own? (1 CORINTHIANS 6:19).

No man ever yet hated his own flesh; but nourisheth and cherisheth it, even as the Lord the church (EPHESIANS 5:29).

When we came to Christ in faith, along came our bodies. We surrendered all to Him, body, soul, and spirit. Our bodies that were once Pizza Huts are now God's temple.

In the past we may have been less than kind to our temples, but it's never too late to refurbish a weathered structure. Treat your body with respect. Eat right, get some exercise, sleep well, and maintain a positive attitude. Our body is one of God's great gifts.

"It is the part of a Christian to take care of his own body for the very purpose that by its soundness and well-being he may be enabled to labor for the aid of those who are in want, and thus the stronger member may serve the weaker member."
—MARTIN LUTHER

God's Call on Your Life

Who hath saved us, and called us with an holy calling, not according to our works, but according to his own purpose and grace, which was given us in Christ Jesus before the world began (2 TIMOTHY 1:9).

As our years pass, it may be hard to remember the call God has on our lives. Despite our busyness, there are prayers to be prayed, work to be done, hungry to be fed, young Christians to be taught. There is always work to be done in God's kingdom, and every man has his place of service.

It's up to each man to step up to the plate and fulfill his calling from God. When we're unsure of God's calling, we can pray, we can ask others what they see as God's calling in us, and we can simply begin filling needs we notice around us. The years will still pass, but like a bank account with compound interest, the work of God continues onward, building up God's house.

"Worldliness is a spirit, a temperament, an attitude of the soul. It is a life without high callings, life devoid of lofty ideals. It is a gaze always horizontal and never vertical." —JOHN JOWETT

THE HOLY GHOST

Now the God of hope fill you with all joy and peace in believing, that ye may abound in hope, through the power of the Holy Ghost (ROMANS 15:13).

There is no Christian life apart from a relationship with each member of the Trinity. We come to know God as our Father, Jesus Christ as Savior, and the Holy Ghost as comforter, teacher, helper, and guide.

Many men know God as their father and Jesus as their Savior but may be shaky when it comes to the Holy Ghost. And yet, in God's plan, our power for living comes from this third member of the Godhead. Never underestimate the privilege of a relationship with the Holy Ghost, for He brings joy, boldness, and guidance for living.

"If there be one God subsisting in three persons, then let us give equal reverence to all the persons in the Trinity. There is not more or less in the Trinity; the Father is not more God than the Son and Holy Ghost. There is an order in the Godhead, but no degrees; one person has not a majority or super eminence above another, therefore we must give equal worship to all the persons." —THOMAS WATSON

THE PRAYING CHRISTIAN MAN

Verily I say unto you, If ye have faith, and doubt not, ye shall not only do this which is done to the fig tree, but also if ye shall say unto this mountain, Be thou removed, and be thou cast into the sea; it shall be done. And all things, whatsoever ye shall ask in prayer, believing, ye shall receive (MATTHEW 21:21-22).

A Christian man is a praying man. Prayer is the essential tool of the Christian life. Not only is it our means of communing with our Lord, but prayer is the means by which God has chosen to attend to our needs.

The Bible is chock-full of answered prayers. The people of God repeatedly prayed for deliverance from enemies and were saved. Barren women prayed for children and became mothers. Sinners prayed for forgiveness and became men who changed not only the course of their lives but the course of history.

Sadly, many men pray far too little. But if we could realize the power of a praying man—we would fall to our knees more often.

Pray much. Believe much. Move mountains.

"The story of every great Christian achievement is the history of answered prayer." —E.M. BOUNDS

ALL FOR CHRIST

Then one of them, which was a lawyer, asked him a question, tempting him, and saying, Master, which is the great commandment in the law? Jesus said unto him, Thou shalt love the Lord thy God with all thy heart, and with all thy soul, and with all thy mind (Matthew 22:35-37).

There's no such thing as a partial Christian. A man either is or is not a Christian. The requirement is to love God with all one's heart, soul, and mind and to seek first the kingdom of God. This is total commitment. It means all a man does, plans, or desires is related to God's plan for that man. We must often ask ourselves, Are we seeking God first, trusting all else will be added to us?

"May not a single moment of my life be spent outside the light, love and joy of God's presence and not a moment without the entire surrender of myself as a vessel for Him to fill full of His Spirit and His love." —Andrew Murray

THE LOVE OF GOD

Behold, what manner of love the Father hath bestowed upon us, that we should be called the sons of God (1 JOHN 3:1).

The contemplation of God's love for us can change us. As we "behold" the manner of God's love, we realize it far surpasses human love. God saw us before time began. He saw to our conceptions, our births, and oversees every day of our lives—and then His love ushers us into eternal existence with Him. There is nothing about God's love for us that can leave us in want. When we are consumed by this divine love God has for each of us, we need have no fear, no worry—and we are able to forgive and truly love others, even our enemies.

"Behold, what manner of love is this, that Christ should be arraigned and we adorned, that the curse should be laid on His head and the crown set on ours." —THOMAS WATSON

THE FAVOR OF GOD

Thou, LORD, wilt bless the righteous; with favor wilt thou compass him as with a shield (PSALM 5:12).

The lines are fallen unto me in pleasant places; yea, I have a goodly heritage (PSALM 16:6).

It's no small thing to acknowledge the blessing of God on the righteous man. Our heavenly Father delights to bring blessing to His children. He also bestows favor on the Christian man, sometimes openly and sometimes in secret.

A man who is benefitting from God's favor may never really know how God worked His plan behind the scenes to bring about a desired end. Even now, God has blessings for you, and He bestows favor on you. This is the heritage of those who trust in God and are busy in His vineyard. The lines fall in pleasant places for you.

"The devil visits idle men with his temptations. God visits industrious men with His favors." —MATTHEW HENRY

God's Promises for a Man

The promise is unto you, and to your children, and to all that are afar off, even as many as the Lord our God shall call (ACTS 2:39).

The promise of God—indeed all the promises of God—are for those of us who are "afar off" from when Luke wrote the book of Acts. The godly man prospers as he searches the Bible for the appropriate promises that relate to his life and his trials. The unprepared man who knows little of God's promises may find himself adrift without an anchor in times of trouble and uncertainty.

What promises of God will you bring to bear today on your present need? Read them, repeat them, believe them.

"Furnish thyself with arguments from the promises to enforce thy prayers, and make them prevalent with God. The promises are the ground of faith, and faith, when strengthened, will make thee fervent, and such fervency ever speeds and returns with victory out of the field of prayer. The mightier any is in the Word, the more mighty he will be in prayer."
—WILLIAM GURNALL

Let God Choose

He shall subdue the people under us, and the nations under our feet. He shall choose our inheritance for us, the excellency of Jacob whom he loved. Selah (Psalm 47:3-4).

Many Christian men have made the discovery that God knows far better than they do how to choose among life's decisions. Our human way of choosing is often at variance with God's way.

We know for certain that a decision that in some way violates God's Word is a wrong decision. Many men have also discovered that when God chooses, He often doesn't work on our timetable. The Bible is full of cautions to "wait on the Lord." Waiting is hard, but if we are to reap God's superior choice, it will be worth it. We must not get ahead of God, but neither must we lag behind. Pray, wait in faith, and see what God chooses for you. It will be a sweet "inheritance."

"The sweetest lesson I have learned in God's school is to let the Lord choose for me." —D.L. Moody

GODLY PROSPERITY

Blessed is the man that walketh not in the counsel of the ungodly, nor standeth in the way of sinners, nor sitteth in the seat of the scornful...he shall be like a tree planted by the rivers of water, that bringeth forth his fruit in his season; his leaf also shall not wither; and whatsoever he doeth shall prosper (PSALM 1:1,3).

God never desires for a man to fail at life. Instead, God offers every man a way to succeed, though that success may not duplicate what the world calls success.

If a man doesn't walk in the counsel of the ungodly (the world), nor live sinfully, nor scorn God's ways, that man can reckon himself a fruitful tree planted by rivers of water.

Be cautioned though. Never expect your prosperity to be accepted as such by those who measure prosperity with the wrong gauge.

"There are great positives as well as refusals necessary for him who would find real prosperity. He must not only say no to the wrong, he must say yes to the right. He must not only avoid the seat of the scornful, but his delight must be in the law of the Lord." —CLOVIS CHAPPELL

THE RETURN OF CHRIST

Ye men of Galilee, why stand ye gazing up into heaven? this same Jesus, which is taken up from you into heaven, shall so come in like manner as ye have seen him go into heaven (ACTS 1:11).

Looking for that blessed hope, and the glorious appearing of the great God and our Savior Jesus Christ (TITUS 2:13).

Christian men differ on the timeline of Christ's return, but most do look forward to that "blessed hope" with anticipation. Every generation has this hope and sees clear signs that the great day will soon arrive. The return of Christ holds significant meaning for every Christian man. It's an incentive to live a pure, unstained life in the midst of a crooked generation. It's a guard against fear as troubling world events unfold, and it's a motive to support worldwide evangelism—and personal evangelism too. With this blessed hope within us, we must be prepared to share with others the source of our hope.

"When He returns is not as important as the fact that we are ready for Him when He does return." —A.W. TOZER

UNIQUELY YOU

O Lord, thou hast searched me, and known me. Thou know-est my downsitting and mine uprising, thou understandest my thought afar off. Thou compassest my path and my lying down, and art acquainted with all my ways. For there is not a word in my tongue, but, lo, O LORD, thou knowest it alto-gether. Thou hast beset me behind and before, and laid thine hand upon me. Such knowledge is too wonderful for me; it is high, I cannot attain unto it (PSALM 139:1-6).

The imprint of God is upon every Christian man. God designed us in His image. He prepared a plan for us in order to have a blessed life. God knows our very thoughts before we think them. He knows the next words out of our mouths. He is acquainted with all our ways.

Such knowledge must change us—and for the better. Our God is, of all things, an intimate God. We can be who we are with Him because He knows us better than we know ourselves. Comprehending God's intimacy in our lives is too wonderful to grasp…and yet it is so.

"You are the only you God made…God made you and broke the mold." —MAX LUCADO

Waiting on God

Wait on the LORD: be of good courage, and he shall strengthen thine heart: wait, I say, on the LORD (PSALM 27:14).

Few men enjoy waiting on God. Truth be told, if we ran things, we would be far hastier than we judge God to be. And we'd be all the poorer for it. We may think we need our answer *now*, but God knows the exact timing to bring our lives' plans to pass.

As we wait, we must remember we're not waiting passively. We're waiting with anticipation, knowing God *will* bring to pass that needful event. He asks only that we be of good courage, and He shall strengthen our hearts. Whatever it is you're waiting to hear from God, pray with expectancy, and it shall come to pass in His time and in His way.

"The prayer that begins with trustfulness, and passes on into waiting, will always end in thankfulness, triumph, and praise." —ALEXANDER MACLAREN

By the Grace of God

The grace of our Lord was exceeding abundant with faith and love which is in Christ Jesus (1 Timothy 1:14).

We often sing of God's "amazing grace," but do we stop to think that part of our amazement is at the depth of God's grace toward us? It's not that His grace barely saves us; no, it's that His grace *abundantly* saves us. And having saved us, His grace follows us through life to our dying day. The supply simply never runs dry. It never will. It cannot. God's grace sustains us with every word we speak, every step we take, every thought we think.

On the following page, you'll find all the verses to the most sung hymn of all time. Take a few moments to read and ponder each stanza. Experience afresh the amazing grace of our God.

"Through many dangers, toils and snares, I have already come; 'Tis grace hath brought me safe thus far, And grace will lead me home." —John Newton

Amazing Grace

Amazing grace! How sweet the sound
that saved a wretch like me!
I once was lost, but now am found;
was blind, but now I see.

'Twas grace that taught my heart to fear,
and grace my fears relieved;
How precious did that grace appear
the hour I first believed.

Through many dangers, toils and snares,
I have already come;
'Tis grace hath brought me safe thus far,
and grace will lead me home.

The Lord has promised good to me,
His Word my hope secures;
He will my Shield and Portion be,
as long as life endures.

Yea, when this flesh and heart shall fail,
and mortal life shall cease,
I shall possess, within the veil,
a life of joy and peace.

When we've been there ten thousand years,
bright shining as the sun,
We've no less days to sing God's praise
than when we'd first begun.

GOD'S PRESENCE

Thou wilt show me the path of life: in thy presence is fulness of joy; at thy right hand there are pleasures for evermore (PSALM 16:11).

A Christian man is never without the presence of God. Our Lord surrounds us moment by moment; we are never out of His care.

And in His presence, what do we find? We discover "fulness of joy." What do we *not* find in His presence? We do not find anger (having made peace with God through the Cross), we do not find fear (for He has told us time after time to "fear not"). We find no hatred (save the hatred of sin). We find no burden (for He bears our burdens for us).

"Fulness of joy," indeed! And pleasures forevermore!

"We should go into His presence as a child goes to his father. We do it with reverence and godly fear, of course, but we should go with a childlike confidence and simplicity." —MARTYN LLOYD-JONES

TIME

Whereas ye know not what shall be on the morrow. For what is your life? It is even a vapor, that appeareth for a little time, and then vanisheth away (JAMES 4:14).

What a precious gift is time! Hours, weeks, months, and years in which we live and thrive in the presence of God. We live by the power of the Holy Spirit, moment by moment. Every second we breathe is accounted for by God—and is given to us as a gift to enjoy but also as a charge to act as stewards. How then can we best allot our time on earth so as to maximize our usefulness? James has the right idea when he reminds us our lives are but vapors. He says we do not know what will happen tomorrow. The implication is that we have only today to be sure of, so if we will use our time wisely, we will use it *today*. A useful day includes prayer, taking in God's Word, obedience to anything we know we must do today, and trusting in guidance from the Holy Spirit. If we fill our days thus, we will arrive at life's end with contentment. Even if that day is tomorrow.

"O God, impress upon me the value of time, and give regulation to all my thoughts and to all my movements."—THOMAS CHALMERS

A Man's Good Memories

The memory of the just is blessed: but the name of the wicked shall rot (PROVERBS 10:7).

As we move through life, we are accumulating memories. For many, those memories may consist of failure, sin, and missed opportunities. But to dwell on those past failures does us no good. We must always remember to put *all* our sins and missteps of the past under the blood of Christ. The recalling of a painful past is only of use to our enemy, Satan, who will continue to accuse us as long as we allow him to do so—even for years. God, on the other hand, would have us cleanse our memories of that regretted past and dwell on memories of His faithfulness.

What is past is simply what He has brought us through and now can only be recalled as a monument to His goodness. Store up your godly memories. Discard forever the memories that stab you afresh with each recollection.

"Gratitude changes the pangs of memory into a tranquil joy."
—DIETRICH BONHOEFFER

MIRACLES

He that believeth on me, the works that I do shall he do also; and greater works than these shall he do; because I go unto my Father. And whatsoever ye shall ask in my name, that will I do, that the Father may be glorified in the Son (JOHN 14:12-13).

Do miracles still happen? Do you need a miracle? I suspect all Christian men need a miracle at various times. We have God's promise of provision throughout our lives even when that provision requires a miracle. But we must remember that not all miracles are instantaneous. God works fast miracles, and He works slow miracles. If you need a miracle, pray for it. Then wait and see how God brings it about without your dictating how it must be performed. Trust is always the key to experiencing a miracle.

"Have you been asking God what He is going to do? He will never tell you. God does not tell you what He is going to do, He reveals to you who He is. Do you believe in a miracle working God, and will you 'go out' in complete surrender to Him until you are not surprised one iota by anything He does?"
—OSWALD CHAMBERS

THE WIDE-OPEN
DOOR OF MERCY

Mercy unto you, and peace, and love, be multiplied (JUDE 1:2).

The matter of sin—perhaps ongoing sin—must be dealt with severely in the man who desires to rise up before God. Sin in a Christian man can delay the work of God in our lives. Yes, the door of mercy remains open if we sin, but our days of ongoing sinful selfish living must be considered as behind us.

If there is sin, we need only apply God's remedy: repentance, confession, and an understanding that Christ has paid for *all* our sin. We need never wallow in the sad aftermath of sin. Once sin is repented of and confessed, the Christian man has only to rise up as a ransomed man and walk confidently forward, enjoying the mercies of God.

Is there any sin you have yet to deal with? Don't delay. Don't allow sin to hold you back from your destiny any longer.

"Every ransomed man owes his salvation to the fact that during his days of sinning, God kept the door of mercy open by refusing to accept any of his evil acts as final." —A. W. TOZER

CHRIST IN US

I am crucified with Christ: nevertheless I live; yet not I, but Christ liveth in me: and the life which I now live in the flesh I live by the faith of the Son of God, who loved me, and gave himself for me (GALATIANS 2:20).

There is a secret to living the Christian life, though it's really not so secret, since God has revealed it to us in His Word. That secret is to see ourselves—our old fallen lives—as crucified with Christ. And though we live on, we do so by Christ living in us and through us.

This is no abstract symbolism. This is God's reality for the Christian. We die to self in order to find true life in Christ. We die; He lives in us.

How is this accomplished? As all God's truth is accomplished in the believer—by faith.

Classic books have revealed this secret in more depth. One of the best is *Hudson Taylor's Spiritual Secret* by Dr. and Mrs. Howard Taylor.

"Christ liveth in me. And how great the difference…instead of bondage, liberty; instead of failure, quiet victories within; instead of fear and weakness, a restful sense of sufficiency in Another." —HUDSON TAYLOR

BE GLAD AND LAUGH

A merry heart doeth good like a medicine: but a broken spirit drieth the bones (PROVERBS 17:22).

Our present world has much that rends our hearts and can bring tears to the manliest of men. But amid the pain of a suffering world, there are men to be found who remember how to have a joyful heart—how to laugh despite adversity. God is looking for more men who are willing to be dispensers of heavenly joy in an often hellish world. We're told in Ecclesiastes 3:4 that there's a time to weep…but also a time to laugh.

A godly man knows the difference between the two. When his friend is in pain, he will weep with him. But when a joyful heart is the prescribed medicine, the Christian brings the joy of the Lord to bear on the situation.

Today, may your life bring you something about which you can laugh. Even in a tough situation…find joy. This too shall pass.

"Be glad and laugh from the low bottom of thine own heart."
—WILLIAM TYNDALE

LOVE NOT THE WORLD

Love not the world, neither the things that are in the world. If any man love the world, the love of the Father is not in him (1 JOHN 2:15).

Every Christian man has his weaknesses when it comes to "the world." At every turn we're tempted to love the things of this world. And one man's worldly temptation is easily discounted by another man who has his own worldly battles.

But to love the world is to *not* love the Father. Our hearts must not be divided. We give our allegiance to God and count the world as God's enemy.

After having been burned by flirtations with the world, many men come to realize this world is simply a place to pass through on our way to eternity. For sure, God gives us pleasures in this life, but they are pleasures of His choosing, not of our own fleshly appetites.

Though we are *in* the world, we are not of the world, which will eventually—with all its attractions—dissolve in flames.

*"Christianity removes the attraction of the earth; and this is one way in which it diminishes men's burden. It makes them citizens of another world." —*HENRY DRUMMOND

KINGDOM LIVING

As ye know how we exhorted and comforted and charged every one of you, as a father doth his children, that ye would walk worthy of God, who hath called you unto his kingdom and glory (1 THESSALONIANS 2:11-12).

A Christian man is a kingdom man. He has been uprooted from this present world and replanted in God's kingdom. Forever after his conversion, his life is lived as one who is becoming more and more acquainted and comfortable as a resident of God's kingdom—a kingdom to which we were called. A kingdom for which we were each personally chosen by God.

Learning kingdom living is a man's greatest joy on earth, influencing all he does. For that reason, we must walk worthy of God, eternally grateful for our place in His kingdom.

"I will place no value on anything I have or may possess except in relation to the kingdom of Christ." —DAVID LIVINGSTONE

REST

Come unto me, all ye that labor and are heavy laden, and I will give you rest. Take my yoke upon you, and learn of me; for I am meek and lowly in heart: and ye shall find rest unto your souls. For my yoke is easy, and my burden is light (MATTHEW 11:28-30).

Is there any burden a man can have that's beyond the power of Christ to bear? No, there is not. He bids us take up His easy yoke. He invites us to find rest for our souls. No matter how heavy *our* burdens, His is light.

Every day we're invited to enter a burden-free day, trusting all to Him.

Have you laid down today's burden? Have you taken up His light load? Have you found rest for your soul? His offer is to "come unto me." It's an offer no burdened man should refuse.

"Abide in Me says Jesus. Cling to Me. Stick fast to Me. Live the life of close and intimate communion with Me. Get nearer to Me. Roll every burden on Me. Cast your whole weight on Me. Never let go your hold on Me for a moment…Do this and I will never fail you." —J.C. RYLE

Redeemed by the Blood

Forasmuch as ye know that ye were not redeemed with corruptible things, as silver and gold, from your vain conversation received by tradition from your fathers; but with the precious blood of Christ, as of a lamb without blemish and without spot (1 PETER 1:18-19).

Throughout the Bible, blood is a means of salvation. We read this in the Passover story where the blood of an innocent lamb was the means of escaping the angel of death. It was a foreshadowing of the true Lamb of God, Christ who saves us from the penalty for our sins.

For many people, the blood of Christ is a topic to avoid. And yet the blood of Christ is central to our salvation. Never disparage the bloody sacrifice on the Cross. Never apologize for claiming the blood. Ponder the irony of the innocent Lamb dying to save the guilty. The Lamb who suffers death so we may live.

Yes, the blood is that important.

"I am ready to meet God face to face tonight and look into those eyes of infinite holiness, for all my sins are covered by the atoning blood." —R.A. TORREY

FIRSTFRUITS

Honor the LORD with thy substance, and with the firstfruits of all thine increase: So shall thy barns be filled with plenty, and thy presses shall burst out with new wine (PROVERBS 3:9-10).

Christian men are givers. We give to the poor, to the church, but above all, we give to God. And not just what's left over at the end of the month. No, we give from the firstfruits of our labors. We give God from the best of the crop before we take for ourselves. Besides money, our giving includes our time, attention, talents… whatever the need, if we can fill it, we're there.

Whether the giving is of ourselves or our finances, it should be at the forefront of our offering. Leftovers are not good enough for the Lord. Every man must consider *how* God can best use him and his resources. What among our "firstfruits" are we able to give generously and without regret?

"God, who is the first and best, must have the first and best of everything; his right is prior to all other, and therefore he must be served first." —MATTHEW HENRY

THE FEAR OF THE LORD

The fear of the LORD is the beginning of knowledge: but fools despise wisdom and instruction (PROVERBS 1:7).

The fear of the LORD is to hate evil: pride, and arrogancy, and the evil way, and the froward mouth, do I hate (PROVERBS 8:13).

It has been rightly said that the fear of the Lord is the fear that banishes all other fears. But even more, the fear of God is the beginning of knowledge and wisdom. On the reverse side, fearing God means to hate evil, pride, and arrogance.

When the fear of God is absent in a man's life, he loses out on the knowledge and wisdom God has provided for him. Likewise, an acceptance of evil and pride in a man's life not only shows a lack of godly fear; it also opens the door to unwise choices and destructive behavior.

Fearing God gives a man a right reason to rejoice, for it's then he knows he's protected by his wisdom and able to avoid Satan's evil traps set for his destruction.

"The fear of God is the cornerstone of all blessedness. We must reverence the ever-blessed God, before we can be blessed ourselves." —CHARLES SPURGEON

ADVERSITY

If thou faint in the day of adversity, thy strength is small
(PROVERBS 24:10).

There are times in a man's life when he faces adversity. It could be a broken relationship, a health crisis, financial loss, or some other tragedy. At such times a man's faith is tested. Will he make it through the trial unscathed and wiser for the experience, or will his faith suffer under the weight of adversity? During good times a man will find it easy to rejoice in God's goodness. But can he also rejoice as he walks through the deep weeds of life?

No matter where you are today, rejoice. If all is well, be grateful. If under the cloud of adversity, let the experience enlarge your trust in God. Every trial has its eventual resolution. Let God lead the way to that end.

"Adversity is not simply a tool. It's God's most effective tool for the advancement of our spiritual lives. The circumstances and events we see as setbacks are oftentimes the very things that launch us into periods of intense spiritual growth. Once we begin to understand this, and accept it as a spiritual fact of life, adversity becomes easier to bear." —CHARLES STANLEY

PEACE WITH GOD

Being justified by faith, we have peace with God through our Lord Jesus Christ (ROMANS 5:1).

In a world that doesn't know peace—real peace—it's all the more important for Christian men to model the peace available to all through Christ. How is it we have this supernatural peace? It's because we're justified by faith. That means God does not count our sins against us. Our records are clean. Expunged. No guilt. No reason to live under the weight of an uneasy conscience.

Every day we freely have this peace. It's not a temporary truce with an adversary with the potential for future skirmishes to resume. No, this peace is ours for today, tomorrow, and forever. This peace is so good, it's something we must share with others who know no peace.

"If you are not at peace with God—then you are at peace with Satan." —JAMES SMITH

A Secure Future

For I know the thoughts that I think toward you, saith the LORD, thoughts of peace, and not of evil, to give you an expected end (JEREMIAH 29:11).

Every man thinks about his future. *Will I be happy? Will I live to a ripe old age? Will my finances last?* All these and more pass through every man's mind. And when that happens, we should think of it as a prompt to reaffirm our trust that God has plans for us that are of peace, to give us an expected end. The road to that end will surely include bumps along the way, but a safe arrival is guaranteed. Even on this very day, God has His plan for you in mind and sees to it that the plan is fully operational, bringing you to the very place God destined you to be.

Confidence in God's ability to bring us to an expected end eliminates worry and needless concern. You have a future with a desired end, designed by God.

"Trust the past to God's mercy, the present to God's love and the future to God's providence."—AUGUSTINE

UNDER THE CIRCUMSTANCES?

For I am persuaded, that neither death, nor life, nor angels, nor principalities, nor powers, nor things present, nor things to come, nor height, nor depth, nor any other creature, shall be able to separate us from the love of God, which is in Christ Jesus our Lord (ROMANS 8:38-39).

When asked how they're doing, some men reply, "Okay, I guess…under the circumstances." But why would we allow ourselves to be *under* a pile of circumstances that render our attitudes as only okay? From God's point of view, we're not to be "under" anything except His care for us.

When you feel circumstances beginning to pile up, take a step back and consider what God would have you do to either change those circumstances or adjust your attitude.

Get on top—stay on top!

"No one can get above circumstances unless he knows that he has the ear of God. The power of intercession is a great thing to the servant of God." —G.V. WIGRAM

THE POWER OF PRAISE

By him therefore let us offer the sacrifice of praise to God continually, that is, the fruit of our lips giving thanks to his name (HEBREWS 13:15).

I will praise thee, O LORD, with my whole heart; I will show forth all thy marvelous works (PSALM 9:1).

Praising God brings power to the Christian man. And while it's great to develop an attitude of praise, don't let it stop there. Vocalize your praise. If you're alone, perhaps in your car or in your office, speak aloud your praise of God. Let the fruit of your lips give thanks to the God who created you and sustains you. Let your whole heart praise God for His marvelous works. Praise Him not just for what He does in your life, but praise Him simply for who He is.

Throughout the day, busy or not, try to take short praise breaks and find yourself renewed.

"Praise lies upon a higher plain than thanksgiving. When I give thanks, my thoughts still circle around myself to some extent. But in praise my soul ascends to self-forgetting adoration, seeing and praising only the majesty and power of God, His grace and redemption." —OLE HALLESBY

Boundaries

I have set the LORD always before me: because he is at my right hand, I shall not be moved (PSALM 16:8).

Many Christian men find themselves in trouble because they have violated boundaries that were designed to keep them safe.

Boundaries are like guardrails on a mountainous highway. How foolish to skirt the guardrails and hope nothing calamitous happens.

What boundaries are in place for you? What boundaries guard your eyes against pornography? What boundaries guard your mouth? Your feet? If your boundaries are weak, it's time for either a reset or to establish them for the first time. If you already have firm boundaries, hold fast to them. A boundaryless man is on the trail of danger.

"You will often have observed, while walking along some footpath that winds its way amid the fields, a flock of sheep quietly feeding within an enclosure made by portable fences. Instead of roaming the whole field over, they are located on one small spot, until the shepherd shifting the simple fence, makes the furthest boundary the commencement of another plot of feeding ground—and so on, until every portion of the field has, in its turn, yielded food and sweetness to the flock."
—ARCHIBALD BROWN

ADDICTED TO JOY

The joy of the LORD is your strength (NEHEMIAH 8:10).

Addictions have been around for centuries, and always with the same goal—to try to fill the joy-starved centers of our beings. But God has a better solution: find our joy in Him. Allow His joy to be our strength. Of necessity, this means turning from our addictions, turning from all that would enslave us, and accepting the joy that comes from above. This joy fills us, never leaving us unsatisfied. It's a supernatural joy—one that is eternal. In this joy we find treasures far beyond the carnal and momentary pleasures our addictions offer us.

Be done with addictions. Seek only true spiritual joy. Let it be the source of your strength.

"Man cannot live without joy; therefore when he is deprived of true spiritual joys it is necessary that he become addicted to carnal pleasures." —THOMAS AQUINAS

A MAN WHO SERVES

If it seem evil unto you to serve the LORD, choose you this day whom ye will serve (JOSHUA 24:15).

Every man faces the crucial choice of who he will serve. Will it be self, by amassing a fortune, becoming well-known, or indulging in the pleasures of this life? God's alternative is a life dedicated to serving Him and Him alone. The irony is that those who choose the former are faced with often unexpected detours from true happiness.

Serving God, on the other hand, also provides many unexpected detours in life. But God's detours take us by the fountains of joy, the streams of right living, the glories of a reward for a life well-lived.

Every day a man must consciously or unconsciously be living out his choice. Today may offer opportunities to remind yourself of the choice you've made.

"Thanks be to God, there is hope today; this very hour you can choose Him and serve Him." —D. L. MOODY

FULL SURRENDER

My son, give me thine heart, and let thine eyes observe my ways (PROVERBS 23:26).

A man may be a Christian, may even be looked up to as a man of great faith, and yet he alone knows he's kept a part of his heart for himself. Oh, he may not think of it like that, but when pressed by the God who is seeking his whole heart, he will confess to that hidden closet where his secret abides.

God's plea for our hearts isn't just because God is collecting hearts. No, it's because God knows that true happiness and fulfillment are found when a man's entire life—closets and all—are His and His alone.

"Unless you have made a complete surrender and are doing his will it will avail you nothing if you've reformed a thousand times and have your name on fifty church records."
—BILLY SUNDAY

QUICK TO HEAR

My beloved brethren, let every man be swift to hear, slow to speak, slow to wrath (JAMES 1:19).

Aman in a race will want to go as fast as he can. A sick man wants to be well *now*. A man seeking wealth will take shortcuts if it will fatten his bank account. But a man of God knows that when it comes to the ears, tongue, and temper, slow is better than fast.

A good man will slow down and listen, not just hear. He will measure his words before speaking. His wrath, if stirred, is subject to a cooling-off period.

God's call to men is to slow down in all aspects of life, but especially in those areas where we rush to judgment, speak unwisely, or make later regrettable decisions.

"God has given us two ears, but one tongue, to show that we should be swift to hear, but slow to speak. God has set a double fence before the tongue, the teeth and the lips, to teach us to be wary that we offend not with our tongue." —THOMAS WATSON

HEAVEN

Blessed be the God and Father of our Lord Jesus Christ, which according to his abundant mercy hath begotten us again unto a lively hope by the resurrection of Jesus Christ from the dead, to an inheritance incorruptible, and undefiled, and that fadeth not away, reserved in heaven for you, who are kept by the power of God through faith unto salvation ready to be revealed in the last time (1 PETER 1:3-5).

While here on earth, we can only ponder what heaven will be like. We know our heavenly inheritance will be incorruptible, undefiled, and eternal. Until then, we're confident in God's ability to keep us by His power, through our faith. Whatever our thoughts of heaven, they're way too modest. Consider our God and His ability to create. Consider His great love for each of us. Consider an eternity with God and all those who have gone before us.

Ponder heaven today. Take a moment here and there to consider your future abode.

Is it any wonder our hope for heaven is a *lively* hope?

"I wonder many times that ever a child of God should have a sad heart, considering what the Lord is preparing for him."
—SAMUEL RUTHERFORD

ABIDING

Abide in me, and I in you. As the branch cannot bear fruit of itself, except it abide in the vine; no more can ye, except ye abide in me. I am the vine, ye are the branches: He that abideth in me, and I in him, the same bringeth forth much fruit: for without me ye can do nothing (JOHN 15:4-5).

Foolish is the man who thinks he can bear fruit by simply exerting himself. Such fruit, should it exist, isn't fit for consumption. And yet we're commanded to be fruit-bearing Christians, so how is this to be? Clearly, there's only one way—and that's to abide in Christ, just as a branch abides in the vine. It is through Him that we not only bear fruit, but bear *much* fruit. Apart from Christ, we can do nothing.

Today, relax in your connection to the vine. Let there be much fruit that comes from simply abiding.

"We shall never abide in Christ as we ought, unless we hear more of Christ, read more of Christ, and think more of Christ. But we must not stop at thinking, hearing, or reading of Christ—we must actually commune with Christ." —J.R. MILLER

THE STRAIT GATE

Enter ye in at the strait gate: for wide is the gate, and broad is the way, that leadeth to destruction, and many there be which go in thereat (MATTHEW 7:13).

It's astonishing that so many men take the broad way leading to destruction. To do so, they must pass by the narrow gate and either ignore it or miss seeing it entirely.

They have chosen the broad way that seems right. Yet we have chosen the narrow way that leads to life.

Through our journey, we're presented with additional versions of the broad way: the lucrative job offer filled with compromise, the sexually immoral invitation, the purchase of material goods we can't afford.

The Christian life is a continual passing succession of gate after gate until we find the right one—the narrow gate of God's will.

"He that will be knighted must kneel for it, and he that will enter in at the strait gate must crowd for it—a gate made so on purpose, narrow and hard in the entrance, yet, after we have entered, wide and glorious, that after our pain our joy may be the sweeter." —THOMAS ADAMS

THE LIFE OF PRAYER

[Jesus] cometh unto the disciples, and findeth them asleep, and saith unto Peter, What, could ye not watch with me one hour? (MATTHEW 26:40).

The Christian man who rises up for the Lord knows that prayer—diligent prayer—is crucial to fulfilling his calling. The seeds of his ministry—whether large or small—are sown in the prayer closet. Short prayers are welcome. But so are lengthy prayers. Every great man of God has been a man of prayer first—and then came his usefulness to God.

How God will use you is up to Him. You may not yet see how He's leading you, but if you wait on Him in prayer, the road ahead will become clearer and clearer.

When in prayer, whether short or long, simply stay on your knees until you're satisfied that God has uttered His "Amen" before you offer your own.

"Hurry is the death of prayer." —SAMUEL CHADWICK

STRENGTH OUT OF WEAKNESS

And he said unto me, My grace is sufficient for thee: for my strength is made perfect in weakness. Most gladly therefore will I rather glory in my infirmities, that the power of Christ may rest upon me (2 CORINTHIANS 12:9).

Wise is the Christian man who's willing to own his weaknesses. We all have them—and not just a few. Thank God we also have our strengths too. And many of the latter are actually found when we look to our weaknesses as a means of trusting in the power of Christ within us.

We can glory in our infirmities only when we see them as opportunities to allow Christ's power to make our strength perfect through our weaknesses. Thank God that today, right now, this very moment, the power of Christ rests on us. We're thus enabled to face anything, especially our weaknesses.

"Before He furnishes the abundant supply, we must first be made conscious of our emptiness. Before he gives strength, we must be made to feel our weakness. Slow, painfully slow, are we to learn this lesson; and slower still to own our nothingness and take the place of helplessness before the Mighty One."
—A.W. PINK

The Man of Vision

Where there is no vision, the people perish (Proverbs 29:18).

A visionless Christian man is like a boat without a rudder, drifting aimlessly along life's long river. How much more rewarding is the Christian life with a God-given purpose.

What vision has God given you for your life? It need not be spelled out in its entirety—in fact, it rarely is. Yet like a headlight on the highway shining just so far, as we move along following the headlight, we can make it safely home.

A vision may begin very small, like a planted seed. Nourished by prayer and with proper follow-through (only as far as the headlight shows the way), the vision for usefulness by God can be attained.

Your vision may be to be a godly husband raising a wholesome family or to own a business that prospers enough to support Christian workers. Truth to tell, there are as many diverse visions for Christian men as there are Christian men.

"We need a baptism of clear seeing. We desperately need seers who can see through the mist—Christian leaders with prophetic vision. Unless they come soon it will be too late for this generation." —A.W. Tozer

THOROUGHLY HIS

Ye are not your own…For ye are bought with a price (1 CO-RINTHIANS 6:19-20).

The man who soon learns he belongs to God, not to himself, is on the road to happiness. It's in our own ownership that we find trouble. We find our natural desires are at war with the man God has called us to be. When we no longer claim ownership of ourselves, we become free to be better men—God's men in this broken world.

In every facet of our lives, we must surrender our right to self to the one who has purchased us. We must allow Him to do His will with us—and lead us to greater depths of true happiness.

We are His. Wholly His.

Relish in His ownership of you.

"I am His by purchase and I am His by conquest; I am His by donation and I am His by election; I am His by covenant and I am His by marriage; I am wholly His; I am peculiarly His; I am universally His; I am eternally His."—THOMAS BROOKS

Cleansed from All Sin

If we walk in the light, as he is in the light, we have fellow-
ship with one another, and the blood of Jesus Christ his Son
cleanseth us from all sin (1 John 1:7).

All sin? Many men would love to believe that all their
sins have been cleansed by the blood of Christ, yet
guilt for past misdeeds lingers on, often simply lurking
in the background of their consciousness.

They may even give mental assent to God's forgiveness of all their sins. And yet, even a molecule of remaining guilt can keep a man from enjoying the truth of full
forgiveness for all sins.

Whether you have this nagging sensation of remaining sins to be forgiven or not, it's always a good thing to
contemplate the vastness of God's love for us in pouring out the blood of Christ so all our sins could be forever removed.

Contemplate today this vastness with profound
thanks for such an atonement.

"It's Satan's delight to tell me that once he's got me, he will keep
me. But at that moment I can go back to God. And I know
that if I confess my sins, God is faithful and just to forgive me."
—Alan Redpath

SMALL THINGS

Even the very hairs of your head are all numbered. Fear not therefore: ye are of more value than many sparrows (LUKE 12:7).

Every life has its ups and downs, its large things and small things. But does God see anything in our lives as "small"? If He troubles Himself to number the hairs on our head, if He cares when the sparrow falls, will He not watch over our so-called small things with the same attention as if they were large?

Nothing about God's care for us is minor—it's all major. His attention to the details of our lives goes mostly unnoticed by us, but in eternity, we may find that some very small things were the pivotal points at which God worked a large thing without our knowing it.

Trust God for all things, large and small.

"There's no such thing as 'chance,' 'luck,' or 'accident' in the Christian's journey through this world! If we profess to be believers in Jesus Christ—then all is arranged and appointed by God...Let us seek to have an abiding sense of God's hand in all that befalls us. Let us strive to realize that our Father's hand is measuring out our daily portion."—J.C. RYLE

DO THE WORD

Be ye doers of the word, and not hearers only, deceiving your own selves (JAMES 1:22).

To hear something takes very little effort. We can sit passively and listen to a message, program, or even the Bible on Audible. But *doing* what we've heard—well, that's a different story.

We can hear and *not* do—which the Bible labels as self-deception. And while it's true we're never saved by our works but only by faith, it's a faith that bears fruit.

It's up to each of us to hear from God and then do what we've been told. For some, the doing is about helping others. For others, it's about supporting those who are helping others. No man is left with nothing to do while he's here on earth. All Christian men are fruit-bearing trees.

"The man who hears Christian teaching, and practices what he hears…doesn't content himself with listening to exhortations to repent, believe in Christ, and live a holy life. He actually repents. He actually believes. He actually ceases to do evil, learns to do well, abhors that which is sinful, and cleaves to that which is good. He is a doer as well as a hearer." —J.C. RYLE

A Man's Anger

A wrathful man stirreth up strife: but he that is slow to anger appeaseth strife (PROVERBS 15:18).

Be ye angry, and sin not: let not the sun go down upon your wrath (EPHESIANS 4:26).

Anger in a man is a valid emotion. God experiences anger (though He's slow to anger). Jesus certainly demonstrated anger. Anger has its uses. But when we allow anger to fester, it turns into sin. Anger issues need to be resolved quickly—or as Paul tells us—before the sun goes down.

A Christian man has ways of handling anger that many men do not. For instance, if we are sinned against and hold a grudge or find a grudge against us, we go to that brother or to the church for resolution (Matthew 18). Another option is an appropriate compromise. Repentance and forgiveness are, of course, the ultimate resolutions to anger.

In any case, a Christian man is to control his anger, not be controlled by it—or by any emotion. Today, monitor your emotions—particularly if anger has been a problem in your life.

"Anger is short-lived in a good man."—THOMAS FULLER

A Thankful Spirit

In every thing give thanks: for this is the will of God in Christ Jesus concerning you (1 THESSALONIANS 5:18).

Thankfulness is necessary for true happiness. Many of us express our gratitude to God when things are going well. But having a thankful spirit means we've learned to be thankful at all times and in all circumstances. When the circumstances are adverse, we know we can be thankful because God will bring us through in His time. It's during these times of circumstantial famine that we most need the continual feast of a thankful and contented spirit.

It can take time to learn true thankfulness. But God is patient and continues to send circumstances our way in which we can practice thankfulness—no matter how we feel.

Feast on contentment. Feast on thankfulness to God.

"A thankful and a contented spirit is a continual feast. We ought to be contented, and we shall be contented, if we are in the habit of seeing God in everything, and living upon Him day by day. Oh, for a spirit of true thankfulness!"
—ASHTON OXENDEN

FRIENDS

Iron sharpeneth iron; so a man sharpeneth the countenance of his friend (PROVERBS 27:17).

The soul of Jonathan was knit with the soul of David, and Jonathan loved him as his own soul (1 SAMUEL 18:1).

Solid male friendships seem to be rare these days. The closeness of David and Jonathan seems unattainable. And yet most men would welcome more and deeper friendships with other men. They desire the kind of iron-sharpening-iron friendships that make each man stronger.

Often, time is the enemy of friendship. We have our jobs and our family responsibilities…so *when* is the time for developing friendships?

It's like anything else we deem important. If it's something we truly want, we'll make time for it, even if it means cutting back on something else. It also takes initiative. Someone has to suggest a next move toward friendship. A fishing trip? Bowling? Guys' movie-night out? Prayer and Bible study? The best options are those that allow time to simply talk to one another, getting to know the other guy as he probably wants to be known.

What part can you play in fostering a deepening relationship with some man you suspect would make a good friend?

"A good friend is my nearest relation." —THOMAS FULLER

Only God...

Jesus beheld them, and said unto them, With men this is impossible; but with God all things are possible (Matthew 19:26).

Every Christian man experiences hard times and intense trials when nothing but a miracle will do. What seems impossible for us can only be made possible by a God who is all-powerful and at the ready to oversee our victories.

Never be alarmed at "only God" circumstances. They build our faith and, as a by-product, they produce compassion in us for others who suffer through the rough patches of life.

If we know the power of God in our lives, we practice turning "only God" situations over to Him.

"God loves with a great love the man whose heart is bursting with a passion for the impossible." —William Booth

THE ULTIMATE MAN CAVE

He that dwelleth in the secret place of the most High shall abide under the shadow of the Almighty (PSALM 91:1).

Psalm 91 is the perfect spiritual man cave and a great go-to portion of Scripture for men who have been shaken by life's events and who yearn for unshakeable stability during tough times. It's printed on the next two pages.

Christian men become unshakeable by being protected by an unshakeable God. We know nothing can harm us that doesn't pass through God's notice first. We are confident in knowing God has our backs. He's our fortress, our refuge, our man cave. He covers us with His feathers, His truth is our shield and buckler. We're not afraid of terror by night nor daytime's poisoned arrows aimed at us. No pestilence can touch us, nor can destruction alarm us.

This unshakeable confidence is our legacy, and we will live and die by it.

"Faith is a living and unshakable confidence, a belief in the grace of God so assured that a man would die a thousand deaths for its sake."—MARTIN LUTHER

Psalm 91

He that dwelleth in the secret place of the most
   High shall abide under the shadow of the
   Almighty.

I will say of the LORD, He is my refuge and my
   fortress: my God; in him will I trust.

Surely he shall deliver thee from the snare of the
   fowler, and from the noisome pestilence.

He shall cover thee with his feathers, and under
   his wings shalt thou trust: his truth shall be
   thy shield and buckler.

Thou shalt not be afraid for the terror by night;
   nor for the arrow that flieth by day;

Nor for the pestilence that walketh in darkness; nor for the destruction that wasteth at
   noonday.

A thousand shall fall at thy side, and ten thousand at thy right hand; but it shall not come
   nigh thee.

Only with thine eyes shalt thou behold and see
   the reward of the wicked.

Because thou hast made the LORD, which is my
   refuge, even the most High, thy habitation;

There shall no evil befall thee, neither shall any plague come nigh thy dwelling.

For he shall give his angels charge over thee, to keep thee in all thy ways.

They shall bear thee up in their hands, lest thou dash thy foot against a stone.

Thou shalt tread upon the lion and adder: the young lion and the dragon shalt thou trample under feet.

Because he hath set his love upon me, therefore will I deliver him: I will set him on high, because he hath known my name.

He shall call upon me, and I will answer him: I will be with him in trouble; I will deliver him, and honor him.

With long life will I satisfy him, and show him my salvation.

DELIGHTING IN GOD

Delight thyself also in the LORD: and he shall give thee the desires of thine heart (PSALM 37:4).

O taste and see that the LORD is good: blessed is the man that trusteth in him (PSALM 34:8).

God has a wonderful way of giving us the desires of our hearts. He encourages us to delight ourselves in Him and in those things that delight Him. He invites us to taste of Him and be satisfied.

Delighting in God is no sour chore.

Delighting in God is its own reward and is the avenue to the desires of our own hearts.

To delight in God is to simply and earnestly *enjoy* Him.

"To wait on God is to live a life of desire toward Him, delight in Him, dependence on Him, and devotedness to Him."
—MATTHEW HENRY

LIVING TO THE GLORY OF GOD

Whether therefore ye eat, or drink, or whatsoever ye do, do all to the glory of God (1 CORINTHIANS 10:31).

God, in His infinite creativity, has chosen a specific way for each of us to glorify Him through our lives. Perhaps it's by being a creator—a writer, painter, sculptor, inventor. Or maybe our way to glorify God is by living to help others. Or by being a faithful husband and father.

Take a moment and consider how your calling in life can best glorify God.

It's when others see Christ glorified in you that they will be drawn to Him. Sometimes the best witness we can be simply involves living righteously.

"We glorify God by living lives that honor Him." —BILLY GRAHAM

I Can Do This!

I can do all things through Christ which strengtheneth me (PHILIPPIANS 4:13).

We all encounter times when we must do what we don't want to do or feel we can't do. We don't feel up for the challenge. And yet what is our faith worth if it doesn't enable us to triumph during the worst of times?

A man with small faith may skate through an easy life. A man of true faith puts aside his fears and displays bravery in the face of adversity. His knees may be shaking, but he's up for this challenge because he knows his God will strengthen him through all things.

If this is not your day for a challenge, don't rest so easy. Your day, like mine, like that of all men, will soon be upon you. And you will prevail as you do "all things."

"If we desire our faith to be strengthened, we should not shrink from opportunities where our faith may be tried, and therefore, through trial, be strengthened." —GEORGE MÜLLER

PREPARING OUR WAYS

[Jotham] did that which was right in the sight of the LORD, according to all that his father Uzziah did…So Jotham became mighty, because he prepared his ways before the LORD his God (2 CHRONICLES 27:2,6).

Jotham was a young man of twenty-five when he took the throne. Following in his father Uzziah's footsteps, he did that which was right in the sight of the Lord. Further, he became mighty for one reason: *He prepared his ways before the Lord.*

Who among us would be mighty in God's eyes? It's no small reward to be pleasing to God. The reward is eternal and in many cases, such as Jotham's, also temporal. He became a rich man and the winner of many wars. Though he only served sixteen years and then died, he is, to this day, reckoned as a mighty man.

Let each of us take care to prepare our ways—and our days—before the Lord.

"[Jotham] walked circumspectly and with much caution, contrived how to shun that which was evil and compass that which was good. He…established or fixed his ways before the Lord, that is, he walked steadily and constantly in the way of his duty, was uniform and resolute in it." —MATTHEW HENRY

HE IS WORTHY!

The four and twenty elders fall down before him that sat on the throne, and worship him that liveth for ever and ever, and cast their crowns before the throne, saying, Thou art worthy, O Lord, to receive glory and honor and power: for thou hast created all things, and for thy pleasure they are and were created (REVELATION 4:10-11).

John, in his exile to Patmos, wrote the book of Revelation and there offers us the words of praise the four and twenty elders uttered. It's not a bad place for us to start our own praise session. We simply declare His worthiness and verbally ascribe honor and power to Him for His creation. Then we keep going by offering praise for specific blessings, but most of all we praise Him for who He is…for His very worthiness.

A day without praise is a day to regret.

"If you had a thousand crowns you should put them all on the head of Christ! And if you had a thousand tongues they should all sing his praise, for he is worthy!" —WILLIAM TIPTAFT

THE CREATIVE MAN

Moses said unto the children of Israel, See, the LORD hath…
filled [Bezaleel] with the spirit of God, in wisdom, in under-
standing, and in knowledge, and in all manner of workman-
ship; and to devise curious works, to work in gold, and in
silver, and in brass, and in the cutting of stones…and in carv-
ing of wood, to make any manner of cunning work (EXO-
DUS 35:30-33).

It pleasures God to invest talent in His sons. Some talents are in the arts (painting, music, poetry), some are in the manual arts (woodworking, metalworking, masonry), and some are design-related or mechanical in nature. Often, these talents are overlooked as being gifts from God, but happy is the man who perceives his gift and uses it in ways that please God.

If your gift isn't apparent to you, ask God. It may have yet to unfold in your life, or it may be dormant for lack of use. It need not be flashy—God provides talents large and small. It's not the size, it's the giving out of one's gift that counts.

"Time is lost when we have not lived a full human life, time
unenriched by experience, creative endeavor, enjoyment, and
suffering." —DIETRICH BONHOEFFER

GENEROSITY

He that hath pity upon the poor lendeth unto the LORD; and that which he hath given will he pay him again (PROVERBS 19:17).

A stingy or miserly Christian man is an oxymoron. God has so designed His godly men to be cheerful givers—even lavish givers. This is often counter to what the world expects us to be. We're told by our culture to become rich, to accumulate more money...but to what end? A rich man dies and takes nothing with him to the grave. A godly man dies and finds an investment in heaven that has earned significant interest.

What needs do you see that you can help meet? Who in your church needs an anonymous gift? Make it your practice to give more than to get more.

God will show you where to give.

"We sometimes forget that nothing is given to us for ourselves alone. When abundance of blessing or prosperity in any form comes to us, we may not shut ourselves in with it, and use it only for ourselves. We are to think of those outside who have no such blessing or favor as we are enjoying, and are to send portions to them." —J.R. MILLER

SAFE MEN

This is the will of God, even your sanctification, that ye should abstain from fornication: That every one of you should know how to possess his vessel in sanctification and honor (1 THESSALONIANS 4:3-4).

A godly man is a *safe* man. Safe around women, children, and even other men. We guard the personhood of anyone who is threatened, especially those who are threatened sexually through abuse or rape. We are protectors of the vulnerable, never perpetrators. Our common fellowship with other believing men is a fellowship with other safe men.

When innocence is violated, we do not let it pass unnoticed. Sin is not hidden by the safe man. Not only are *we* safe, but we see to it that we're raising safe sons and teaching young men to be safe.

Take pride in being a safe man. For to protect others is to emulate the divine protection God affords us. He is a safe God, and we are His safe men.

"The most critical need of the church at this moment is men, bold men, free men. The church must seek, in prayer and much humility, the coming again of men made of the stuff of which prophets and martyrs are made." —A.W. TOZER

LIGHTS IN THE WORLD

That ye may be blameless and harmless, the sons of God, without rebuke, in the midst of a crooked and perverse nation, among whom ye shine as lights in the world (PHILIPPIANS 2:15).

A Christian man doesn't have to search for evil. Rather, evil searches out the godly man. The influences are all too close to us in the form of TV, movies, song lyrics, books...But are we just men focused on uncovering evil?

No, we must be men who both avoid evil and pursue good. We're to be blameless and harmless sons of God in the midst of a perverse generation. We're to overcome evil with good. So let's train our eyes to look for righteousness and goodness in our world.

Evil may be easier to spot, but it's more rewarding to see and affirm the good.

Watch for a way today to affirm goodness around you.

"The great and important duty which is incumbent on Christians, is to guard against all appearance of evil; to watch against the first risings in the heart to evil; and to have a guard upon our actions, that they may not be sinful, or so much as seem to be so." —GEORGE WHITEFIELD

Vying for the Crown

Henceforth there is laid up for me a crown of righteousness, which the Lord, the righteous judge, shall give me at that day: and not to me only, but unto all them also that love his appearing (2 Timothy 4:8).

The secret to getting through a rough patch in life is to look longingly ahead to eternity. We are on this earth but a scant few years compared to what awaits us after we move on to our heavenly home. Paul suffered much for the gospel, including stoning, whippings, scarcities, rejection, and ultimately a martyr's death. But he counted it all worthwhile for the reward that awaited him. Paul goes on to say that the same reward awaits all who love Christ's appearing.

So yes, we look ahead to that day of His appearing, and the crown that shall be ours.

"There are no crown-wearers in heaven who were not cross-bearers here below." —Charles Spurgeon

Generation to Generation

One generation shall praise thy works to another, and shall declare thy mighty acts (PSALM 145:4).

Every Christian man has a duty to the generations below him. Even if we're not a father of sons, we can be father-like to younger men coming up in the faith. A thirty-something-year-old man can have a strong influence on a ten-year-old. A man in his fifties can help a twenty-year-old become all he's meant to be. A man in his seventies and beyond can influence several generations below him.

Consider how God has orchestrated events in your life for your good. Tell your story to other men, including younger men. Be willing to teach the younger men around you—at church, in the home, in the workplace. Reach out with a hand to help the younger man up the mountain. You may think you're influencing just one man, but through his future influence, you may be reaching more than you think. Take up the task of helping other males into manhood.

"Oh! young men, learn to be thoughtful. Learn to consider what you are doing—and where you are going. Make time for calm reflection. Commune with your own heart—and be still." —J.C. RYLE

A MAN'S CONSCIENCE

Let us draw near with a true heart in full assurance of faith, having our hearts sprinkled from an evil conscience, and our bodies washed with pure water (HEBREWS 10:22).

One crucial prerequisite for confidence in the presence of God is a clear conscience. At no time should we be aware of unrepented sin. Keep short accounts with God. When you've violated your conscience, own up to it. Confess it to God and, by faith, accept His forgiveness—and then move on. Once sin is forsaken and confessed, the deed is done. You never have to ask for forgiveness for the same sin twice. (The second asking only reveals a lack of faith that God forgave you at the first asking.)

Then *do* draw near. Do pray with confidence. As sure as God heard your confession, He now hears your requests. There is a righteous boldness before God that belongs to every Christian man, and God loves spiritual boldness in His sons.

"Preserve your conscience always soft and sensitive. If but one sin force its way into that tender part of the soul and dwell there, the road is paved for a thousand iniquities." —ISAAC WATTS

The Love of Money

The love of money is the root of all evil: which while some coveted after, they have erred from the faith, and pierced themselves through with many sorrows (1 Timothy 6:10).

Coveting money is a shortcut to spiritual suicide. If we desire riches, we'll surely find ways to have them. But we'll eventually discover that on the other side of our pot of gold is a bucket of sorrows money can't buy our way out of.

A wise man will avoid the inevitable piercing of many sorrows by seeking God first and foremost, trusting that all needed material goods, including finances, will be supplied through the work God gives us to do or from the hands of those who care for us.

The word "love" is best used in reference to God and to other people, never to money.

"Do not think me mad. It is not to make money that I believe a Christian should live. The noblest thing a man can do is, just humbly to receive, and then go amongst others and give."
—David Livingstone

GOSSIP

A talebearer revealeth secrets: but he that is of a faithful spirit concealeth the matter (PROVERBS 11:13).

A froward man soweth strife: and a whisperer separateth chief friends (PROVERBS 16:28).

Women often suffer from the accusation of being gossipers. The truth is, men, too, can be guilty of gossip. Many men say things that should remain unsaid. Rumors, unsubstantiated accusations, and innuendoes are all ways some men fall prey to the sin of gossiping. Friendships suffer, innocents are besmirched, reputations suffer…and all from needless talk.

Most men value the ear of a trusted friend who will never betray a word spoken in confidence. Every man must ask himself if he's that kind of friend. And when gossip or rumor comes to your ears, let it stop there. It need go no farther.

"A gossip is one who tells stories which ought not to be told, whether true or false, whether fairly or unfairly represented. The worst kind of gossips are those who tell their stories to those who are most likely to be provoked by them, and at the same time do not wish to be mentioned as authors of the story, or witnesses in it." —GEORGE LAWSON

MUTUAL CONFESSION

Confess your faults one to another, and pray one for another, that ye may be healed (JAMES 5:16).

Who in your life can you freely confess your faults to? Who will pray for you when you need God's intervention? Are you the man other men can rely on for brotherly confession and healing prayer?

Many men mistakenly believe it's a weakness to confess their faults to another man, but the opposite is true. A weak man harbors his secrets to himself, unwilling to open up to another man. A strong man finds it easier to admit his failings and seek prayer. He knows that God works through his brothers in Christ.

It doesn't take much to be a faithful man to other faithful men. Be that man. Someone needs your prayers. And you need someone to know your faults prayerfully.

"Sometimes it may be of good use to Christians to disclose their…weaknesses and infirmities to one another, where there are great intimacies and friendships, and where they may help each other by their prayers to obtain pardon of their sins and power against them. Those who make confession of their faults one to another should thereupon pray with and for one another." —MATTHEW HENRY

JUDGING OTHERS

Therefore thou art inexcusable, O man, whosoever thou art that judgest: for wherein thou judgest another, thou condemnest thyself; for thou that judgest doest the same things. But we are sure that the judgment of God is according to truth against them which commit such things. And thinkest thou this, O man, that judgest them which do such things, and doest the same, that thou shalt escape the judgment of God? (ROMANS 2:1-3).

It's freeing to realize that the responsibility for judging others isn't up to us. We will therefore neither judge others nor expect others to judge us. Our judge and theirs is God alone. Paul points out to the believers in Rome that they're especially guilty of misjudging others because they're doing the very same things they're judging others for!

May God give us a clear eye to not only forgive others who may offend but also not judge them. The burden of judging is a heavy one. Too heavy for any of us.

"In judging of others, a man laboreth in vain, often erreth and easily sinneth; but in judging and examining himself, he always laboreth fruitfully." —THOMAS À KEMPIS

AMBITION

Whosoever shall exalt himself shall be abased; and he that shall humble himself shall be exalted (MATTHEW 23:12).

Ambition, rightly understood, is a good thing. There are aspects of a man's life in which he should be ambitious. The use of spiritual gifts, for instance. He may be ambitious in sports, desiring to best his record. He may be ambitious at his job as he does his work as unto the Lord. He may be ambitious in ministry, helping others in their Christian walk. Certainly in his family life, a godly man is ambitious to be the best dad and husband he can be.

There is, of course, the wrong use of ambition. The source of wrong ambition is *self*. A man who aspires to greater things to satisfy his ego is approaching ambition in the wrong spirit.

Godly ambition will be motivated by thinking of others or by seeing God glorified through achievement. This involves humbling oneself and allowing God to promote us in our field of ambition as we work hard and wait hard for God to do the promoting.

"Sin comes when we take a perfectly natural desire or longing or ambition and try desperately to fulfill it without God."
—AUGUSTINE

SPEAK TRUTH

Ye shall know the truth, and the truth shall make you free (JOHN 8:32).

Wherefore putting away lying, speak every man truth with his neighbor: for we are members one of another (EPHESIANS 4:25).

We, of all men, must be men of the truth. We are done with falsehoods and compromises with the truth. Yes, being a man of truth will sometimes be hard. Many of our acquaintances don't want to hear the truth if it contradicts what they already believe. In order for the truth we speak to have gravitas, we ourselves must be men with gravitas. Our lives must be examples of the truths we speak and live.

Today you may find a chance to speak a truth that's not popular. If speaking up is appropriate, do so with grace and integrity. The worst response to hearing a lie is to passively give the impression you agree with the untruth being spoken or acted upon.

Remember that the truth will set us free. It's the lies we encounter that lay us low.

"He that takes truth for his guide, and duty for his end, may safely trust to God's providence to lead him aright." —BLAISE PASCAL

Corrupt Speech

Let no corrupt communication proceed out of your mouth, but that which is good to the use of edifying, that it may minister grace unto the hearers (EPHESIANS 4:29).

But now ye also put off all these; anger, wrath, malice, blasphemy, filthy communication out of your mouth (COLOSSIANS 3:8).

When we were saved, our mouths were saved along with the rest of us. Every part of our being is to be submitted to God. When it comes to our tongues, submission to God means we weigh our words before we speak. We do not speak corruption, lies, anger, blasphemy, or filthiness. Instead, we speak good words that edify and bring grace to those with whom we speak.

If, due to long-held habit, our words have not been edifying, we can establish a new habit—by *learning* to speak affirming words (and corrective words too) when appropriate. One way to ingrain the habit of speaking that which is good is to consciously look for opportunities to compliment or affirm someone else. Seek such an opportunity today.

"In our manner of speech, our plans of living, our dealings with others, our conduct and walk in the church and out of it; all should be done as becomes the gospel." —ALBERT BARNES

RACISM

For there is no difference between the Jew and the Greek: for the same Lord over all is rich unto all that call upon him (ROMANS 10:12).

God's method of dividing mankind has nothing to do with race. God saves all who trust in Christ, with no racial distinction. Christians, by virtue of their new nature, should know this instinctively.

A Christian cannot be a racist. It violates the very idea of a God who is "Lord over all, and is rich to all what call upon him." Neither can a Christian affirm those who espouse or support racism. With God, every racial barrier is down. Jews, Gentiles of all colors, are accepted based on their faith in Christ. To erect any other kind of barrier where God has torn down a barrier is to foolishly try to trump God Himself.

Christian men rejoice in the God who sees the heart, not the color of a man's skin. Such men also rejoice in their brothers of another color.

"Be not proud of race, face, place, or grace." —CHARLES SPURGEON

SECRET SIN

Thou hast set our iniquities before thee, our secret sins in the light of thy countenance (PSALM 90:8).

What a man does publicly is important, but what a man does in secret reveals his true character. When we're tempted to commit a sin no one will ever know about, what's our response? For some, the decision is easy. We can sin, no one will know, and God will forgive.

That sort of thinking is selfish, self-wounding, and presumptuous. When we sin in the dark, we hurt our souls by partaking of actions or attitudes that war against our better selves.

Will God forgive secret sin? Yes, but inherent in God's forgiveness is repentance on our part. True sorrow works a repentant attitude in us. Such an attitude rebels at the next thought of secret sin and rejects it. This is the building of true character in a man. Too, we must be aware that secret sin will eventually lead to open sin.

"There are no sins so pernicious to the souls of men as those that are most inward and secret. Secret sins often reign in the souls of men most powerfully, when they are least apparent!"
—THOMAS BROOKS

Spiritual Gifts

Every man hath his proper gift of God, one after this manner, and another after that (1 Corinthians 7:7).

As every man hath received the gift, even so minister the same one to another, as good stewards of the manifold grace of God (1 Peter 4:10).

It seems remarkable that so many men wonder what their "proper gift" from God is. Many may even wonder if indeed they have such a gift. But we're reminded by Scripture that "every man hath received the gift," with the responsibility to minister that gift for the benefit of others.

How then does one discover and develop their spiritual gift? First, by simply asking God. Then by considering where we find joy in serving. What do others see as our giftedness? Though the "proper gift" may be given at the moment of conversion, it may be revealed to us over the course of time. But we must be desiring our gifts and willing to use them. God will not give us gifts we will not use.

"Do not bury the gifts and talents which have been given to you, but use them, that you may enter into the joy of your Lord."
—Sadhu Sundar Singh

GROUNDED MEN

Be not conformed to this world: but be ye transformed by the renewing of your mind (ROMANS 12:2).

Before we knew Christ, we were fashioned after the course of the Christ-rejecting world. We took our cues on manhood from sitcoms, glossy magazines, social media, and ad campaigns promoting a sense of manhood far different from God's design. And it's in God's design for us as men that we find happiness, purpose, and a fruitful destiny.

We never fully grasp all God has for us as men, but as we pursue Him and His purposes, He reveals more and more of His plan. We have only to respond to God—the Great Initiator of our destiny. We need only to be assured of our place as God's men in the unfolding of history.

"Uncertainty as to our relationship with God is one of the most enfeebling and dispiriting of things. It makes a man heartless. It takes the pith out of him. He cannot fight; he cannot run. He is easily dismayed and gives way. He can do nothing for God. But when we know that we are of God, we are vigorous, brave, invincible. There is no more quickening truth than this of assurance." —HORATIUS BONAR

In Understanding Be Men

Brethren, be not children in understanding: howbeit in malice be ye children, but in understanding be men (1 CORINTHIANS 14:20).

Every man faces circumstances that are, at the time, not understandable. We may have doubts about God's way of doing things. We may question His goodness. We may wonder at His motives. But as we mature as men, as we become more acquainted with His ways, we grow into men of understanding. Not necessarily the circumstances God has arranged, but the character of God Himself. He who can do no wrong always works out His will to our ultimate benefit.

"Faith is the deliberate confidence in the character of God whose ways you may not understand at the time." —OSWALD CHAMBERS

OUR INHERITANCE

And if children, then heirs; heirs of God, and joint-heirs with Christ; if so be that we suffer with him, that we may be also glorified together (ROMANS 8:17).

Because we are God's children, we are also his heirs. We have obtained a divine inheritance and that inheritance is priceless. All we have in this life and the next is found in Christ. As we learn to dwell by faith in Him, we learn more and more about our inheritance. We discover we don't need money to be rich—the High King of heaven is our treasure. When we make Him so, we prosper. Not necessarily monetarily, but according to God's definition of prosperity. But if we are to inherit and share His glory, we will also share His suffering. Learning to suffer is not pleasant, but when we suffer for any reason—whether it's our own foolish mistakes, addictions, or unforeseen circumstances—we have "glory" waiting for us on the other side of our suffering.

"Riches I heed not, nor man's empty praise, / thou mine inheritance, now and always: / thou and thou only, first in my heart, / High King of heaven, my treasure thou art." —"BE THOU MY VISION," ATTRIBUTED TO DALLAN FORGAILL

GOD IN CREATION

The heavens declare the glory of God; and the firmament showeth his handywork. Day unto day uttereth speech, and night unto night showeth knowledge (PSALM 19:1-2).

God's glory in creation is dazzling. It brings health and healing to our deepest wounds. Nature isn't always readily accessible, but surely some part of God's creative world can be visited. Allow the beauty of the world outside of man's creations to renew your mind. Stop somewhere and drink in the beautiful surroundings. Then consider the God who created it—and you, as His greater creation. Worship Him silently as you ponder His world and your unique place in it. Give thanks.

"The spiritual mind, fond of soaring through nature in quest of new proofs of God's existence and fresh emblems of His wisdom, power and goodness—exults in the thought that it is his Father's domain which he treads! He feels that God, his God, is there." —OCTAVIUS WINSLOW

PERFECT AND COMPLETE

Knowing this, that the trying of your faith worketh patience.
But let patience have her perfect work, that ye may be perfect
and entire, wanting nothing (JAMES 1:3-4).

The perfect and complete Christian is so because he or she has found their true full, perfect, and complete self in Christ. Men and women without Christ are imperfect and incomplete—no matter how successful they appear on the outside—a fact borne out by the many ways they try to complete their personhood. To be complete is to lack nothing and thus seek happiness in nothing other than Christ. This is the road to the full effect of the measure of perfection we're allowed on earth.

"Through the death of Christ on the cross, making atonement
for sin, we get a perfect standing before God. That is justifi-
cation, and it puts us, in God's sight, back in Eden before sin
entered. God looks upon us and treats us as if we had never
sinned." —A. C. DIXON

Owned by God

Whether we live, we live unto the Lord; and whether we die, we die unto the Lord: whether we live therefore, or die, we are the Lord's (Romans 14:8).

There is great joy in being owned by God. Most Christian men have already come to the conclusion that ownership of oneself is a nonstarter. Perhaps we suffer a failure or two relationally, vocationally, or financially, or maybe we go through a season of seriously poor health. For some, addiction reveals our inability to be our own keepers. Praise God when our eyes are finally opened to the joy that comes from knowing God owns us and we are here to glorify Him in our bodies, souls, and spirits.

There is no part of us God is unwilling to claim as His own. Every day we have the opportunity to remind both ourselves and God that we belong to Him. How then shall we not rejoice in His care?

"God owns all; He owns me; He owns my home; He owns my children; He owns my property... The Christian idea is this: that God is the absolute owner of all things." —Clovis G. Chappell

THE GOLIATH OF LUST

So David prevailed over the Philistine with a sling and with a stone, and smote the Philistine, and slew him; but there was no sword in the hand of David (1 SAMUEL 17:50).

Facing the Goliath of lust within us can mean only one thing: We will prevail without swords or earthly weapons. We need only to be confidently wielding the sling of faith, filled with the stone of prayer, and our Goliath of lust will fall like a redwood in the forest.

David's mighty brothers weren't up to the job of facing Goliath. It took David, the smallest of the siblings, to defeat the giant. God chooses His warriors among the small, those who will simply have faith. Even against the Goliath of lust.

"Do as David when he was to go up against Goliath. He said, 'I come to you in the name of the Lord!' So say to your Goliath lust, 'I come to you in the name of Christ!' Then we conquer, when the Lion of the tribe of Judah marches before us!"
—THOMAS WATSON

Temptations

Watch and pray, that ye enter not into temptation: the spirit indeed is willing, but the flesh is weak (Matthew 26:41).

Temptations will always come, and we must be ready for them. Prayer preparation is key to overcoming, for every temptation finds its resistance in prayer. However, we must pray far ahead of the temptation to be fully prepared. To be "prayed up" is to be temptation resistant.

One of the unexpected pluses of temptation is that it creates great prayer warriors. Take your place among God's army of intercessors. Let temptation have the positive effect of exercising your faith. Overcome temptation through prayer to a mighty God.

"Temptation exercises our faith and teaches us to pray."
—A.B. Simpson

Obey What You
Know You Need to Do

Samuel said, Hath the Lord as great delight in burnt offerings and sacrifices, as in obeying the voice of the Lord? Behold, to obey is better than sacrifice (1 Samuel 15:22).

Sacrifice can be a positive part of our Christian life— if it's done in faith and not out of legalism. But better than sacrifice is obedience. Obedience to what? First of all to what we know is right, defined by the words of Scripture. Second, we must obey the promptings God has given us for our own lives. Many men sense God's calling in one direction only to head off in another direction. Ask Jonah how that turns out.

Obeying, like sacrifice, is done by faith. Obeying God keeps us firmly in God's will and on the right track. Contrarily, disobedience to God's known will can only bring setbacks in our walk with God. Stay the course of obedience and be blessed.

"The Bible recognizes no faith that does not lead to obedience, nor does it recognize any obedience that does not spring from faith. The two are at opposite sides of the same coin." —A.W. Tozer

Enjoy the Banquet!

He brought me to the banqueting house, and his banner over me was love (Song of Solomon 2:4).

The gospel is like a lavish banquet to which all are invited. Sadly, not all come to the table the Lord has spread for them. Even some Christians will sometimes feast on spiritual junk food rather than eat from the healthy and tasty banqueting table. It's true the table isn't easily seen, as is the junk food. God has so arranged the table that one must be hungry for the delicacies He has spread for us.

You may see others content with the lesser food, but your steps should take you beyond the trough. Keep walking and you'll soon be there—worth the effort.

"Jesus has a table spread / Where the saints of God are fed, / He invites His chosen people, 'Come and dine'; / With His manna He doth feed / And supplies our every need: / Oh, 'tis sweet to sup with Jesus all the time! / 'Come and dine,' the Master calleth, 'Come and dine'; / You may feast at Jesus' table all the time; / He Who fed the multitude, turned the water into wine, / To the hungry calleth now, 'Come and dine.'" —CHARLES B. WIDMEYER

SILENT STRENGTH

Be silent, O all flesh, before the LORD: for he is raised up out of his holy habitation (ZECHARIAH 2:13).

There is wisdom in the old adage "Better to be silent and thought a fool rather than to speak and remove all doubt." In a world full of words, a godly man finds strength in silence—both when alone or with others. In silence, we can hear better than when we fill the air with our words. Make silence a strength, not a weakness. When you do speak, let it be seasoned with grace.

"A man who lives right, and is right, has more power in his silence than another has by his words." —PHILLIPS BROOKS

RIGHT THINKING

For God hath not given us the spirit of fear; but of power, and of love, and of a sound mind (2 TIMOTHY 1:7).

Our thoughts can take us where we want to go...or where we don't want to go. In the latter case, a random but undesired thought may occur to us—often out of nowhere—and if we allow that thought to take root, we can end up turning those thoughts into actions we later regret.

Wise is the man who controls his thoughts, rejecting negative or destructive thoughts the second they occur. Wise, too, is the man who welcomes life-affirming thoughts that likewise can turn into actions that advance his spiritual, vocational, or family life. Learn, then, to discipline your mind—the result will be a well-lived life.

"The secret of living a life of excellence is merely a matter of thinking thoughts of excellence. Really, it's a matter of programming our minds with the kind of information that will set us free." —CHUCK SWINDOLL

HAPPY IS THE MAN

Happy is he that hath the God of Jacob for his help, whose hope is in the LORD his God (PSALM 146:5).

Does God desire us to be happy? Let's turn the question around and maybe the answer will be evident. Does God desire us to be *un*happy? I think most would agree that God's will is not a life of unhappiness. But what of adversity that brings unhappiness into our lives? For the Christian man, adversity must be endured with an end in sight.

Unhappiness is counterproductive, while happiness enhances productivity. True happiness, we know, comes from God, and the happy man is the man who trusts in God, even during adversity. He knows that God can even bring a positive result at the end of any trial. Trust in the final outcome, not in the dubious unfolding of adversity.

"No man in the world should be so happy as a man of God. It is one continual source of gladness. He can look up and say, 'God is my Father, Christ is my Savior, and the Church is my mother.'" —D.L. MOODY

YOUR WORST ENEMY

Look not every man on his own things, but every man also on the things of others (PHILIPPIANS 2:4).

Most men who have had a good look in the mirror will admit that's where they met their greatest enemy. History has seen many a good man falter under the weight of obsessive self-interest. God's prescription for overcoming this mortal enemy is to adopt the habit of turning our eyes toward the needs of others. There are people in every man's life that can benefit from his influence, his presence, or his support. Be that man. Become your own best friend by befriending others.

"I have had more trouble with myself than with any other man I have ever met." —D.L. MOODY

SEALED!

Now he which stablisheth us with you in Christ, and hath anointed us, is God; Who hath also sealed us, and given the earnest of the Spirit in our hearts (2 CORINTHIANS 1:21-22).

Every man in Christ has a seal about him. This seal was given by the Holy Spirit and is one of the markers of belonging to God. From what are we sealed? We're sealed *from* the world and its anti-Christian influence and sealed *to* God and His kingdom.

When temptations arise, it's imperative to remember that though we're not sealed from temptations, we are sealed from having to act on them. We are given ways of escape. We have the ability to remind Satan that our seal is like a boundary he cannot cross. Our seal, then, becomes yet one more advantage we have in living a positive Christian life.

"Come, blessed and eternal Spirit, into my heart; make it a temple, now and forever, for Your abode worthless though the offering be, yet it is all I have to present You; enter, with all Your humbling, sanctifying, sealing and comforting influences, and take full possession for Yourself." —OCTAVIUS WINSLOW

GOD CONFIDENCE

And now, little children, abide in him; that, when he shall appear, we may have confidence, and not be ashamed before him at his coming (1 JOHN 2:28).

A foolish man who doesn't know his God will trust in himself to get through life successfully. The Christian man knows better. He knows his weaknesses and has confidence in God. This confidence enables him to make the right decisions, keep his temper, act appropriately in every situation, and flourish under pressure. Confidence in God is often learned over the course of time. It's been appreciated when circumstances remind us of our own fallibility.

Confidence in God comes, too, through simple faith. Faith that God knows all, sees all, and that His hand is working behind the scenes in every aspect of our lives.

"The ultimate ground of faith and knowledge is confidence in God." —CHARLES HODGE

LIVE BY THE POWER

But ye shall receive power, after that the Holy Ghost is come upon you: and ye shall be witnesses unto me both in Jerusalem, and in all Judaea, and in Samaria, and unto the uttermost part of the earth (ACTS 1:8).

Many Christian men live by the power of their own human strength. Human strength is good, but it's not enough. The believing man has access to power beyond his natural strength. That power is found in the indwelling Holy Spirit. When we rely on Him, we're able to access resources beyond what the natural man can obtain. Sadly, many men neglect to use it.

Christian men, in a darkening age, must learn to live God-filled and God-led lives. Nothing less will do. How then do we access this supernatural strength? By appropriating each day's strength (and wisdom and discernment) through faith anew every morning. Reading and trusting in the power of God's Word is imperative. As we take in God's Word, we are refueled and enabled to meet every challenge.

"If you look up into His face and say, 'Yes, Lord, whatever it costs,' at that moment He'll flood your Life with His presence and power."—ALAN REDPATH

May God Be Glorified

That God in all things may be glorified through Jesus Christ, to whom be praise and dominion for ever and ever. Amen (1 Peter 4:11).

The wise Christian man is all about glorifying God. He does this through the way he lives, the work of his hands, the family he leads. This part of a Christian man's job description requires great humility. Men who lead out of pride can cause great harm to themselves and those whom they purpose to lead. Glorifying God requires taking oneself down several notches. We esteem others more than ourselves. We search for ways to serve those in our circle of influence.

Today you may find a God-ordained way to glorify God. Watch for it…and act on it.

"We should always look upon ourselves as God's servants, placed in God's world, to do his work; and accordingly labor faithfully for him; not with a design to grow rich and great, but to glorify God, and do all the good we possibly can."
—David Brainerd

THE GREAT RESTORER

He restoreth my soul: he leadeth me in the paths of righteousness for his name's sake (PSALM 23:3).

Our God is the Great Restorer. What we have lost—often due to our own foolishness or by responding to fleshly desires—God desires to heal. The path of healing includes the removal of our painful memories and our guilt over sins long ago forgiven by God as well as the granting of assurance that we have peace with God. Many a man has been held back in life because he has not yet allowed God to restore that which has been lost. Though it doesn't happen in an instant, it happens as God applies His truth as a salve to our wounds.

Don't let another day go by without identifying an area where you need restoration—and then allow God to do His restorative work.

"We often need to have our soul restored, quickened, revived or we would never get safely home, through this evil world."
—J.R. MILLER

SEED THOUGHTS

For out of the heart proceed evil thoughts, murders, adulteries, fornications, thefts, false witness, blasphemies (MATTHEW 15:19).

Our departure from God's will for right living usually starts with just a thought, doesn't it? A seed thought that when watered by our carnal desires blossoms into further wrong thoughts, words, and actions. We don't often realize that the summoning up of evil thoughts is the summoning up of Satan's kingdom, his minions, his lies, his strategies. Soon after, subtly perhaps, will follow his depressions, his mental breakdowns, and other maladies from his bag of destruction.

For victory to reign, every man must be quick to stop evil seed thoughts the moment they appear. To hesitate, to entertain the thought is to give it permission to grow. Hasten to put up a barrier—the shield of faith—to repel the fiery darts of the enemy.

"The heart is the great workshop where all sin is produced before it is exposed to open view. The heart is the mint where evil thoughts are coined, before they are current in our words and actions." —GEORGE SWINNOCK

BLESSED IS HE

Blessed is he whose transgression is forgiven, whose sin is covered (PSALM 32:1).

Dwelling on our past sins, failures, or mistakes is a nonstarter. It accomplishes nothing except to drag us down. Better instead is to allow all those past missteps to serve a positive purpose. One such purpose is to remind us of God's grace toward us. No matter what we name as a past departure from who we want to be, it is all forgiven at the cross. Grace in the life of a Christian man must mean that all our past failures and successes now serve a purpose.

"True happiness consists not in beauty, honor, riches (the world's trinity); but in the forgiveness of sin." —THOMAS WATSON

GOD IS OURS TO ENJOY

He brought me forth also into a large place; he delivered me, because he delighted in me (PSALM 18:19).

Most men probably don't think of "enjoying" God. And yet the noted Westminster Shorter Catechism reminds believers that the chief end of man is to glorify God and to enjoy Him forever. That chief end is not just for one denomination or followers of one particular doctrine—it's a true statement fit for all believers. The first part—glorifying God—is a way to consider all our daily activities as a means of glorifying Him. The latter end makes real our relationship with God. He is to be worshipped, but He is also to be enjoyed. Wondrous is the thought that God not only desires us to enjoy Him but also delights in enjoying us.

"Man's chief end is to glorify God, and to enjoy Him forever."
—THE WESTMINSTER SHORTER CATECHISM

TRUTH IS OUR GUARDIAN

The LORD is nigh unto all them that call upon him, to all that call upon him in truth (PSALM 145:18).

If we don't believe the truth, we're open to believing a lie. Thus the truth is a defense against accepting the premise and false promise of a lie.

Truth is our great guardian against lies. Filling our minds with the truth of God's Word enables us to identify the lies of the world and refute them. When our guard is down and we listen to lies, we become open to their deceit. The longer we listen, the more likely our abandonment of the truth and our acceptance of the lie.

Christian men must be men who hunger for truth and guard it, lest the bountiful lies become as "truth."

"One never errs more safely than when one errs by too much loving the truth." —AUGUSTINE

GOD IS NEVER SURPRISED

O fear the LORD, ye his saints: for there is no want to them that fear him. The young lions do lack, and suffer hunger: but they that seek the LORD shall not want any good thing (PSALM 34:9-10).

Is there enough truth in the Bible to meet any and every need? Yes, but we must believe this, preach this, live this. Every circumstance in our lives is known by God. He is never surprised. He never thinks, *Wow, I didn't see that coming.* Or *Whoops, how did that happen?*

When we are in an uncomfortable place—when we're going through a rough patch—it's enough for us to bend our knees to God and ask Him to resolve it according to His perfect will. Then we wait and watch—without worry.

"Pray, and let God worry." —MARTIN LUTHER

Our Great Sin-Bearer

Cast thy burden upon the LORD, *and he shall sustain thee: he shall never suffer the righteous to be moved* (PSALM 55:22).

Only a truly merciful and loving God would invite His children to cast their burdens on Him. If we have sinned, we need not run away from God but instead run toward Him. Though God hates our sin, He has compassion for us and knows the weight our sin bears down on us. Therefore, He bids us cast all our sin upon the Lamb of Sacrifice, our Great Sin-Bearer. Only a true son of God—Jesus—could bear the weight of the world's sin...including *our* sin. Yes, it's all on Him now. Not on us. Rejoice and praise your Great Sin-Bearer.

"Oh, forbid that we should live looking at sin as though it was not removed, instead of looking to you as our great sin-bearer, and sin-remover! Oh, to live assured that our sins are gone, and gone forever; that the eye of justice will rest upon them no more, that the record in the Divine debt-book is perfectly erased, and that when sought for—they shall not be found!"
—JAMES SMITH

There's Power in Praise

Blessed be the LORD God, the God of Israel, who only doeth wondrous things (PSALM 72:18).

God delights in our worship of Him. But as a bonus, when we worship God, there is inherent in our worship a blessing for us too. When we focus on God in worship, we're taking our minds off our problems. We can't be fully worshipping if we are still clutching our problems and worries to our chests. Praise allows us to release all our burdens.

In addition, praising God somehow brings us fresh spiritual energy—and often physical energy too—to meet life's demands.

Spend time in worship today. Release all your troubles to Him. Give Him thanks for your many victories too. But most of all, praise Him simply for who He is.

God has so arranged it that when we give thanks and gratitude and praise to God, we receive a blessing.

"Trying to work for God without worshipping God results in joyless legalism. Work minus worship magnifies your will power not God's worth. If you try to do things for God without delighting in God you bring dishonor upon God. Serving God without savoring God is lifeless and unreal."
—JOHN PIPER

PURPOSE: THE
SECRET TO HAPPINESS

In whom also we have obtained an inheritance, being pre-destinated according to the purpose of him who worketh all things after the counsel of his own will (EPHESIANS 1:11).

The secret of happiness is to covet no higher plan in the universe than that which is allotted to us—and at the same time, to be content with no *lesser* place than that to which God has purposed for each of us.

To have a happy life, make each day an ongoing discovery and appropriation of God's unique purpose for you. Trusting that God has such a purpose is critical—but it must then result in seeking that purpose also. For to not seek is to not find.

"God has a purpose in every life, and when the soul is completely yielded and acquiescent, He will certainly realize it. Blessed is he who has never thwarted the working of the divine ideal." —F.B. MEYER

THE FEAR OF THE LORD

The fear of the LORD is clean,
enduring for ever (PSALM 19:9).

The fear of God is a wonderful thing. It's a fountain of life, the beginning of knowledge, the hatred of evil, the source of wisdom, and the basis for confidence. Why then would a man not make it a priority to grasp the fear of the Lord…to make that great fear the cornerstone of life?

The fear of God is also "clean, enduring for ever." To know the fear of the Lord is to know the only thing that endures forever. Fear God, but never be afraid of Him.

"Some may think the fear of God breeds sadness; no, it is the inlet to joy! The fear of God is the morning star, which ushers in the sunlight of comfort: 'Walking in the fear of the Lord, and in the comfort of the Holy Spirit' (Acts 9:31). The fear of God has solid joy in it, though not frivolity. God mixes joy with holy fear, that fear may not seem slavish." —THOMAS WATSON

Grace's Lesson

The grace of God that bringeth salvation hath appeared to all men, Teaching us that, denying ungodliness and worldly lusts, we should live soberly, righteously, and godly, in this present world (Titus 2:11-12).

Among the many benefits of the grace of God is its ability to teach us to deny the ungodliness and worldly lusts that surround us daily. We know for certain that legalism fails to teach us to deny ourselves. We see God's law, and though we may wish to obey, our own lusts lead us into the deep weeds of sin.

Grace first restores us and then teaches us, but we must first each be teachable and willing to learn grace's lesson.

"Grace in the heart prevents us from abusing grace in the head—it delivers us from making grace the lackey of sin. Where the grace of God brings salvation to the soul, it works effectually. And what is it that grace teaches? Practical holiness. Grace does not eradicate ungodliness and worldly lusts—but it causes us to deny them." —Arthur Pink

YOUR CALLING

We are his workmanship, created in Christ Jesus unto good works, which God hath before ordained that we should walk in them (EPHESIANS 2:10).

Every man has some aspect of God's will for him for which that man must assume responsibility. We must be attracted to God's plan for us, knowing without a doubt that God's will trumps any ideas we may have for ourselves. Success, then, is fully leaning into and living out God's call, whether it be visible or quiet. There are no large or small callings of God. Your calling is as large as your hopes and dreams.

"Good works are not to be an amusement, but a vocation. We are not to indulge in them occasionally: they are to be the tenor and bent of our lives." —CHARLES SPURGEON

STRENGTH AND BEAUTY

Honor and majesty are before him: strength and beauty are in his sanctuary (PSALM 96:6).

God is beautiful—did you realize that? We often gaze at a glorious sunset or flowers and marvel at their loveliness. But if we look beyond the evidence of God's beauty in creation, we will see the beauty of God Himself.

Today, ponder gazing upon God. No, we can't do that literally—yet. But we can gaze upon Him spiritually. We can, as the old hymn says, "look into His wonderful face."

Wherever God is, beauty is.

"My Father, supremely good, beauty of all things beautiful."
—AUGUSTINE

THE COMPASSION OF THE LORD

When he saw the multitudes, he was moved with compassion on them, because they fainted, and were scattered abroad, as sheep having no shepherd (MATTHEW 9:36).

When we think of Jesus, what words come to mind? We may recall His healing of the sick, His dying on the cross, His forgiveness of sins, His commitment to His disciples. We may think of His anger at the legalistic Pharisees. But when we consider His whole ministry on earth, we find that all His actions were rooted in *compassion*.

When we act on Christ's behalf in loving others, compassion must be at the core of our motives. When Jesus *saw* the crowds, He had compassion. Seeing requires looking.

Today we may come in contact with harassed and helpless people. Let's look for ways to exhibit compassion toward them. When we extend a hand to help others, we are temporarily acting as undershepherds to the Great Shepherd.

"How far you go in life depends on your being tender with the young, compassionate with the aged, sympathetic with the striving and tolerant of the weak and strong. Because someday in your life you will have been all of these." —GEORGE WASHINGTON CARVER

FINDING OUR LIVES BY
LOSING OUR LIVES

*He that findeth his life shall lose it: and he that loseth his life
for my sake shall find it* (MATTHEW 10:39).

Jesus strikes at the heart of every man's need when
He urges us to lose our lives in order to find them.
There is no finding life while keeping our own. To give
up oneself is no loss; it's a gain.

Self without Christ renders us as incomplete men. If
we're still finding value in an unsurrendered life, we have
yet to learn a basic lesson about ourselves. The irony is
that in surrender, we find the power to live and accom-
plish much more than if left to ourselves. Today, feel the
power inherent in losing your life…and finding true life
in Christ.

*"Entire renunciation of the world and self prepares us for the
entire and perfect salvation of God. Leave all and you shall
possess all."* —JAMES SMITH

THE THORN

There was given to me a thorn in the flesh, the messenger of Satan to buffet me, lest I should be exalted above measure. For this thing I besought the Lord thrice, that it might depart from me (2 CORINTHIANS 12:7-8).

When confronted by a thorn, we, like Paul, become eager for the thorn to disappear so we can get on with a thornless life. But God's response to us—as it was to Paul—is that the thorn must stay, perhaps for the rest of our lives.

While the thought sounds discouraging, we must remember that Paul was given strength to bear up under his thorn. God will likewise give us the power to do what we're meant to do.

Ask for God to remove your thorn. And if He does, rejoice. And if He doesn't, rejoice. You will still have all the power necessary to run your race well.

"God will deal out the requisite grace in all time of our need. Seated by us like a kind physician, with His hand on our pulse He will watch our weakness, and accommodate the divine supply to our several needs and circumstances. He will not allow the thorn to pierce too far!" —JOHN MACDUFF

Avoid a Toxic Environment

But every man is tempted, when he is drawn away of his own lust, and enticed (JAMES 1:14).

There are places every Christian man should avoid. There are people Christian men must avoid. These are the places and people that create a hostile and toxic environment for us. Our past history will reveal where and with whom toxicity is bred.

Superman had to avoid kryptonite. We, too, must know the dangers of spiritual kryptonite. If we think there is no danger to us—that we're somehow exempt from toxic exposure—we're dead wrong. Every man alive has his weaknesses. Wise men know this and build safeguards to keep themselves strong. The best safeguard of all is avoidance of danger. It would be good to make a list of the places and people that you know from experience are your kryptonite. Make the list, pray over it, and establish a boundary you will not cross, lest you be exposed to spiritual danger.

"When we pray for the Spirit's help…we will simply fall down at the Lord's feet in our weakness. There we will find the victory and power that comes from His love." —ANDREW MURRAY

ESTABLISH THE PEACE
OF GOD IN YOUR LIFE

And the peace of God, which passeth all understanding, shall keep your hearts and minds through Christ Jesus (PHILIPPIANS 4:7).

I f we have the peace of God, it will squelch all fears and worries. This remedy to life's roller-coaster circumstances is beyond human understanding—but then, we don't really need to understand it. We just need to establish the peace of God in our lives as if it were an anchor... which it is.

Trouble may raise its head today, but you can be prepared by knowing that God's peace will bring you through. Let it guard both your heart and your mind. You will be safe.

"Is the peace of God in the soul disturbed by things down here? No, never! If waters break in stormy currents against a rock, the rock is unmoved; it is only the waters that are disturbed."
—G.V. WIGRAM

BUYER'S REMORSE

Take heed therefore unto yourselves, and to all the flock, over the which the Holy Ghost hath made you overseers, to feed the church of God, which he hath purchased with his own blood (Acts 20:28).

Did you ever buy something and later regret it? That's buyer's remorse. We may encounter it often in our lives, but God never has buyer's remorse. He has purchased us without regret, knowing ahead of time what the purchase involved: a high price (the blood of Christ) for our moth-eaten rags of human righteousness.

We may notice a friend pay a high price for an item we know is worthless and shake our heads in wonder. But when we consider God's "foolish" purchase, we can only rejoice that God always buys wisely, especially when we're the purchased ones.

"Safe! Yes! Will God part with the objects of His highest love? Never! Will Jesus surrender the purchase of His own heart's blood? Never! Happy! Yes; if anything can render us happy, this should: that we are God's choice and the Savior's purchase; that the Father and the Son jointly claim us, and highly value us!" —James Smith

Fulfilling the Law of Christ

Bear ye one another's burdens, and so fulfill the law of Christ (GALATIANS 6:2).

How does God meet the needs of His people? More often than not, the miracle comes *through* His people. In the book of Acts, we see a church where needs were met by believers voluntarily pooling their resources. Needs were seen and then needs were met.

How is it with us, twenty centuries later? No doubt in God's mind we're still to be the channel through which God's gifts flow. When we withdraw from meeting the needs of others, the channel is dammed up and needs remain unmet.

Every Christian man has the charge to care for others. In so doing, we fulfill the law of Christ.

"We all need each other. Not one of us could carry on without others to share his burdens. And we begin to be like Christ only when we begin to help others, to be of use to them, to make life a little easier for them, to give them some of our strength in their weakness, some of our joy in their sorrow. When we have learned this lesson we have begun to live worthily." —J.R. MILLER

Consider What Great Things

Only fear the LORD, and serve him in truth with all your heart: for consider how great things he hath done for you (1 SAMUEL 12:24).

Every Christian man has a past with the Lord. If a new believer, the past may be short; only weeks or months. For many men, their past spans the course of years or even decades. During that time—long or short—God has proven Himself faithful. Through trials galore, through temptations aplenty, through health and sickness, God has been there. Often, though, we pass on through life barely recalling the "great things" He has done.

God asks that we fear Him, serve Him, and consider our past with Him, recalling the miracles we've experienced. What miracle can you bring to mind today to rejoice over God's faithfulness?

"There is nothing good in my daily life but has come by His blessing and gift. There is no deliverance from danger, no sudden incoming of joy, no softening and mellowing and sanctifying through trial which He did not devise and send."
—ALEXANDER SMELLIE

God's Supply

When they were filled, he said unto his disciples, Gather up the fragments that remain, that nothing be lost (JOHN 6:12).

When we were children and were delighted by candy or a new toy, we might have said—or even demanded—"More! More!" But we're men now, no longer children. We learn from Scripture that God gives us enough. If we truly need more, God will multiply what we have—just as He did with the loaves and fishes. There is no scarcity with God. Let your needs be known to Him and watch for His perfect supply. It will be enough, with pieces left over.

"Have you been holding back from a risky, costly course to which you know in your heart God has called you? Hold back no longer. Your God is faithful to you, and adequate for you. You will never need more than He can supply, and what He supplies, both materially and spiritually, will always be enough for the present." —J.I. PACKER

Hidden in Christ

Thou art my hiding place; thou shalt preserve me from trouble;thou shalt compass me about with songs of deliverance. Selah (PSALM 32:7).

During times of danger or just daily stress, God desires to be our hiding place. Here is where we are preserved from trouble. We are surrounded by songs of holy deliverance. Here we can be safe from temptation. Here the evil one cannot approach us. Here we rest and regain our strength for daily living. Here is where we live with God.

"All those who in time of danger are duly sensible of it, and make use of God as their refuge and hiding place shall find him to be that to them, which their faith expects from him."
—ROBERT LEIGHTON

HEALTHY AND WHOLE

Beloved, I wish above all things that thou mayest prosper and be in health, even as thy soul prospereth (3 JOHN 1:2).

As the apostle John prayed for the readers of his letter that all would go well with them, so too can we believe God desires for all to go well with us. Yes, there will be life's rough patches, but the secret is that when we are going through adversity, we keep walking until we come out on the other side. God's will leads us on to wholeness. It's not God's will for us to be living below the level of His perfect plan for each of us.

God desires us to be healthy and whole.

"These three things, so necessary to the comfort of life, every Christian may in a certain measure expect, and for them every Christian is authorized to pray; and we should have more of all three if we devoutly prayed for them." —ADAM CLARKE

Tender Mercies

*Remember, O L*ORD, *thy tender mercies and thy lovingkind-nesses; for they have been ever of old* (PSALM 25:6).

Many Christian men have a history that portrays God as less than merciful, not an example of loving-kindness. For these men, God was a hard taskmaster, and their performances were seemingly measured by God's yardstick and always came up short. What a miserable way to live. It's like the poor donkey who only moves ahead as he tries to catch up with the carrot on the string in front of him.

Blessed is the man who has discovered that God is full of tender mercies and offers at every turn the benefits of His loving-kindness. They are "of old" and yet never grow old. Daily we're invited to feast on His mercy and loving-kindness.

"It is the multitude of His mercies that makes Him so merciful a God. He does not give but a drop or two of mercy—that would soon be gone, like the rain which fell this morning under the hot sun. But His mercies flow like a river! There is in Him…a multitude of mercies, for a multitude of sins, and a multitude of sinners!" —J.C. PHILPOT

THE NEED TO FORGIVE AND MOVE ON WITH YOUR LIFE

And when ye stand praying, forgive, if ye have ought against any: that your Father also which is in heaven may forgive you your trespasses (MARK 11:25).

Some Christian men…perhaps you…have suffered needlessly because of someone else's actions or words. These wounds are surely painful and, yes, God sees the hurt. But if there is unforgiveness due to ill-treatment, the pain will only linger and perhaps end up in bitterness. For our own sakes, God calls us to forgive others. It doesn't really matter if they see their part in an offense. If they will not or cannot be involved in righting a wrong, you must deal with it yourself.

Forgiveness brings us out of the rut we're in. It stops the tape from endlessly replaying the offense in our heads. Best of all, when we forgive, our heavenly Father is able to forgive us for our many trespasses.

"He that cannot forgive others, breaks the bridge over which he himself must pass if he would ever reach heaven; for everyone has need to be forgiven." —GEORGE HERBERT

THE MIND OF CHRIST

For who hath known the mind of the Lord, that he may instruct him? but we have the mind of Christ (1 CORINTHIANS 2:16).

Need wisdom? Need an answer to a tough problem? If so, remember that we're not left to figure things out with our own human (and fallible) wisdom. We have the mind of Christ. We're able to think things through with godly reason. We can weigh our options against the Word of God.

Is one of our options questionable or inappropriate according to God's Word? If so, we have our answer. When the Bible doesn't give clear counsel, we can pray and ask God to reveal the right course—and then make that decision in faith. In some matters, it's wise to share your situation with a trusted Christian friend. Talking about it may reveal the answer. Never rush toward an answer. Give God time to reveal the correct path.

"True religion is having the mind of Christ."—JOHN ANGELL JAMES

Fire in Our Bosoms?

Can a man take fire in his bosom, and his clothes not be burned? (Proverbs 6:27).

We Christian men can make a mess of things when we figuratively carry fire in our bosoms by flirting with temptation. During temptation, a false promise presents itself to us, and we must decide whether to believe this false promise and act on it or refuse to accept it, knowing both its source and its end. Many men have been severely burned by the fire in their bosoms when they fanned the flame with their consent to temptation. A wise man will quickly discern the kindling fire and put it out without a second thought. *No good thing can result from fire in a man's bosom.*

"The temptation once yielded to gains power. The crack in the embankment which lets a drop or two ooze through is soon a hole which lets out a flood." —Alexander Maclaren

ACCOUNTABILITY

Obey them that have the rule over you, and submit yourselves:
for they watch for your souls, as they that must give account,
that they may do it with joy, and not with grief: for that is
unprofitable for you (HEBREWS 13:17).

Accountability for many men is like having a parent watching over you once again. And yet, God does appoint people in the Bible and in the church to whom we should be accountable without reluctance. Accountability is a blessing, not a curse.

Consider the many Christian men caught up in some form of addiction. Such men often find an accountability partner essential to their recovery. What if those men had a person to whom they were accountable *before* they fell into addiction?

Every growing Christian man should desire to have someone to whom he can be accountable. He should also be available as someone to whom someone in need can be accountable.

"It is one of the severest tests of friendship to tell your friend his
faults. So to love a man that you cannot bear to see a stain
upon him, and to speak painful truth through loving words,
that is friendship." —HENRY WARD BEECHER

ENCOURAGING OURSELVES
IN THE LORD

David was greatly distressed; for the people spake of stoning him, because the soul of all the people was grieved, every man for his sons and for his daughters: but David encouraged himself in the LORD his God (1 SAMUEL 30:6).

There are times when a man must face serious situations alone. No one is able to help. At such times it's up to that man to encourage himself in the Lord his God.

How so? One way is to resort to the encouragement found in God's Word. Find and meditate on Scriptures that bless you. Another way is to recall God's past faithfulness. Perhaps David encouraged himself by recalling his victory over Goliath. Or simply turning to praise is yet another way of encouraging ourselves in the Lord. No matter the situation, praise always lifts our burdens.

The bottom line is that in the alone times when we must be encouraged, we have the power to do so.

"Encourage yourself in God. Whatever you lose, whatever you lack, He will supply all you need. All things in earth and Heaven are His, and if you trust in Him, no good thing will He withhold." —GEORGE EVERARD

Good Counsel

Thy testimonies also are my delight and my counselors (Psalm 119:24).

No man is free from the need of counseling. Life often presents dilemmas that require wisdom beyond ourselves. In such situations, a man's first resort for counseling is God's Word. This is especially true if we have learned to *delight* in God's Word, knowing it will never lead us astray. God often allows circumstances that require us to lean hard on His Word.

It may come as no shock to think of the book of Proverbs as one of the fountains of wisdom in the Bible. With thirty-one chapters, many men have found it beneficial to read a chapter a day throughout the month and then begin again the next month. The wisdom of Solomon can help us in our present situations and caution us against the mistakes that require us to make hard choices or that will prompt repentance.

"If honest of heart and uprightness before God were lacking or if I did not patiently wait on God for instruction, or if I preferred the counsel of my fellow-men to the declarations of the Word of God, I made great mistakes." —George Müller

SELF-ACCEPTANCE

I will praise thee; for I am fearfully and wonderfully made: marvelous are thy works; and that my soul knoweth right well (PSALM 139:14).

Few men are aware of their own giftedness. And yet we know every man *is* gifted by God. Every man is created in God's image and has been deemed of great value to God as evidenced by Christ's death on the cross. It seems strange then that some men devalue themselves or are unaware of their importance in God's unfolding will.

Some men find it hard to accept their lot in life, and yet for every man born from above, indwelt by God's Holy Spirit, there is great acceptance by God. How then can we who are the children of God question our worth? God has answered that question with total resolve. Self-esteem in every Christian man should be off the charts. We are accepted, acceptable, deeply loved, and deeply valued.

"The saints are God's jewels, highly esteemed by and dear to him; they are a royal diadem in his hand." —MATTHEW HENRY

It's All by Faith

For therein is the righteousness of God revealed from faith to faith: as it is written, The just shall live by faith (ROMANS 1:17).

The Christian life is begun by faith…and sustained through our whole lives by that same faith. Most of us learned fairly early that faith is the ever-present Miracle-Gro for our lives.

This faith is what began God's work in us, and it's by this faith that He will continue to perform the work until the day of Jesus Christ.

That means we continue to believe in God for our entire lives and all that pertains to them. We believed in God first for salvation, but then we also must go on believing in Him for our sustenance, our finances, our health, our relationships, our jobs…It all comes from His hand through faith. Even faith that carries us through the cloudy days when we can't really get a handle on what God's doing with us. Faith knows God has the handle. We'll be fine.

"Daily living by faith on Christ is what makes the difference between the sickly and the healthy Christian, between the defeated and the victorious saint." —A.W. PINK

Epistles to a
World of Lost Men

And the angel of the LORD appeared unto him, and said unto him, The LORD is with thee, thou mighty man of valour (JUDGES 6:12).

Are we a weakened generation of men? If so, we must consider that in our present weakness there is hidden great opportunity. For too long we have allowed our appetites to rule us. Have we not misused the gifts of God…or left them unused? Have not our sexual lives been more patterned after the world than patterned after God's plan for sexuality?

There are men who watch us as Christians, wondering if we truly have answers that could benefit them. Thus we are God's epistles to a world of lost men. But in order to reach them, we ourselves must be truly found. May no man within our circle of influence be lost without our witness being real to him.

"Soon we shall be up there with Christ. God did not mean us to be happy without Him; but God would first have us to be witnesses for Him down here, to hold out as much light as we can." —G.V. WIGRAM

THE EQUIPPING COMES
WITH THE CALLING

Wherefore I put thee in remembrance that thou stir up the gift of God, which is in thee by the putting on of my hands (2 TIMOTHY 1:6).

God is faithful in calling each of us to a specific work. And what we are called to do, we are equipped to do. For many men, fear or feelings of inadequacy keep them from stepping out and believing in God for an effective life.

A man's calling in life may be large or small, but it is never without the means to fulfill it. Prayer opens the door to our assignment, but we must move one step at a time toward our purpose. The result will be much fruit, and when our lives end, we will look back and be satisfied that we didn't miss out on the blessing of our personal calling in life.

"Next to faith this is the highest art—to be content with the calling in which God has placed you." —MARTIN LUTHER

The Depth of God's Love

But God commendeth his love toward us, in that, while we were yet sinners, Christ died for us (ROMANS 5:8).

Isn't it remarkable that God should love us so fully? Isn't it a miracle to be considered by God as valued enough to send His Son to die for us?

Truth be known, we may never fully grasp the depth of God's love in this lifetime. We can only marvel and give thanks.

We may think we're just one in eight billion that God loves—and that His love is diffused among the many. But no. God's love is focused on each of us. *Focused!* We exist to receive His love as if each of us was the only creation He loves. What manner of love is this!

"Believe God's love and power more than you believe your own feelings and experiences. Your rock is Christ, and it is not the rock that ebbs and flows but the sea." —SAMUEL RUTHERFORD

GOD'S TIMING IS PERFECT

So teach us to number our days, that we may apply our hearts unto wisdom (PSALM 90:12).

If we were to plan the events in our lives, we would no doubt speed things up a bit. We don't like waiting, especially if it's for something we truly want. But God, not us, sets the timetable for our lives' events. And when He seems slow, we can know that "waiting on the Lord" is a valuable learning tool God loves to use. The Bible is full of men who waited. Noah waited. Moses waited. David waited. Joseph waited. Jacob waited. Even Jesus waited until the fullness of time. Let us, then, be patient and wait for God to bring to pass His promises.

"The prayer that begins with trustfulness, and passes on into waiting, will always end in thankfulness, triumph, and praise." —ALEXANDER MACLAREN

OUR INTERIOR VOICE

Bless the LORD, O my soul: and all that is within me, bless his holy name (PSALM 103:1).

Every man has an interior voice that speaks to him throughout the day. Much of what we say to ourselves relates to the mundane matters of life. But then every man has that voice that accuses him of not measuring up or of having failed in the past. Sometimes the voice provokes fear and anxiety. But when that voice starts to repeat the condemning or fearful tapes we've heard time and again, it's up to us to stop that voice and replace it by speaking affirming words to ourselves. David spoke to himself and benefited from his words. Each of us can do likewise. Today, when your interior voice starts to speak destructive thoughts, shut it down by speaking thoughts of faith and courage.

"Most unhappiness comes from listening to ourselves instead of talking to ourselves." —MARTYN LLOYD JONES

COMPARING OURSELVES
WITH OTHERS

For we dare not make ourselves of the number, or compare ourselves with some that commend themselves: but they measuring themselves by themselves, and comparing themselves among themselves, are not wise (2 CORINTHIANS 10:12).

It may bolster our self-esteem to compare ourselves positively with some other men who are not as successful, strong, handsome, or smart as we are. It may also bring us down to compare ourselves negatively with men who we may envy for their apparently happy lot. But in either case, we're on the wrong track. Measuring ourselves by comparison with others is not God's way. We are all unique men with distinct personalities, strengths, and weaknesses, and specific callings in life.

Be the man you know you're called to be. That will bring about contentment and the end of faulty comparisons.

"Men compare themselves with men, and readily with the worst, and flatter themselves with that comparative betterness. This is not the way to see spots, to look into the muddy streams of profane men's lives; but look into the clear fountain of the Word, and there we may both discern and wash them; and consider the infinite holiness of God, and this will humble us to the dust." —ROBERT LEIGHTON

WHERE DID GOD FIND YOU?

He found him in a desert land, and in the waste howling wilderness; he led him about, he instructed him, he kept him as the apple of his eye (DEUTERONOMY 32:10).

God's love for Israel is pictured as a man found by God in a desert land. God led him, instructed him, and kept him as the apple of His eye. In short, God found Israel in its great need—and He meant to fill that need. He still does that today...searching each of us out in our great need with the goal of leading us out of our personal desert, instructing us in life, and yes, keeping each of us as the apple of His eye.

Where did God find you when you first met Him? Was it in the desert? Or did the desert come later? Where does God find you today? Wherever you are, God is there to lead you out.

You are the apple of His eye.

"Christian! God has found you! God is leading you! God is instructing you! Oh, then, leave to Him to choose your path in life!" —JOHN MACDUFF

MISTAKES

The LORD will perfect that which concerneth me: thy mercy, O LORD, endureth for ever: forsake not the works of thine own hands (PSALM 138:8).

Every man makes mistakes. Some make many mistakes daily. But whether our mistakes are few or many, big or small, God has the power—and the will—to override our errors in such a way as to turn the situation around for our ultimate good, though that may not be seen immediately. Many a man's seeming mistake became the pivot God used to bring that man into a new place of blessing.

When you suffer from the effects of a wrong turn in life, let prayer and faith make that wrong turn a turn onto the perfect path of God's will. As a bonus, when we must suffer from the mistakes of another, God is also willing to turn that to our good. But faith and often patience are key. Don't be rattled when God is pivoting you into a new phase of life.

"We serve a gracious Master who knows how to overrule even our mistakes to His glory and our own advantage." —JOHN NEWTON

A Man's Limits

And he said unto them, Come ye yourselves apart into a desert place, and rest a while: for there were many coming and going, and they had no leisure so much as to eat (MARK 6:31).

Every man must know his limits and honor them. They are there to keep him safe. Stress is a huge killer of men, and that stress is often caused by men exceeding their capacity for work or some other activity that consumes time and energy.

We are built by God to be useful and to stay busy. But God has also set limits on what our bodies and brains can handle. Learn your limits the easy way—by marking how far you can go before anxiety sets in. Don't learn the hard way through deteriorating health or a meltdown.

Limits are your friends.

"Man's spiritual life consists in the number and fulness of his correspondences with God. In order to develop these he may be constrained to insulate them, to enclose them from the other correspondences, to shut himself in with them. In many ways the limitation of the natural life is the necessary condition of the full enjoyment of the spiritual life." —HENRY DRUMMOND

God Has Your Back

My little children, these things write I unto you, that ye sin not. And if any man sin, we have an advocate with the Father, Jesus Christ the righteous (1 John 2:1).

One of the truest tests of commitment comes during hard times. Who has our back when we're under attack? Who will watch over us with true loyalty? Who will be in our corner when we mess up?

Only Christ. He is our permanent and loyal brother. He will never fail us…especially during those times when our earthly friends do.

What then is our response to this overwhelming loyalty? Isn't it that we return that loyalty to Christ? When He is under attack, do we speak up in His defense? Do we recommend Him to our acquaintances going through tough times? Loyalty should beget loyalty. And loyalty is based on commitment. Are we as fully committed to Christ today as He is to us?

"Faith does not grasp a doctrine, but a heart. The trust which Christ requires is the bond that unites souls with Him; and the very life of it is entire committal of myself to Him in all my relations and for all my needs, and absolute utter confidence in Him as all sufficient for everything that I can require."
—Alexander Maclaren

Sin Is Leaven

A little leaven leaveneth the whole lump (GALATIANS 5:9).

In the Bible, sin is likened to leaven. During the Passover, leaven was removed from the house as part of God's directive to keep the angel of death at bay. In the New Testament, the Lord's Table is celebrated with unleavened bread—typifying a renunciation of sin.

The analogy is fitting. Sin is like leaven in its ability to enlarge its place in our lives in the same way leaven enlarges the loaf. And doesn't a little sin often lead to additional sin? A pinch of sin, like leaven, expands easily; and if we give way to sin, sin becomes our master.

Let every man, then, remove the leaven of sin from his life. May every celebration of the Lord's Table remind us of the necessary absence of the leaven of sin in our lives.

"Little sins are very dangerous! A little leaven, leavens the whole lump. A little knife, may kill. A little leak in a ship, may sink it. Though the scorpion is little—yet will it sting a lion to death! Just so, a little sin may at once bar the door of Heaven, and open the gates of Hell!" —THOMAS BROOKS

A Divine Nature

Whereby are given unto us exceeding great and precious promises: that by these ye might be partakers of the divine nature, having escaped the corruption that is in the world through lust (2 PETER 1:4).

In Christ we find not just a Savior from the dire penalty of sin but also a deliverer from the power of sin. At our conversion we were given a new nature that doesn't recognize the power of sin. Abiding in our new nature enables us to overcome the sins that cause us to fall prey to our "old man."

True, we may not always *feel* as though we have a new nature, but then, there's no place in the Bible where we are told to reckon according to our feelings.

Today and always, live according to God's promises, and reckon yourself alive by virtue of your new nature.

"If we had the tongue of the mightiest of orators, and if that tongue could be touched with a live coal from off the altar, yet still it could not utter a tenth of the praises of the exceeding great and precious promises of God." —CHARLES SPURGEON

THE SCULPTING OF GOD

It is God that girdeth me with strength, and maketh my way perfect (PSALM 18:32).

Left to ourselves, we might design our lives differently from the way God has designed them. We would certainly allow for less sorrow, fewer run-ins with sin, and a more carefree existence. But when we realize that God is always doing something behind the scenes of our circumstances, we can bear the ups and downs of life more easily.

Every seeming adversity has its redemption when accepted by faith as God's tool for sculpting us into the image of Christ. Praise God for life's happy times, but praise Him also during the valleys. It's there that we truly grow as we learn submission to the sculpting of God.

"The divine Sculptor must do with us, as the sculptor did with the stone. He must bring to bear upon us the sharp chisel of affliction, of disappointment, of trial. It seems that these things will destroy us...But all the time, the Master Sculptor with His sharp chisel of pain, is only carving His own image in their natures and characters." —CHARLES NAYLOR

Our Limited Vision

O Lord God, thou hast begun to show thy servant thy greatness, and thy mighty hand: for what God is there in heaven or in earth, that can do according to thy works, and according to thy might? (Deuteronomy 3:24).

We men often have such limited vision when it comes to who we are. Especially who we are in Christ. God simply doesn't make second-rate men. Every man has more potential than he'll ever use. Of course, this man knows well enough that his potential comes from God, not from any merit of his own. And seldom do we really comprehend the power of God when it comes to animating our own lives. When it gets down to it, we men are more than we think we are because our God is more than we think He is.

"If a Christian remains in a carnal condition long after experiencing new birth, he hinders God's salvation from realizing its full potential and manifestation. Only when he is growing in grace, constantly governed by the spirit, can salvation be wrought in him." —Watchman Nee

LIFE TO THE HILT

A wise man is strong; yea, a man of knowledge increaseth strength (PROVERBS 24:5).

Jim Elliot lived a short life of twenty-nine years…but he lived it to the hilt and died a martyr for Christ. The tribe he had hoped to reach for Christ became his murderers. But that wasn't the end of the story. Eventually, many of those who killed Jim became followers of Christ. His influence continues today through the story of his life as written by his widow, Elisabeth Elliot. If we could talk to Jim and tell him how sorry we are for his tragic end, he would surely tell us not to waste our tears—that he did indeed live his life to the hilt by fulfilling God's purpose in his death.

We're not likely to have the same calling as Jim Elliot, but whatever our calling and however short or long our earthly lives, we can and must live them to the hilt. Anything less is an insult to God—the one who desires us to be all there, wherever we find ourselves.

"Wherever you are, be all there. Live to the hilt every situation you believe to be the will of God." —JIM ELLIOT

GOD'S INVESTMENT

Thou oughtest therefore to have put my money to the exchangers, and then at my coming I should have received mine own with usury (MATTHEW 25:27).

God has something invested in you, and He will not let that investment fail to yield its dividends. What, though, do we have invested in God? Are they eternal investments? Will there be generous dividends? Or will our investments fail to yield a profit?

Just as God has invested in us, so too must we invest in Him. We do this by *daily* responding to the gospel afresh, anticipating another day of profit.

Our response may be that of prayer, it might mean a literal financial investment with someone in need, or it might mean laying down our lives in some meaningful way that brings benefit to another person. Count on it: There will be a way to invest in God today.

"It is the very essence of true religion, to feel that God is ours. To have him for our portion, yields the highest comfort, and invests with the greatest wealth in time and in eternity."
—WILLIAM NICHOLSON

Give Diligence

Wherefore the rather, brethren, give diligence to make your calling and election sure: for if ye do these things, ye shall never fall (2 Peter 1:10).

Every man has a distinct calling. But by calling, we don't need to think of heading off to seminary or the mission field (unless that is indeed God's calling for you). A laborer, a teacher, a banker, a store manager, a cement mason—no matter the label we put on our day's work, it can be as important a calling as Billy Graham's. Why? Because it's *our* calling, and it will use our talents, strength, and time to the best advantage. So let us be bold in our day's work, whatever it is. And if we can't be bold and confident in our calling, maybe we should ask ourselves, *Is this indeed my calling?*

"Take care of giving up your first zeal; beware of cooling in the least degree. Ye were hot and earnest once; be hot and earnest still, and let the fire which once burnt within you still animate you. Be ye still men of might and vigour, men who serve their God with diligence and zeal." —Charles Spurgeon

A Man and His Brothers

Two are better than one; because they have a good reward for their labor. For if they fall, the one will lift up his fellow: but woe to him that is alone when he falleth; for he hath not another to help him up (ECCLESIASTES 4:9-10).

Our culture likes to portray genuine manhood as the rugged "can-do-anything" individualist attitude. But for Christian men, we understand the power of our brotherhood with other believers. We are not complete in ourselves; we need the rest of the Body of Christ, particularly our brothers in Christ. Often our inadequacies can be filled by the strengths in other men, just as we may supply our strengths to complete a brother's weakness.

Brotherhood is by God's design. Friendship is God's gift to men. Don't go alone in life. Bring your brothers along. The pleasures of the journey will be multiplied when shared with other men.

"There is a brotherhood within the body of believers, and the Lord Jesus Christ is the common denominator. Friendship and fellowship are the legal tender among believers."
—J. VERNON MCGEE

BIBLICAL PRINCIPLES

But this I say, He which soweth sparingly shall reap also sparingly; and he which soweth bountifully shall reap also bountifully (2 CORINTHIANS 9:6).

The Bible is more than a revelation of God and His kingdom. In its pages we're given various principles that when followed will enhance our likelihood of success. Every major life event—marriage, vocation, finances, parenting—and even manhood itself will be safeguarded as we obey what God's Word tells us. When we neglect godly principles, we venture into dangerous territory.

We may find broken relationships, financial loss, parenting failures, and health problems in the wake of our disobedience of God's Word. But even then, one of God's principles involves restoration when we have exceeded the boundaries of Scripture. If one or more areas of your life are suffering due to a violation of a biblical principle, search out in God's Word the violation and its remedy. As you reintroduce the principle in your life, give God time to bring about healing. Like a seed planted, your restoration will sprout and grow like a mighty oak.

"The safe place lies in obedience to God's Word, singleness of heart and holy vigilance."—A.B. SIMPSON

OPEN THE GIFT THAT
IS YOUR FUTURE

These things I have spoken unto you, that in me ye might have peace. In the world ye shall have tribulation: but be of good cheer; I have overcome the world (JOHN 16:33).

We live in perilous times. There can be great cause for fear among men who will not trust in God, but to be a Christian man is to expect a blessed future. We look forward to success, not failure. We seek and receive favor from God in our endeavors. When the headlines report dire circumstances, we know to exalt God's Word above the latest prediction. Trouble may come through financial reverses, scarcity of resources, weather-related events, or personal setbacks. But in every case, God sees and God provides. We must never give in to fear in the light of world events. Trust in God for both small and large changes.

"Faith, which is trust, and fear are opposite poles. If a man has the one, he can scarcely have the other in vigorous operation. He that has his trust set upon God does not need to dread any-thing except the weakening or the paralyzing of that trust."
—ALEXANDER MACLAREN

THE GOD WHO IS NEEDY

Verily I say unto you, Inasmuch as ye have done it unto one of the least of these my brethren, ye have done it unto me (MATTHEW 25:40).

It's odd to imagine God being needy. And yet Jesus tells us that as we tend to the needy, we're tending to Him. In short, God cares for people through each of us. Thus the needs of others are the needs of God.

If we want to see God while on this earth, we can see Him in the faces of the lonely, the sick, and the poor. And when we tend to the needs of God by helping others (irony of all ironies), we're more blessed than those to whom we give.

If every Christian man would tend to the needs of those around him, what an impact it would make on the unbelieving world.

"Giving of alms is a glorious work, and let me assure you it is not unfruitful work. Whatever is disbursed to the poor brethren, is given to Christ!... The poor man's hand is Christ's treasury, and there is nothing lost that is put there." —THOMAS WATSON

God Is the Dad
You Never Had

We have had fathers of our flesh which corrected us, and we gave them reverence: shall we not much rather be in subjection unto the Father of spirits, and live? (Hebrews 12:9).

How was it with your dad? Was he a good or even great dad? Or was there something missing from your paternal relationship? For many men, there was no dad on the scene. For others, Dad was physically present but emotionally absent. If your dad was missing in action, you can know that God is the dad you never had.

As adult men, we forgive our less-than-perfect dads and transfer our primary allegiance to our heavenly dad. If our father on earth is or was a good dad, his attributes should point us to the One who exhibits those attributes in full measure.

Whether your relationship with your dad was good, poor, or nonexistent, you can now trust in the true father of us all.

"God is the archetypal Father; all other fatherhood is a more or less imperfect copy of his perfect fatherhood." —F.F. Bruce

THE DISCORDANT NOTE

Speaking to yourselves in psalms and hymns and spiritual songs, singing and making melody in your heart to the Lord (EPHESIANS 5:19).

My friend plays the guitar as he leads worship in our church. One day he said, "If I make a mistake as I'm playing, I have to go on. If I keep thinking about the mistake I made a measure ago, I can't play the music."

There's a lesson there. We're all making music with our lives. And when we've hit the wrong note, we have to let it go and play the present notes. There's no recapturing a wrong note once played.

If your life's symphony has hit some wrong notes, keep playing your music and forget the discordant life behind you. The music in the next measure is up. Play it.

"It is with life as with music. The rests on the staff in one sense are not part of the music…yet they're as important…as if they were notes to be struck or sung… There are rests in life which are quite as important in the melody of life, as any notes on the staff. To overlook them…is to mar the music. We should mind the rests." —J.R. MILLER

BE SURE OF GOD

And we know that all things work together for good to them that love God, to them who are the called according to his purpose (ROMANS 8:28).

As Christian men, we naturally believe in the existence of God. But is that enough to get us through? No, it isn't. To really get the most out of our Christian lives, we must be as certain of His goodness, His promises, His moment-by-moment presence as we are of His existence.

The whole of our lives can be spent happily becoming more and more certain of God each day. When trials come, we can be sure God sees and is active in resolving our situation. When we're in a season of blessing, we can know God is the source of that blessing. Being sure of God in every aspect of life bolsters our confidence that no matter what happens, everything will turn out for the best.

"We must learn to live on the heavenly side and look at things from above. To contemplate all things as God sees them, as Christ beholds them, overcomes sin, defies Satan, dissolves perplexities, lifts us above trials, separates us from the world and conquers fear of death." —A.B. SIMPSON

Forks in the Road

Show me thy ways, O LORD; teach me thy paths (PSALM 25:4).

Every man is often faced with serious decisions, some of which could alter his life forever. How then to decide which fork in the road to take? Poet Robert Frost would tell us to take the path less traveled. And sometimes that is the best choice. But we can't reduce our decision-making to such a simplistic tactic. Instead, for the Christian man, there are barometers that can nudge us toward the right path. First, any decision must be supported by Scripture. Another test is to ask, Do those who know me best have an objective opinion? Then ask, Do the circumstances lead in one direction over another? Finally, we can trust our own God-given inner instincts (not to be confused with emotional influence) by asking, How do we truly feel about the choices?

In the final analysis, make all your decisions by faith. You'll never go wrong.

"It is the characteristic excellence of the strong man that he can bring momentous issues to the fore and make a decision about them. The weak are always forced to decide between alternatives they have not chosen themselves." —DIETRICH BONHOEFFER

A MAN'S TONGUE

If any man among you seem to be religious, and bridleth not his tongue, but deceiveth his own heart, this man's religion is vain (JAMES 1:26).

Whoso keepeth his mouth and his tongue keepeth his soul from troubles (PROVERBS 21:23).

Face it, for many Christian men, our tongues often betray us before we can formulate the most appropriate words to say. Anger, oversensitivity, and disappointment often result in harsh words that can't change our circumstances or even our mood. Instead, the situation is often made worse. If we would like to avoid troubles today, let's take a lesson from Solomon's playbook of Proverbs and "keepeth" our tongues, and thus our souls, from trouble. Choose to speak good words today, even if in the midst of adversity or turmoil.

"O Lord, keep our hearts, keep our eyes, keep our feet, and keep our tongues." —WILLIAM TIPTAFT

THE BOOK OF MY LIFE

Thou tellest my wanderings: put thou my tears into thy bottle: are they not in thy book? (PSALM 56:8).

Your life is like a book God has written just for you. Each day is the next page in the story, and you keep turning the pages, day by day, page by page, to see what happens next. You keep reading, too, to find out if the book of your life is a drama, comedy, or tragedy. Eventually, you realize it's a little of all three, measured out by God's timetable. And for every Christian man, no matter the measure of sadness or gladness in this life, the book of his life has a very happy ending.

"Every man is an original and solitary character. None can either understand or feel the book of his own life like himself."
—RICHARD CECIL

BUILDING A TOXIC
ENVIRONMENT FOR SATAN

Be sober, be vigilant; because your adversary the devil, as a roaring lion, walketh about, seeking whom he may devour (1 PETER 5:8).

Is your life toxic? It should be. Toxic, that is, to Satan. Some men mistakenly give little credence to the craftiness of our ruthless enemy and thus allow him unfettered influence in their lives. But wise Christian men not only refuse Satan any influence in their lives; they build safeguards that repel Satan. These safeguards are toxic to Satan, and he no longer assails the man whose very presence threatens him. Do not belittle your enemy. Be wise in keeping yourself from his clutches. Make your life toxic to the enemy.

"Satan trembles when he sees the weakest saint upon their knees."—WILLIAM COWPER

GOD IS AT WORK

Being confident of this very thing, that he which hath begun a good work in you will perform it until the day of Jesus Christ (PHILIPPIANS 1:6).

God is actively (not passively) at work in the life of every believing man. Our daily thoughts may for a brief while not include God, but God's thoughts of us and all that concerns us never cease. As you read these words, God, your Father, is performing the work of maturation in you and will do so for the rest of your life. And the work He performs, as Paul tells us, is a *good* work. When this realization becomes firmly affixed in our minds, we may be confident in all that God does in us and for us. Even as we read these words, His plans are moving us forward, never backward.

"The work of grace is but begun and carried on in this life—it is not finished here—it is not perfect here. As long as we are in this imperfect state, there is still something more to be done. We shall always find cause to go forward, to grow, to increase, to abound more and more." —WILLIAM NICHOLSON

A Shining Lamp

Thy word is a lamp unto my feet, and a light unto my path (PSALM 119:105).

The Bible isn't a textbook. Nor is it a theology thesis. For the Christian man, the Bible is a lamp shining on his path. No man really knows what his future holds. Will there be joys? Yes. Will there be trials? Of course. But in every circumstance, God illuminates a path only seen by the light of His Word. When we neglect or disobey the Word, we're prone to walking off the lighted path. But when we stay on the lighted path and follow where it leads, we will come through just fine.

Read the Word, certainly. But more than reading it, we must follow the path it illuminates for us.

"One who carries a lantern on a country-road at night, sees only one step before him. If he takes that step, he carries his lantern forward, and thus makes another step plain. At length he reaches his destination in safety, without once stepping into darkness. The whole way has been made light for him, though only a single step of it at a time. This illustrates the usual method of God's guidance." —J.R. MILLER

REPENTANCE

Despisest thou the riches of his goodness and forbearance and longsuffering; not knowing that the goodness of God leadeth thee to repentance? (ROMANS 2:4).

What causes a man to repent? Regret plays a part. So does the conviction of the Holy Spirit. But Paul reminds us that one strong motivation for repentance is the goodness of God.

While some people will always carry a grudge against those who offended them, God isn't like that. Instead, God is like the father of the Prodigal Son. He eagerly yearned for the repentant son—and as the lad returned, the father welcomed him home. Not a word of reproach came from the father, though the son expected it. Such unwarranted goodness had to bring a sigh of relief to the son who hoped for no more than to be taken on by his father as a hired hand. A party was out of the question—and yet a party was on the father's mind.

When we have something from which we need to repent, let's remember that the goodness of God is waiting to accept our repentance by throwing a party.

"The goodness of God is a spiritual sunbeam to melt the heart into tears." —THOMAS WATSON

Pray, Lest You Become Prey

For the eyes of the Lord are over the righteous, and his ears are open unto their prayers: but the face of the Lord is against them that do evil (1 Peter 3:12).

Prayer is many things, but one of the most vital is its function as a spiritual weapon against the forces of evil. In the hour of great need, there is prayer. In the hour of temptation, there is prayer. In the hour of financial reverses, there is prayer. Relationship problems? Pray! Health issues? Pray! Even before all these and other dire situations arise, prayer is the wall that keeps the enemy without. Every man is called to pray and pray hardily. There are no exceptions.

Never let prayer become plan B, nor should prayer be a matter of neglect. As the old saying goes, seven days without prayer makes one weak.

"Oh, how strenuous is life! I know a little of it…How fierce the battle! I know something of the conflict, but I ought not to faint, because I can pray." —G. Campbell Morgan

GOD'S TIME

Humble yourselves therefore under the mighty hand of God, that he may exalt you in due time (1 PETER 5:6).

It's a fact that spiritual growth takes time. There are no instantly mature Christians. And those who claim to be so will find their roots shallow and likely will wither away in a short time. True Christian men know that the measure required to grow strong like a mighty oak takes time. Even years. And such men, though seemingly content with the time factor, know that as they wait, they must water their spiritual life with the Word. They know prayer sends down strong roots. Adversity builds muscle. Fellowship and community with other believers bring comfort and encouragement. The secret to growth isn't rocket science. Follow what you know you should do, and wait and watch. Growth always comes to those who seek it.

"He who waits on God loses no time." —VANCE HAVNER

Our Divine Helper

So that we may boldly say, The Lord is my helper, and I will not fear what man shall do unto me (HEBREWS 13:6).

One of the functions of the Holy Spirit is to be our divine Helper. One way He helps is to guide us into the right paths and detour us around the wrong ones. But for this to happen, we must develop the habit of listening. The boundaries the Holy Spirit establishes for us are divinely ordered and are given for our safety. The Holy Spirit speaks to us through the Word and occasionally through our spirit. But in the latter case, it will always be in accordance with the Word of God. The Holy Spirit never leads us in a way that contradicts what the Bible teaches.

Learn to listen today. Is God speaking through His Word, through prayer, through others you encounter? Are there boundaries the Holy Spirit has established for you that you have ignored or violated? Get back on the right path today, and trust the leading of the Holy Spirit.

"Faith never knows where it is being led, but it loves and knows the One who is leading." —OSWALD CHAMBERS

WEAKNESS IS STRENGTH

Therefore I take pleasure in infirmities, in reproaches, in necessities, in persecutions, in distresses for Christ's sake: for when I am weak, then am I strong (2 CORINTHIANS 12:10).

When circumstances shed light on our weaknesses, we can rejoice that the same light will also shed the light of God's strength. It's easy to defend ourselves or complain about a weakness revealed, but admitting weakness opens the door for God to move in strength.

What weakness is being revealed in you? Can you see this as an opportunity for God to enter into your weakness with His power and might? Weakness is never meant to embarrass us or make us feel less than. From God's perspective, the revelation of weakness is a good and necessary thing.

"Real true faith is man's weakness leaning on God's strength."
—D.L. MOODY

Your Spiritual Footprint

For even hereunto were ye called: because Christ also suffered for us, leaving us an example, that ye should follow his steps (1 PETER 2:21).

Much is being said these days about the size of our carbon footprint. Are we careless with our use of energy and natural resources? That's a valid question, but more importantly, are we careless with our spiritual footprint?

There will always be new generations of young men coming up behind us, looking at the spiritual footprints we've left behind. What will they see? What will they say? Is our spiritual footprint worthy of someone else's steps? Can future generations look to what we've left behind and walk as we've walked?

Today and every day, we leave yet another print as we walk through our lives. Make today's footprint worthy of emulation.

"A Christian should be both a magnet and a diamond! A magnet in drawing others to Christ; a diamond in casting a sparkling luster of holiness, in his life. Oh let us be...so just in our dealings, so true in our promises, so devout in our worship, so unblamable in our lives; that we may be the walking pictures of Christ!" —THOMAS WATSON

CELEBRATING FAILURE

For a just man falleth seven times, and riseth up again: but the wicked shall fall into mischief (PROVERBS 24:16).

When we succeed, it's fun to celebrate our successes. But what do we do when we fail at something? It may be hard to do, but perhaps we should celebrate our failures too. Every failure has within it the seeds of wisdom. We probably learn more from failure than from success. The one thing we mustn't do in the light of failure is beat ourselves up over it. If we let it, the tape of accusation will loop over and over in our minds endlessly, bringing with it the useless and counterproductive guilt that can paralyze us from future attempts at success.

Celebrate success, but find a way to commemorate failure too.

"God may allow His servant to succeed when He has disciplined him to a point where he does not need to succeed to be happy. The man who is elated by success and is cast down by failure is still a carnal man. At best his fruit will have a worm in it." —A. W. TOZER

REMEMBERING

After the same manner also he took the cup, when he had supped, saying, this cup is the new testament in my blood: this do ye, as oft as ye drink it, in remembrance of me (1 CORINTHIANS 11:25).

An important part of Christians coming together is for remembrance. When Christians gather together to partake of Communion (the Lord's Supper in some churches), we're asked by Jesus to "remember." Remembering, for the Christian man, is a means of affirming over and over the reality behind the taking of the bread and the cup.

As a man ages, he has more and more of the Lord's work in his life to remember. Slowing our lives down so we actually take time to remember the Lord and what He's done is crucial. Today, call to mind some of God's greatest blessings in your life. Where has He brought you from and where is He taking you? Then the next time your fellowship enjoys the Lord's Supper, make sure to remember Him. Remember all His goodness to you.

"Memory is the treasure house of the mind wherein the monuments thereof are kept and preserved." —THOMAS FULLER

A Channel of Blessing

Give, and it shall be given unto you; good measure, pressed down, and shaken together, and running over, shall men give into your bosom. For with the same measure that ye mete withal it shall be measured to you again (Luke 6:38).

Some Christian men seem gifted to become financially successful. Others, not so much. Their gifts lie elsewhere. But what are we to do with our gifts, whether they be large or small? The clear answer is that we're to pass on our blessings to others. If we have the gift of finances, we can surely voluntarily share with those in need. If our gifts are as simple as listening ears, those too can be put to good use. Virtually every gift God gives to man is meant to be shared. We're to become channels of God's blessings to others. Today identify a gift you have and figure out how you might pass it on to someone who needs it.

"Every good gift that we have had from the cradle up has come from God. If a man just stops to think what he has to praise God for, he will find there is enough to keep him singing praises for a week." —D.L. Moody

LIFE AS A SERIES OF MIRACLES

For whoso findeth me findeth life, and shall obtain favor of the LORD (PROVERBS 8:35).

Through happy times and sad times, through the highs of life and the lows, life itself is a series of miracles. Every man's presence on earth is the first miracle of existence. Then day by day as life unfolds, so do the everyday miracles that make up a man's life. True, these miracles are best identified as a man ages. But even younger men can pause and take notice of the work of God in their lives so far. A man's conversion to Christ is the greatest miracle, but in most cases, surely not the last. To truly appreciate the daily miracles, we need to watch for them. Though some may be smaller than others and harder to notice, they are still there. If nothing else, consider that every breath you take today is a miracle. A wise friend once said, "You're alive, so live!" That's the best way to experience today's miracle.

"A Christian is a perpetual miracle." —CHARLES SPURGEON

AMBASSADORS FOR CHRIST

*We are ambassadors for Christ, as though God did beseech you
by us: we pray you in Christ's stead, be ye reconciled to God*
(2 CORINTHIANS 5:20).

Every Christian man has a story. Whether converted
as a child, a teen, or an adult, a man's testimony
is one of his greatest assets. But like any asset, a man's
story must be invested. Paul referred to us as ambassadors for Christ, and so we are. When appropriate times
to share our stories present themselves—often divinely
appointed by God—we should speak of Christ in the
same way an ambassador speaks of his home country. Our home country is heaven, but though we enter
heaven upon our death, it's fair to say we inherit eternal
life the moment we say yes to Christ. We become citizens of heaven though we are not yet residents of heaven.
How we each came to Christ is a story we should rehearse
in our minds frequently and be prepared to share with
ease and conviction. Watch for such moments. Just
make sure your testimony rings true to those who are
observing your life.

*"If lips and life do not agree, the testimony will not amount to
much."* —HARRY IRONSIDE

THE PROMISES MUST BE BELIEVED

And this is the promise that he hath promised us, even eternal life (1 JOHN 2:25).

Ours is a life built on the promises of God. When we're doubtful about our future, we can know God has already secured it, both here and in eternity. When faced with adversity, we can claim various promises of God. When tempted, we must lay a firm hold on the promises of God.

We must be strong in the Lord, knowing "He will not allow you to be tempted above that you are able to bear." "With the temptation he will provide a way of escape." The promises, when believed, are fatal to Satan's suggestions. "My grace is sufficient for you" rendered harmless all the buffetings of Satan in the case of Paul. Know God's Word. Beware of ignorance.

"Prayer, like faith, obtains promises, enlarges their operation, and adds to the measure of their results." —E.M. BOUNDS

Search Out the Promises

Let us hold fast the profession of our faith without wavering; (for he is faithful that promised) (Hebrews 10:23).

God is more aware of His promises to us than we are. He has them memorized while we yet seek them out, one by one. And the search for God's promises is a lifelong pursuit. We never run out of the need for the secure promises of God, and the promises never have an expiration date. God delights in our ongoing search for and faith in His promises. If you wish to delight God today, identify a need in your life and find the corresponding promises to claim.

"To believe that He will preserve us is, indeed, a means of preservation. God will certainly preserve us, and make a way of escape for us out of the temptation, should we fall. We are to pray for what God has already promised. Our requests are to be regulated by His promises and commands. Faith embraces the promises and so finds relief." —John Owen

OUR LAST ENEMY

The last enemy that shall be destroyed is death (1 CORINTHIANS 15:26).

Every Christian man will eventually face death. How he handles the coming end of his days is important. First, he must set aside all fear. The sting of death is removed for the believer. Second, he must leave the timing of his departure to God. Third, all practical matters must be settled so he leaves no unwieldy burden to his loved ones.

If you think it's too early to think about death, the reality is that it's never too early to be ready. We may rightly wish for many more years of service. We may pray, like Jesus, for the cup to pass from us. But also like Jesus, we must finally acknowledge, "Not my will, but yours be done."

"Take care of your life and the Lord will take care of your death." —GEORGE WHITEFIELD

SELF-WORTH

If ye fulfil the royal law according to the scripture, Thou shalt love thy neighbor as thyself, ye do well (JAMES 2:8).

Some Christian men fall prey to the enemy's attacks that lead to low self-worth. It may come from an abusive childhood, broken relationships, vocational failure, health crises, or some other genesis. But God's love of each of us as manifested in His creating us should spur us on to proper self-worth and also enable us to truly love one another. It ends all comparisons with others and all competition to best our brother in Christ.

Today, give thanks to God for *you.* Do not accept any suggestions that you are less than. You're *more than* in God's eyes.

"There is a self-love which is corrupt, and the root of the greatest sins, and it must be put off and mortified; but there is a self-love which is the rule of the greatest duty: we must have a due concern for the welfare of our own souls and bodies." —
MATTHEW HENRY

Our Shortcomings

Let your conversation be without covetousness; and be content with such things as ye have: for he hath said, I will never leave thee, nor forsake thee (HEBREWS 13:5).

What a mixture is every man! Part warrior, part thinker, part planner, part doer—and so much more. We're often partly successful and…often partly *unsuccessful*. When the latter is our lot, we must remember that God's presence within us always trumps our many shortcomings. Focusing on our lacks—and every man has them—can only bring us down. Trusting God to fill in the many spaces we lack takes away the burden of "performance." We are who we are, shortcomings and all, and God is good with that—and so must we be.

"O slow of heart to believe and trust in the constant presence and overruling agency of our almighty Savior!" —ADONIRAM JUDSON

Spirit and Life

It is the spirit that quickeneth; the flesh profiteth nothing: the words that I speak unto you, they are spirit, and they are life (JOHN 6:63).

What do we see when we read the Bible? Words on a page? Ink on paper? Yes, that's what we see on the surface, but if we mix what we read with faith, we find life in those words of Scripture. As we feed on the Word, we feed on life itself—spiritual life. As we meditate on the day's reading of Scripture, we internalize the very Word of God. We then find that being filled with the written Word of God is a giant step toward being filled with the Living Word. As the apostle John wrote in recording Jesus's words, we find spirit and life in the words of Christ. And as every man has learned, the flesh is, indeed, no help at all.

"The Bible is alive…it speaks to me…it has feet, it runs after me…it has hands, it lays hold of me." —MARTIN LUTHER

LEANING IN

The wicked flee when no man pursueth: but the righteous are bold as a lion (PROVERBS 28:1).

Increasingly we are leaning into a fallen world that accepts and even enjoys the corruption that comes with sin. But Christian men play an important role in holding back the forces of evil. To do so, we must lean into personal righteousness. We must cleave to that which is good and rebel against all that is evil. Silence and apathy aren't options. Prayer warriors must fall on their knees. Leaders must lead in righteousness. Compassion must be our badge as we become first responders to those hurt by sin and corruption.

If we listen hard, we can hear the cries of the captives and the victims of a fallen humanity. We hear the call of God to come alongside those who hurt. We must not flee from our responsibility; we must be as bold as lions.

"What does love look like? It has the hands to help others. It has the feet to hasten to the poor and needy. It has eyes to see misery and want. It has the ears to hear the sighs and sorrows of men. That is what love looks like." —AUGUSTINE

DUTY

He hath showed thee, O man, what is good; and what doth the LORD require of thee, but to do justly, and to love mercy, and to walk humbly with thy God? (MICAH 6:8).

A Christian must quickly discern his duty while here on earth. Duty to God, to self, to family, to church, to country, to his brothers and sisters in Christ. Duty, in fact, is the railroad track of God's will for us. When we find and assume our duties on our shoulders, we discover they automatically broaden to accommodate the weight of the new responsibilities. When Christian men abscond from their duties, they leave a hole they alone can fill. When we find our duties here on earth, we will discover that their geneses are simply to do justly, love mercy, and walk humbly with our God.

"The soldier is summoned to a life of active duty and so is the Christian." —WILLIAM GURNALL

Being Countercultural

Beware lest any man spoil you through philosophy and vain deceit, after the tradition of men, after the rudiments of the world, and not after Christ (Colossians 2:8).

This present time is crying out for Christian men to be thoroughly Christian and thoroughly countercultural. Sunday Christians won't do in a society that is increasingly hostile to Christianity. The time to "go along to get along" is long past. Men must step up to the plate at home, in the workplace, and in the church.

God is seeking such men today. Men who refuse to be swayed by the latest emerging trends that continue to lower the standard that is manhood.

Even today may present a temptation to go along with the crowd. But the time to prepare to take a stand is before the pressure to cave presents itself.

Today, be thoroughly Christian. Tomorrow too.

"Manhood is made in the field of struggle and hardship, not in ways of ease and luxury. Hindrances are opportunities. Difficulty is a school for manhood. Strength is the glory of manhood." —J.R. Miller

ORDER OUT OF CHAOS

By him were all things created, that are in heaven, and that are in earth, visible and invisible, whether they be thrones, or dominions, or principalities, or powers: all things were created by him, and for him: And he is before all things, and by him all things consist (COLOSSIANS 1:16-17).

It's man's privilege to—like God in whose image he is created—bring order out of chaos. Many men spend their lives in jobs bringing order into being. Others have hobbies requiring the often slow talent of bringing beauty and order into existence where there was previously disorder. A stump of wood under the carver's hand becomes an object of art. A composer takes the twelve notes of music and produces a symphony. A house painter brings restoration to the chaos of a dilapidated fixer-upper. A wise counselor helps a tormented soul sort out the causes of his mental disorder.

What sorts of chaos in your life can you work to bring about order to? When you do, you're engaged in God's work.

"The Spirit brings order out of chaos and beauty out of ugliness. He can transform a sin-blistered man into a paragon of virtue. The Spirit changes people." —R.C. SPROUL

Prayer Is Not
Wishing on Steroids

I exhort therefore, that, first of all, supplications, prayers, intercessions, and giving of thanks, be made for all men (1 Timothy 2:1).

When tragedy happens, we hear the call for "thoughts and prayers." And yes, prayer is certainly called for. But are our prayers simply thoughts that reach no higher than the ceiling? A Christian man is by necessity a praying man. He prays with genuine concern for those he intercedes for. His prayers are not mere thoughts, nor are they simply wishes for a happy outcome.

Today's Christian man knows the furtherance of God's will is influenced by his prayers. He prays boldly. He prays with faith. He prays with clarity. And God hears and answers that man's prayers.

"The more praying there is in the world, the better the world will be; the mightier the forces against evil everywhere."
—E.M. Bounds

Moving Forward

Without faith it is impossible to please him: for he that cometh to God must believe that he is, and that he is a rewarder of them that diligently seek him (Hebrews 11:6).

The Christian life isn't a static life. We never stand still in our growth in Christ. Rather, from day to day, week to week, year to year, we move forward in our walk with the Lord. We come upon stumbling blocks and walk past them. We go through dark tunnels and emerge into the light. We take a misstep backward but then take two recovery steps forward.

God never stops tending to our growth. He sets in motion the very circumstances we need to move ahead. Nothing can stop us from growing, for we are Christian men.

"The Christian life is very much like climbing a hill of ice. You cannot slide up. You have to cut every step with an ice axe. Only with incessant labor in cutting and chipping can you make any progress. If you want to know how to backslide, leave off going forward. Cease going upward and you will go downward of necessity. You can never stand still."
—CHARLES SPURGEON

LIFE MANAGEMENT

He that hath no rule over his own spirit is like a city that is broken down, and without walls (PROVERBS 25:28).

Every Christian man needs to learn to be a good manager of his own life. Managing oneself effectively eliminates one of the major causes of stress. Thank God we have within us by the Holy Spirit the ability to manage our lives successfully. That is, *if* we're managing what God has called us to and not *more* than God has called us to.

Take a brief inventory of your life. Is it manageable? Manageable without stress? If the answer is no, consider prayerfully where to cut loose time-robbing activities that are not as productive as others. If the answer is yes, consider how you may have time to help take on some responsibilities of others—including family members.

Manage well, live well, and finish well.

"We can easily manage if we will only take, each day, the burden appointed to it. But the load will be too heavy for us if we carry yesterday's burden over again today, and then add the burden of the morrow before we are required to bear it."
—JOHN NEWTON

No Condemnation!

There is therefore now no condemnation to them which are in Christ Jesus, who walk not after the flesh, but after the Spirit. For the law of the Spirit of life in Christ Jesus hath made me free from the law of sin and death (ROMANS 8:1-2).

Satan is a reality, and we must not be unaware of his devices and strategies for our fall. But to be honest, most men are more likely to fall into sin or even apathy from their own fleshly desires than from Satan's enticements. Christian men can and must become winners in the battle between their flesh and their desire to live holy and wholly. If the apostle Paul fought this battle (see Romans 7), we can be sure we will too. Temptation and sin are not unique to each of us. We are all prone to obey the flesh's siren call. But we must remember Paul won his battle, and so can we.

"What ground is left for accusation since sin's penalty has been fully paid? The blood of the Lord has atoned for all the sins of a believer; hence there is no more condemnation in the conscience." —WATCHMAN NEE

GOD'S UNSEEN HAND

That the trial of your faith, being much more precious than
of gold that perisheth, though it be tried with fire, might be
found unto praise and honor and glory at the appearing of
Jesus Christ (1 PETER 1:7).

Happy is the man who perceives the unseen hand of God in every aspect of his life. Nothing can touch us that does not pass through the knowledge of God first. And when embraced by faith in God's goodness and His ability to work out His perfect plan for our lives, even trials turn to gold eventually. Trust in the unseen hand of God today. Just as He is always present, even when we don't perceive His presence, so too is He always at work even when we're unaware.

"When all nature is at rest, not a leaf moving, then at evening
the dew comes down—no eye to see the pearly drops descend-
ing, no ear to hear them falling on the verdant grass—so does
the Spirit come to you who believe. When the heart is at rest
in Jesus—unseen, unheard by the world—the Spirit comes,
and softly fills the believing soul, quickening all, renewing all
within." —ROBERT MURRAY MCCHEYNE

Our Eternal Deposits

He that hath a bountiful eye shall be blessed; for he giveth of his bread to the poor (PROVERBS 22:9).

What would it be like if every Christian would look upon money as something he gives more than something he earns or spends? Welfare as we know it might cease. Missionaries would have better tools to reach the lost. The homeless could find shelter. Happy is the man who isn't a slave to mammon but instead searches out new ways to give—often anonymously. If we would be good investors of our money, we would find there is no greater investment than the eternal deposits we make in our heavenly retirement account.

"Do not think me mad. It is not to make money that I believe a Christian should live. The noblest thing a man can do is just humbly to receive, and then go amongst others and give."
—DAVID LIVINGSTONE

Our Ever-Present God

We love him, because he first loved us (1 John 4:19).

Though we may think we have searched for God and found Him in Christ, the truth is before we searched for Him, He searched for us and found us. He wanted us from day one in eternity past, and He wants us for every day in eternity future. We are His. He is ours. We are engraved on the palms of His hands. He is always with us and always *for* us.

"I am graven on the palms of His hands. I am never out of His mind. All my knowledge of Him depends on His sustained initiative in knowing me. I know Him, because He first knew me, and continues to know me. He knows me as a friend, One who loves me; and there is no moment when His eye is off me, or His attention distracted for me, and no moment, therefore, when His care falters." —J.I. Packer

PERSECUTION

Blessed are they which are persecuted for righteousness' sake: for theirs is the kingdom of heaven. Blessed are ye, when men shall revile you, and persecute you, and shall say all manner of evil against you falsely, for my sake. Rejoice, and be exceeding glad: for great is your reward in heaven: for so persecuted they the prophets which were before you (MATTHEW 5:10-12).

A Christian need not look for opposition—it will surely find him. It has always been so and will continue in the future, perhaps with an accelerated pace. The time to prepare for opposition isn't at the moment of confrontation but much earlier. In fact, *now* is always the best time to prepare for opposition.

There are two ways to prepare. One is to consider the opposition, scorn, and rejection the Lord Jesus went through for us. The second way is to focus on eternity, where all opposition will no longer exist. There is, then, an end to opposition, though there is not an end to our lives in Christ.

"If you are going to walk with Jesus Christ, you are going to be opposed. In our days, to be a true Christian is really to become a scandal." —GEORGE WHITEFIELD

Think on These Things

Finally, brethren, whatsoever things are true, whatsoever things are honest, whatsoever things are just, whatsoever things are pure, whatsoever things are lovely, whatsoever things are of good report; if there be any virtue, and if there be any praise, think on these things (Philippians 4:8).

It is right to hate evil. But it's not right to focus so much on hating evil that we fail to love and approve that which is good. Some men are temperamentally predisposed to look for the half-empty glass, to expect the worst, to find fault. Sometimes our words of negativity are out of our mouths before we realize how unnecessary it was to offer our opinion. Speak that which is good. Think of the best things. See the glass not half empty nor half full but overflowing with the goodness of God. For each of us, our cup truly runs over.

"Our souls must not merely hate what is evil; we must love what is good." —Thomas Chalmers

Overcoming Failure

My flesh and my heart faileth: but God is the strength of my heart, and my portion for ever (Psalm 73:26).

If you've ever experienced colossal failure—and who hasn't—you know the aftermath is one of life's occasions when our flesh and our heart faileth. Our spirits couldn't be lower. We forget failure is the road to success.

For every man who reaches the pinnacle of success, there are others who, having failed, gave up their dreams. The difference between the two is that the former didn't fear failure; they knew that failure had its purpose in their quest, and they persisted despite failure after failure. Essentially, these men failed their way to success. The latter—those who have given up—couldn't see past their present or past failures to try again. Sometimes failure produces fear of future failure and stops the man in his tracks. Try. Fail. Try. Fail. Succeed. It's the way God brings us to maturity and allows us to see our dreams fulfilled.

"Trying, failing, and trying again is called learning."
—Henry Cloud

BE GLAD AND LAUGH!

Then was our mouth filled with laughter, and our tongue with singing: then said they among the heathen, The LORD hath done great things for them (PSALM 126:2).

Laughter is one of God's greatest gifts to man. A man who can find the humor in life—especially in life's darker moments—has God on his side. An easy laugh comes from a heart that is perpetually *glad*. If we are without gladness of heart, it can be cultivated. How? One place to start is ruminating on the goodness of God. Calling to mind the ways God has worked in our past to bring about a desired end. Another way to cultivate gladness of heart is to simply practice praising God no matter the circumstances. God is no less God during our rough patches than He is during our mountaintop experiences. Rejoice and be glad, Christian man! You are the possessor of all good things!

"Be glad and laugh from the low bottom of thine own heart."
—WILLIAM TYNDALE

Our One True Commitment

Seek ye first the kingdom of God, and his righteousness; and all these things shall be added unto you (MATTHEW 6:33).

We men are most likely to be successful at that to which we're totally committed. The problem is that many men try to be committed to too many things. We can only be totally committed to one thing to be effective. There are, of course, lesser commitments we make in life, but the one true commitment to which all other commitments must bow is our commitment to Christ. We must have a single eye for Him and His kingdom. When our curiosity suggests new commitments, we must make sure they won't supplant or diminish our one true commitment. We must weigh carefully new interruptions in our lives and consider whether they will hinder or help our one true commitment. All the important things in life will be added to us if we will seek first Christ and His kingdom.

"None do seek the Lord so earnestly, but they have need of stirring up to seek him more earnestly; neither have any attained to such a measure of communion with God, but they have need to seek for a further measure." —DAVID DICKSON

Nick Harrison is the author of several books, including these in the One-Minute Prayers® series from House Publishers:

One-Minute Prayers® for Husbands

The very best way you can take care of your wife is by praying for her and your marriage. Discover biblical encouragement in this collection of prayers and devotions written for busy husbands like you who need a minute of inspiration.

One-Minute Prayers® for Dads

Take a minute out of your day to thank God for your children, and let Him equip you for the challenges of fatherhood with these brief but powerful prayers that fit into your busy schedule.

One-Minute Prayers® for Those with Cancer

These writings will lead you from fear to faith in the face of illness. Each entry includes a reassuring encouragement as well as a suggested prayer to open your heart to nourishment and understanding.

One-Minute Prayers® When You Need a Miracle

When life looks bleak and you need God to show up in a big way, these prayers will connect your needs to God's promises, increase your faith, and enlarge your view of God.